In-flight

This edition first published in the UK in 2009
By Green Umbrella Publishing

© Green Umbrella Publishing 2009

www.gupublishing.co.uk

Publishers Jules Gammond and Vanessa Gardner

Creative Director: Kevin Gardner

Picture Credits: Shutterstock

Printed and bound by J. H. Haynes & Co. Ltd., Sparkford

ISBN: 978-1-9066-3543-5

In-flight
CONFIDENTIAL

Ladies and Gentleman sit back, relax and prepare to be amused...

Richard Havers and Christopher Tiffney

Contents

Introduction

I t's surprising that so few books have been written about what really happens in the airline business. Perhaps the truth is just too ghastly, amazing, or downright worrying to be told. What's assembled here is a collection of stories, anecdotes, facts, titbits, and pieces of trivia about what is a fascinating business. Most of them are true, and those that are not we thought were just too funny to leave out. We think you'll be able to work out what's true and what's not. The truth is often stranger than fiction which means that some of those that really happened are almost unbelievable.

Why are we fascinated by flying? Well, for a start, it's a pretty amazing concept that something that's heavier than air can stay aloft. What's always been remarkable is how those huge beasts get up there in the first place. The sheer power of the engines, and the technology to allow them to take off is awesome (particularly to me as I was asked to leave physics after getting 'nul points' in an O level mock exam – Richard).

It's not just the science of it all, because what flying offers us is the ability to travel quickly to far-flung places – whether it be for work or for pleasure. Air travel has, to use the old cliché, caused the world to shrink. Whether or not this is a good thing is open to debate. If nothing else it has created employment for millions around the world, which is particularly good for those who are employed by airlines and all the ancillary companies that support the industry – because without air travel they would have to get a proper job.

If you ask a group of teenage girls what they would like to be when they grow up then there's a good chance that some of them will say – 'air hostess'. That obviously excludes those that just want to be famous, but then again it is possible to be both, as you will learn from what follows. Similarly among the boys, pilot probably ranks up there in the top ten of desirable careers. That's possibly because it's usually the pretty girls who want to be hostesses.

In the days before the Second World War it was only the very rich and the very famous who could fly in commercial aircraft; there were exceptions like prime ministers seeking appeasement but in general it was a truism. Of course it was only the very rich, and those who were slightly mad, who flew for pleasure in light aircraft. The concept of flying to Paris or some other nearby destination on board an aircraft that was noisier than hell captured the public's imagination. Those who flew further afield on the flying boats of Imperial Airways were at the very pinnacle of fame, wealth and celebrity. This is what some are expecting to experience when they fly on today's glorified bus services. The Second World War revolutionised aircraft technology making it inevitable that commercial aviation took on a whole new meaning. This was not just as a result of the technical advances, but also because there was a ready supply of ex-military aircraft and the pilots to fly them. Without both, aviation around the world would have been much slower to develop.

It was the pilots who created the illusion of glamour, the gossamer sheen that was reflected in their tanned and rugged faces, which the airline business has traded off ever since – it certainly wasn't the aircraft in the late 1940s and early 1950s. Dashing ex-military types became civilian airline pilots who wore their caps at a jaunty angle, had a devil-may-care attitude and gave the illusion of having the most interesting of lives to the majority of us who were stuck with our feet firmly on the ground.

When I started in the business in the late 1960s there was one particular pilot I knew who exuded everything that was alluring about flying; he even had a name to go with the image – 'Flash' Phillips. He was every inch the ex-RAF officer; debonair, he even wore white cotton gloves to land the aircraft and was fond of playing the harmonica on the boring bits of long-haul flights – although this was for the 'amusement' of those on the flight deck, not the passengers.

As the airline business expanded into something that resembled a real business rather than some kind of hobby, you would think that it would have become more serious. Big jets, rather than ex-military propeller aircraft, radically altered airline operations, but did not fundamentally change the way they behaved – the boys and their toys syndrome continued for many a year.

For the airlines, the challenge was trying to cope with increasing capacity brought about by quantum leaps in aircraft size, particularly when the Boeing 747 came along. It provided a huge increase in seats when compared to a Boeing 707 or DC8. If an airline had a service that operated once a day between two cities it was unlikely, and unwise, to reduce the frequency of flights. It therefore meant that the airlines had to find ways of filling all those extra seats. The answer was simple, at least in theory – encourage holiday travel. For a time this stretched the imagination of the marketing types in the travel business, especially as all this was happening at a time when the fuel crisis and other economic factors conspired against discretionary air travel.

But times have long since changed. During the last 25 years or so the air travel business has seen another revolution. More fuel-efficient engines have radically altered the cost of flying and airlines have also changed. The unionised, fat, dumb and happy approach of the 1960s and 1970s has been replaced by the lean and mean hard-nose ethics of the new entrant carriers – like Southwest in the USA or Ryanair and easyJet in Europe. Not that the switch from the old style industry to the new way has made things any the less interesting. There's been no noticeable downturn in applications for the mile-high club, or reduction in the number of people behaving badly on planes.

Psychologists would no doubt be able to explain, in terms that the rest of us would find difficult to understand; why it is that people and aircraft frequently don't mix. Undoubtedly it's got something to do with the fact that most of us are nervous about flying – to varying degrees. No matter how the statistics shape up the average person can't help thinking, 'How is it those things stay up there?' As often as not people who are travelling are tense about time, particularly that curious breed – the business traveller. Will the flight be late, or will it get me to the next airport to make my connection? Will I make that important meeting? All this is a recipe for conflict. At check-in passengers are not at their most charming, especially if told that their flight is over-booked or that it's late for any one of a hundred seemingly bizarre reasons. This can often result in the strange phenomenon of perfectly reasonable people uttering the immortal line: 'Do you know who I am?'

Once passengers are on board then the desire to have a drink will as often as not kick in. Indeed some can't even wait until they're on board. They start in the airport building, which often precipitates a rather unfortunate downturn in their normal standards of behaviour. There was a period when the scheduled airlines offered free drinks in their economy cabins, which of course did nothing to improve standards of behaviour. One upside of the low fare revolution is the fact that the low-cost carriers charge for drinks, even water, and so the chances of someone getting a little too merry are drastically reduced.

Even in these troubled times for airlines with an increasing number of airlines going bust and the difficulties that it causes for both employees and passengers, aviation still fascinates us.

Always remember one thing, the airline business is cyclical and so in a while we'll be back to the madness once again. In the meantime people behaving badly, or bizarrely will continue to give rise to airlines and air travel being a source of amusement. Despite everything, flying is fun, air travel is fascinating and they will always have more than their fair share of laughs.

Ladies and gentlemen, sit back and relax and prepare to be amused.

Acknowledgements

'd like to dedicate this book to the late Tony Robinson, who worked with me at British Caledonian Airways and Continental Airlines. Tony tragically died in January 2005. One day at a meeting while we were at Continental Airlines I made a suggestion: 'Ah, Tone, I've had this great idea to launch the new route from London to Denver. We'll theme it around the Gold Rush and Wild West.' Quick as a flash, Tony responded with, 'Well, it'll confirm the travel agents' view of us as a cowboy outfit.' I'd also like to mention the great Mike Kay who is probably the funniest man I ever met in the airline business. Some former British Caledonian employees are still recovering from shock after Mike painted one of his company's Viscounts in BCAL's colours.

Richard Havers

Thanks to everyone who generously shared their memories. I'd also like to thank my family and friends, and most of all my wife, Vanessa.

Christopher Tiffney

Chapter**ONE**

The Mile-High Club

'*Remember when sex was safe and flying was dangerous?*'

– ANON.

Get a group of people talking about the airline business, and flying in general, and they will mention one of two things. Either it's the great lost baggage story or the legendary mile-high club. In all honesty there are few who can truly claim to be a member of the club. Even those who are keen to brag of their membership are probably lying, and not just because there are, in reality, so few who have actually done it. The fact is that most commercial aircraft fly at closer to seven miles high. In order to be technically correct, if you are a member of the mile-high club then the chances are you will have needed to have 'done it' either during climb or in the descent, which means that you should have been wearing your seat belt!

A recent survey found that around nine per cent of people admitted to having had sex on board a commercial airliner. The respondents were evenly split between men and women, perhaps indicating that the traditional wisdom – that men tend to brag and women tend to be modest when asked questions about sex – may be fading. Before you start checking around you on your next flight to see if close to one in 10 people are at it, don't forget that only means that they may have done it on one occasion, not every time they fly! What is it that makes talk of sexual exploits on board aircraft so fascinating? It's possibly linked to the whole romance that used to be associated with flying – in the days when aircraft actually had proper bunk beds, and when air travel was for the privileged few. Nowadays, with air travel being more akin to getting on and off a bus, the romance has very definitely gone out of flying.

Another aspect of the whole sex and travel routine is the single guy, and particularly the businessman, who somehow thinks that every air stewardess, flight attendant, trolley dolly, call them what you like, is going to be instantly attracted to him. Watching lonely business travellers chatting up flight attendants is still one of the saddest sights to behold. New research in fact shows that air stewardesses are facing increasing levels of harassment. Even the British Medical Journal has got in on the act, claiming that passengers have pestered one in five stewardesses. The research was undertaken among 2,000 stewardesses who worked between 1965 and 1995 for Alitalia, the Italian airline. We will refrain from making any comment.

PLANE SPEAKING

Cessna: *'Jones tower, Cessna 12345, student pilot, I am out of fuel.'*
Tower: 'Roger Cessna 12345, reduce airspeed to best glide! Do you have the airfield in sight?'
Cessna: *'Uh... tower, I am on the south ramp; I just want to know where the fuel truck is.'*

Mile-High Pioneer

'The Club' owes a huge debt to the pioneers of mid-air hanky panky, Lawrence Sperry and Mrs Waldo Polk. In 1916 Sperry, a daredevil flyer and inventor of the autopilot, was giving flying lessons to Mrs Polk, a wealthy New York socialite. They crashed in the waters of the South Bay and were found, naked, by two duck hunters. After the rescue Sperry claimed that the forces of the crash had divested them of their clothes, but that explanation was not universally accepted. One other point to note: Sperry was piloting a flying boat at the time, which of course proves that they were in at least one respect a badly named flying machine; whatever floats your boat. As a footnote Sperry was killed flying a light aircraft (not a flying boat) across the English Channel a few years later.

> *They say it's better than sex. It's so much better. It's amazing.*
>
> – ANGELINA JOLIE, PILOT AND ACTRESS, TALKING ABOUT FLYING!

Mile-High or Forty Winks

Beds were first put in aircraft years ago, back in the days when flying was just for the elite. On the early flying boats operated by Imperial Airways and Pan American, passengers had dinner at tables and then retired to bed for a jolly good night's sleep. No one complained about the threat to the morals of passengers.

Fast-forward to the 21st century and enter that defender of the nation's morals Miss Ann Widdecombe MP. Sir Richard Branson announced that he was to introduce double beds into some of Virgin's long haul flights – like many other airlines Virgin already has single beds in its first class cabin. Miss Widdecombe was outraged: 'This is unnecessary and unfortunate. There's an immense issue of public decency here because there are other passengers who will not wish to see or hear such things.' Maybe Miss Widdecombe, who has her own website – the Widdy Web – has something to be worried about. Back in 1999 Sir Richard Branson, who is often described by the press as 'a flamboyant businessman', said, 'The legitimate mile-high club is finally aboard... You can do it on cruise ships, you can do it at home, so why shouldn't you be able to have relationships on planes?'

> *It is not necessarily impossible for human beings to fly, but it so happens that God didn't give them the knowledge of how to do it. It follows, therefore, that anyone who claims he can fly must have sought the aid of the devil. To attempt to fly is therefore sinful.*
>
> – ROGER BACON, 13TH CENTURY PHILOSOPHER

Catching an Eyeful

The huge London Eye Ferris wheel on London's South Bank has been an enormous success and gained a lot of publicity for its sponsor, British Airways. Sadly the millennium laser beam display used on it wasn't pilot friendly – a British Midland pilot complained of being temporarily dazzled by a searchlight-style beam from it when on approach to Heathrow.

An even more arresting sight is occasionally to be seen on the Eye. It seems that amorous couples, either seduced by the fact that a 20-minute trip on the wheel is called a 'flight' and hoping that they will qualify for the mile-high club despite the lack of altitude, or simply being shamelessly exhibitionist, have rented out a transparent pod in order to make whoopee in full view of the whole of central London.

The £285 'Cupid's Capsule' private trips are promoted as a 'romantic champagne flight for two' but such has been the attraction to couples intent on some sexual high jinks that British Airways has been forced to employ stewards to keep watch and put a stop to such shenanigans.

‘ *Lovers of air travel find it exhilarating to hang poised between the illusion of immortality and the fact of death.*

– ALEXANDER CHASE, PERSPECTIVES, 1966 ’

Italian Passion

Italians are famous for their high passions, but it is unusual even for them to indulge in sexual acts with total strangers on packed aircraft. However, that is what happened in March 2002 on board a Varig Airlines DC-10 en route from Milan to Rio de Janeiro.

Flight crew noticed a 'very attractive' Italian lady undoing the trousers of her economy class neighbour and attempting to have sex with him. Egged on by the man's friends, the lady, who had allegedly been drinking, climbed on top of him and endeavoured to join the mile-high club.

Their fun was cut short when a flight attendant grabbed the lusty lady by the hair, and she responded to the intrusion by kicking and biting the stewardess. Once the captain announced that he was diverting the flight to make an emergency landing at Salvador de Bahia because of the incident, the bella donna had to be restrained by cabin crew members to prevent her from entering the cockpit. It is not known whether her intention was to remonstrate with the pilot about the inconvenience or whether she thought her urges might be satisfied in peace on the flight deck.

The unfulfilled filly was arrested by the Brazilian police when the plane landed. Her unidentified Italian 'partner' continued on the flight to Rio and presumably still looks back on his trip with fondness.

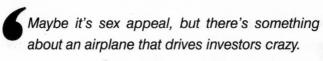

Maybe it's sex appeal, but there's something about an airplane that drives investors crazy.

– ALFRED KAHN, THE 'FATHER OF AIRLINE DEREGULATION'

Love Is in the Air

It will probably come as something of a surprise that one of the most extraordinary stories of drink-fuelled on board sexual gymnastics doesn't involve a major celebrity, or even a minor one. In 1999 two total strangers, who were old enough to know better, found themselves next to one another on an American Airlines flight from Dallas to Manchester.

The 36 year-old woman and 40 year-old man's relationship developed rapidly during the 10 hour flight. To the astonishment of fellow business class passengers they drank heavily, consuming two bottles of wine and numerous glasses of cognac and port before proceeding to have a bit of a fumble under a blanket. But as the court later heard the lady, who was in just her bra and knickers, was asked numerous times to cover herself up. One of the passengers seated in front of the couple apparently saw her flailing feet above her headrest.

Despite the protestations of the cabin crew they continued in their activities. As one witness observed, 'Nothing could stop them. It would have taken a bucket of cold water. They were determined to continue until passions were spent. And they were.' Their excitement subsided rather when the couple, who were both married although not to each other, were arrested on arrival by four policemen and thrown into the cells for six hours. Initially it was not clear whether this was for a 'cooling off' period or outraging public decency, being drunk on board an aircraft and conduct causing harassment, alarm and distress.

They were fined a total of £2,250; the woman ended up losing her job and her partner resigned his position with his company before taking a lesser-paid job. You have been warned!

Perhaps the last word should go to the male half of the randy pair: 'We became a little over-familiar, that's all.'

 An airplane doesn't respond to sex – it only responds to skill.

– 86-YEAR-OLD BETTY JANE WILLIAMS, A FORMER FLIGHT ATTENDANT

Crack in the Toilet

It is certainly not unheard of for couples to sneak off to join the mile-high club in the lavatories of an aircraft. Once the cabin lights dim and most passengers are either asleep or engrossed in the in-flight movie there's ample opportunity to slip into a cubicle and make out. So long as it doesn't disturb anyone else (and don't think they won't have spotted what's going on) the flight attendants sometimes turn a blind eye. However, things can get out of hand, especially in the era of heightened terrorist vigilance.

A gay British couple were looking forward to their visit to New York and decided to get into the mood by smoking crack cocaine and having sex in the toilet of the American Airlines aircraft while in flight from Heathrow. It wasn't long before other passengers became increasingly alarmed as the pair visited the toilet together four or five times during the flight. They might have expected some admonishment from the cabin crew, but they were not prepared for Flight 101 to be escorted into New York's JFK Airport by two F-16 fighter jets as a precaution against a possible terrorist threat. The two red-faced men confessed their 'crime' when taken into custody upon landing and were immediately deported back to London.

> *When it comes to testing new aircraft or determining maximum performance, pilots like to talk about 'pushing the envelope'. They're talking about a two-dimensional model: the bottom is zero altitude, the ground; the left is zero speed; the top is max altitude; and the right, maximum velocity, of course. So, the pilots are pushing that upper-right-hand corner of the envelope. What everybody tries not to dwell on is that that's where the postage gets cancelled, too.*
>
> – ADMIRAL RICK HUNTER, US NAVY

Mile-High in Style

Given that there will always be some who have this uncontrollable urge to engage in sex on board an aircraft but are not prepared to risk a trip to the toilets, are unconvinced by enjoying an intimate moment shrouded in a airline blanket at the back of the cabin, or lack the exhibitionist tendencies of the few bent on performing in front of their fellow passengers, then there is help at hand.

A number of aircraft operators in the US run profitable charter services for amorous couples, allowing them to live out their airborne fantasies in comparative privacy. The Florida-based Key West Mile High Flight Service offers rides in a converted 1968 Piper Cherokee at '5,280 feet – give or take six inches'.

The normally six-seat aircraft has been converted to a two-seater with an open 'lounge' area in the passenger cabin, with a screen behind the pilot providing some privacy. The customer has a choice of 'The Quickie', a 20-minute flight for $199, or 'The Big Bone Islander', 40 minutes of fun for $299. For an extra $50 they can take the trip at sunset. They do a brisk trade, and don't often need to detail the opportunity to their customers; as their advertisement says, 'If we have to explain, you're on the wrong plane.'

Aero Tech of Kentucky have been offering similar flights for 30 years. Although their Cessna aircraft is not specifically configured for the job, they maintain that the presence of seats leads to more fun – rather like doing it in the back of a car, they say.

More luxurious is the offering from TriMotor Air Tours of Fullerton, California, which operates an aircraft equipped with a queen-size bed. A flight with them costs $1,195, but can be priceless; one couple who had tried to start a family unsuccessfully for several years were advised to try something wild and crazy. They took a TriMotor flight and, to paraphrase Johnny Mathis, a child was born. However, it was, as far as we know, not immaculate and it took the normal nine months to see the fruits of their labour.

Not content with the memory, passengers availing themselves of these operator's services can take home a memento like a certificate, badge, mug or T-shirt. Some even offer a video of the event (the exact content of which is not specified). Key West even lets you take home the sheets. However, they may want them back after they've been washed.

No Sex Please, We're Just Nudists

In 2003 an American travel agency specialising in 'clothing-optional vacations' announced that it was organising the first nude flight. However, according to the owners of the travel agency this was not an excuse for naughtiness. 'Inappropriate behaviour is not condoned,' said James Bailey, who owns Castaways Travel with his wife, Donna Daniels. 'This is not a mile-high club, not a bunch of groupies or anything. It's just a fun flight.'

The company chartered a Boeing 727, with 170 seats, for a week's holiday for the nudists in Cancún, Mexico. The crew naturally remained fully clothed, and passengers checked in dressed and had to remain that way for take-off. It was only when the aircraft reached cruising altitude that they got their kit off. Even then, according to Bailey, 'Nude etiquette always requests you take a towel – you always have a towel between you and the seat.' Other precautions on the flight included the fact that no hot drinks or meals were going to be served on board – 'to avoid those nasty little accidents'.

The travel agent, who now books around 50 nudist trips each year, says, 'People are looking for stress relief. In a nudist environment, everyone is the same. There's no culture shock, no hierarchy of social strata, no caste system. Everyone is on the same wavelength.'

The Federal Aviation Administration is taking a hands-off approach: 'We have no regulations pertaining to nudity on board an aircraft.' Does this mean you cannot be arrested on an American aircraft if you take your clothes off? Anyone interested in checking out 'clothing optional vacations' can do so on the web; we'll leave you to find the address!

Renting airplanes is like renting sex: it's difficult to arrange at short notice on Saturday, the fun things always cost more, and someone's always looking at their watch.
– ANON.

Animal House at Altitude

The crew of a charter flight taking US high school students to Mexico to celebrate their graduation knew that their passengers would be in high spirits. The summer post-graduation trip is a rite of passage in American youth culture and is often the first chance the late-teens have to take a trip without teachers, parents or chaperones. Mexico's alcohol laws are more relaxed than in America where the serving of drink to under-21s is usually banned, so it's also a chance to learn about the disinhibiting effects of booze.

Normally the high jinks break out on arrival, but on one Falcon Air flight from Portland, Oregon, with 150 students on board, festivities got under way about halfway through the flight when a crew member and some boys staged a 'wet T-shirt' competition. At the flight attendant's urging, male passengers came up with $60 in prize money and two girls volunteered. The attendant then prowled the aisle pulling further 'volunteers' into the contest. Adding to the sense of excitement, the flight attendant announced, 'We're not going to land this plane until you girls get wet! We've only got so much fuel...'

Once the candidates were assembled and their shirts duly drenched, the judging began. They decided that the captain, as a figure of authority, should judge the contestants. The girls spent about 15 minutes being inspected in the cockpit of the Boeing 727; a shaky video of the event showed them going in and out of the cockpit door.

The question of who was flying the plane during the event was not lost on one of the passengers. Eighteen-year-old Sara Walker of Eugene, who was a student pilot, noted, 'If you have a plane full of irresponsible, unprofessional pilots, crew and students, who the hell's flying the plane?' The FAA launched an investigation after stories of the revelry came out. The winner of the contest is unknown.

 Flying is like sex – I've never had all I wanted but occasionally I've had all I could stand.
– STEPHEN COONTS, THE CANNIBAL QUEEN

Suspect Package

Having gone through the security questions at check-in, had their carry-on bags X-rayed and finally got on board their flight, the passengers on a Monarch Airlines Airbus flying from Goa in India to London's Gatwick Airport in 1999 were not expecting baggage to cause any delays. However, the alarm was raised when suspicious noises were heard from a package and a full-scale alert was triggered. The aircraft diverted to Bombay and the 354 passengers waited tensely for four hours while security services checked the package and aircraft. The aircraft was finally allowed to continue to London when the search revealed the responsible device was a vibrator. The owner of the sex toy didn't volunteer to claim it.

Perhaps it was fear of precipitating a similar mid-air alert that led another passenger to off-load a vibrating toy by dropping it in a rubbish bin at Brisbane Airport Australia, in April 2004. Unfortunately, by avoiding a problem for the aircraft he or she caused an emergency at the airport when the bin was heard humming furiously. Terminal cafeteria manager Lynne Bryant heard the noise and alerted the security staff, who immediately called for the evacuation of the terminal. After three-quarters of an hour the cause of the noise was established and the alert was cancelled. Bryant later said that, in hindsight, the humming had sounded exactly like a vibrator, but, 'You can't afford to take chances.' The incident clearly points to the fact that having a woman in a position of such authority has its advantages.

The issues of travelling with 'personal massagers' are not limited to diverting aircraft or evacuating airports. A Florida resident sued a US airline in 2002 for emotional distress and gender discrimination after she was made to open her luggage and hold up an active vibrator that was inside. The passenger felt humiliated when she was called off the aircraft in Dallas en route from Las Vegas to Florida and asked by a security agent to explain the noise coming from one of her bags. She told the agent that a sex toy that her husband had bought for her in Las Vegas was the cause. The agent requested her to remove it and hold it up for inspection. The passengers on one side of the aircraft and the airline employees nearby had a clear view of proceedings. The airline staff allegedly 'began laughing hysterically' and made 'obnoxious and sexually harassing remarks'. When interviewed by the press about the lawsuit, the lady somewhat surprisingly said, 'I just don't want to be embarrassed any more than I've already been.' So next time you are on a plane and the crew ask you to switch off all portable electrical devices prior to take-off we advise you to take heed.

What Do You Do in a Double Bed?

In 2007 Singapore Airlines took the unusual step of publicly asking passengers flying on its new Airbus A380 aircraft not to engage in any sexual activities. Why is that unusual? The first class area of the superjumbo contains 12 private suites complete with double beds – apparently the suites are not sound-proofed.

It said it did not want anyone to offend other travellers or crew. 'All we ask of customers, wherever they are on our aircraft, is to observe standards that don't cause offence to other customers and crew.' Singapore Airlines have a total of six of the giant planes on order. What's the odds on people not taking any notice of their request.

> *They don't realise that while you're sitting here talking, someone is fucking you. Changing a fare changing a flight, moving something. There's no autopilot, and that's why I've seen a lot of guys come and go.*
>
> – GORDON BETHUNE, CEO OF CONTINENTAL AIRLINES

At a Loose End

Male passengers waiting for their flights in the departure lounge of Israel's Tel Aviv Airport in August 2001 were prepared for a slightly boring wait, perhaps relieved by a drink and a newspaper. They were surprised, therefore, when a naked blonde woman began circulating through the lounge requesting sex. The 25-year-old German tourist decided to fill in the time during the two-hour delay her flight was suffering by enjoying some airport romance with a stranger or two. Sadly the first candidate for a brief encounter wasn't up to scratch and the lusty frau went off in search of a more able partner. Her ardour was finally dampened by the Israeli police when they ordered her to stop her bare-faced display.

And this, ladies and gentlemen, is the very first Fokker airplane built in the world. The Dutch call it the mother Fokker.

– CUSTODIAN AT THE FORMER AVIODOME AVIATION MUSEUM, SCHIPHOL AIRPORT, AMSTERDAM

The Not Mile-High Club

Perhaps intimidated by the confines of the toilets, but certainly not put off by the potential for embarrassment of being caught in flagrante delicto (naturally this is not something purely confined to Italian airlines), a couple of strangers decided to get down to business in Manchester Airport. They thought they would kill some time waiting for a delayed flight by drinking a bottle of Baileys and sneaking off to a quiet spot for romance (we like to think it was not just a drink-inspired lust-fest).

Unfortunately for them, while no other passengers saw them and complained, they were spotted on CCTV by security staff. The British man and Swedish woman had made a bed from their coats and got to know one another a little better. Their passion was doused by a visit from a police officer who broke up proceedings and sent them on their way.

> *Every time we hit an air pocket and the plane dropped about 500 feet (leaving my stomach in my mouth) I vowed to give up sex, bacon, and air travel if I ever made it back to terra firma in one piece.*
> – ERICA JONG

In a Land Down Under

Companies, airline and otherwise, certainly have to worry about their image in this day and age where marketing reigns supreme, which is perhaps why an Australian airline asked a woman to cover her tattoo. The painted lady was made to wear a stewardess' jacket to cover the offending illustration when she flew into Brisbane Airport one day in early 2006. The offending tattoo apparently featured a man and a woman indulging in a sex act. The 36-year-old mother of two reportedly said, 'They're not having sex. No way, I would never get that tattooed on my body,' she said. 'I have children and I do have values.' All in all, it's an indication of how far standards have slipped. In the great days of air travel between the wars no lady would have flown unless she was wearing some of her very best clothes – it was haute couture for the high-flying set.

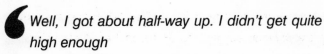

Well, I got about half-way up. I didn't get quite high enough

– SINGER RONAN KEATING WHEN ASKED IF HE HAD JOINED THE MILE-HIGH CLUB

Jamaica? No, She Did It of Her Own Accord

Drink is almost always the precursor to sex on planes, and on a recent British Airways flight to Jamaica it got a couple from Luton into big trouble. At least on this occasion it was a couple and not two strangers who had got acquainted at check-in. They were on board a Boeing 777 with around 200 other passengers and after they were apparently caught 'in the act' they flew into a violent rage and the aircraft had to make an unscheduled stop in Bermuda.

They had paid £2,000 each for their business class tickets to Kingston, Jamaica, and were prepared to take full advantage on what was supposed to be a 10-hour flight. In business class the drinks just keep on coming, whereas, as most of us know, getting a drink in economy seems about as difficult as selling The Big Issue outside the Ivy, and so it wasn't long before they were fully fuelled and ready for action.

This couple opted for the toilet rather than a public show, but the eagle-eyed crew spotted them and, after some banging on the lavatory door, the couple were asked to go back to their seats. Tempers quickly became frayed and the crew were having their work cut out trying to calm things down. When matters became very heated even the captain's intervention failed to get things under control. Eventually the man involved had to be handcuffed – this may normally have been something he liked but on this occasion it made him even more cross, which is what prompted the stop in Bermuda. Here the two offending passengers were off-loaded and then flown back to London. To make matters worse, it was Gatwick and not even 'Luton Airport'.

PLANE SPEAKING

Controller to aircraft that has just landed: *'Bear right, next intersection.'*
Pilot: *'Roger, we have him in sight.'*

Strangers in the Night

On a British Airways overnight flight from Boston to London two business class passengers found themselves in all sorts of trouble after they had sneaked off to the toilet to join the mile-high club. Apparently they were so engrossed in completing their application form that they failed to notice the cabin staff unscrewing the lavatory door, and when they finally removed it the couple were still going at it.

Other apparently embarrassed passengers in the club class cabin had to listen to the couple, who were strangers before they met on board, for an hour groaning, moaning and making thumping noises. A BA spokesman said: 'We do our best to ensure passengers have an enjoyable flight, but we must ensure others are not disturbed or offended.' The couple were given 'a mild rebuke' by flight crew, but no further action was taken against them. When the aircraft landed in London they made a hasty exit.

Apparently the Scots are a nation with more people intent on joining the mile-high club than most others. A couple of years ago randy Scots would rather join the mile-high club than have kids, a survey found. Only 11 per cent of Scots admit to wanting children – the lowest proportion in Britain – but, according to the poll, a fifth dream of making love in a cramped airplane toilet. However, fewer than four per cent have actually plucked up the courage to have sex at 30,000 feet.

The survey, carried out by brewing giants Grolsch, asked 2,000 people what they want to achieve before they die. The most popular choice was swimming with dolphins. A third admitted to dreaming of packing in their jobs and travelling around the world. Almost a quarter of us want to write a best-selling novel before our time is up. And one in five said they wanted to meet their all-time hero. A spokesman for Grolsch said the findings showed Scotland is a nation of thrill-seekers. He added: 'If there's one lesson to learn, it's to throw caution to the wind and live the dream because the only thing you'll regret is not doing it.'

Sex is in the air... again

… see that got you attention. It has also got the attention of Air New Zealand as the airline has designed their new flat bed business premier class seat so that no one else is in sight when you are in your 'bed'. This is all for the benefit of that female corporate traveller who has been 'very badly served', over the years. This is according to their spokesman.

He went on to explain that the airline has taken a leaf out of the book of the Hilton chain that allows female guests to order room service and pay the same price as they would in the hotel restaurant; this is so that they don't feel guilty about eating in their room. Quite how that logic explains how the airline came to think that 'women travellers do not want to find themselves sitting or indeed lying next to a plump, chatty salesman from Iowa so it is trying to avoid these situations.' Salesmen from Iowa, plump or otherwise, should rise up and defend themselves.

Apparently all new Air New Zealand aircraft are being fitted with security cameras so pilots can keep an eye on the cabin. The systems are meant to prevent potential terrorist hijacking threats and also act as evidence in cases of air rage. The president of the New Zealand Airline Pilots' Association said the cameras were 'the way of the future' because the protocol on leaving the flight deck had changed in the past few years.

How long before we're going to have the first case of a video recording of applicants for the Mile-High Club appearing on YouTube?

Chapter**TWO**

Did You Pack Your Own Bag?

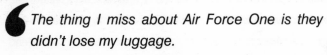

The thing I miss about Air Force One is they didn't lose my luggage.

– PRESIDENT GEORGE BUSH SR.

F or obvious reasons security issues have come to dominate both airline and airport management planning and operational activity. Logically and rationally all of us can see the need for security. The absolute requirement for us all to be vigilant needs no explanation, or justification. So why is it that people often behave so badly and so stupidly when faced with what seem like simple procedures to protect them from danger? Sometimes it seems like the inmates want to run the asylum.

Part of the problem is possibly related to the fact that many people, when travelling, are just a little on edge. Tensions are raised and so it's an ideal opportunity for them to be tipped over that edge by security staff who, while they may just be doing their job, do it with astonishing insensitivity at times.

There is of course a trade-off to be made between security and maintaining the semblance of an efficient air transport system. What irks both the regular and the sporadic traveller are the entrenched views of some of the 'jobsworths' seeking to impose their rules on the general public. This is sometimes not the fault of the individual security zealot; they are merely victims of circumstance. For example, why is it that so many airports seem to have so few of their scanners operating at peak travel times?

Given that we are all totally onside with the idea of secure air travel, some of what follows is at best totally baffling, and at worst astonishingly stupid.

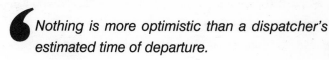

Nothing is more optimistic than a dispatcher's estimated time of departure.

– ANON.

No Laughing Matter

There was a time when the risk of terrorism was taken very lightly. The pre-flight security questions were considered a bit of a joke. One stand-up comedian even had in his act a piece about when he last flew and they asked him if he'd packed his own bag. He replied, 'No, I had my friend from the Hizbollah do it for me.' It's no longer wise to joke about such things, with arrests for bomb 'humour' a regular feature of airport police forces' days.

As the passengers were boarding a 737 in Canada the flight attendant asked to see a lady's boarding pass. The passenger replied, 'I don't have a boarding pass, I'm a hijacker.' She then pushed past onto the aircraft. The flight attendant mentioned this rudeness to the captain, who set about following procedure to the absolute letter of his company's policy. The rude passenger began to regret her behaviour when eight Mounties took her off the aircraft. Once on the jetway the police officers tightly surrounded the passenger, but suddenly all took a step back. The lady was so scared she had wet herself.

Everyone knows that it's unwise to greet a friend on a plane with a loud 'Hi Jack!' for fear of misunderstanding, but the case of one woman illustrates how seriously out of hand things can get. The lady, a 48-year-old librarian, found herself arrested when she tried to explain to her husband why American Airlines would not let them on board a flight.

The couple had been re-routed on American Airlines following the postponement of a USAir flight to Charlotte, North Carolina. They had arrived ready to board the AA flight, but their luggage had remained on board the USAir plane. The airline's security policy prevented passengers and their bags travelling on separate flights, but the husband failed to see the logic of this in the circumstances.

His wife explained the idea to him succinctly: 'This is the way we planned it; that we fly American, that our bags go on USAir and that the bomb in our bags can blow up their airplane. Now do you understand?'

She faced five years in prison for her ill-judged commentary, and spent a great deal of 'time, effort and money' clearing her name.

> *The odds against there being a bomb on a plane are a million to one, and against two bombs a million times a million to one. Next time you fly, cut the odds and take a bomb.*
>
> – BENNY HILL

FLYING FACTS

Women in the Cockpit

The first all-female flight deck crew on a commercial flight were Emily Warner and Barbra Cooke, who operated a Frontier Airlines flight from Denver to Lexington in Kentucky in June 1984.

Fit to Burst

One of the hazards facing the less frequent flyer is the misjudgement associated with the amount of time you may be required to be out of range of a lavatory when flying – notwithstanding the added hazard of being in the window seat when the two people next to you are far too big to be sitting in an economy seat and have both fallen asleep.

In the same vein I well remember flying from Rio de Janeiro to Miami in the 1970s and upon waking I was instantly aware that it wasn't the bottom that was about to fall out of my world and I was trapped in the middle seat of five in the 48th row of economy, but that's a different story.

How much it was a misjudgement on the part of a German student who was flying home from Florida, or just an out and out emergency, is none too clear. He complained that he needed to visit the lavatory, despite the 'Fasten Seat Belts' sign being illuminated, since his bladder was going to 'explode'.

For some inexplicable reason the flight attendant believed he was threatening to bomb the plane. Not so much a case of two people divided by a common language, as simply lost in translation. The aircraft was turned around and flew back to Fort Lauderdale-Hollywood

International Airport where the hapless scholar was arrested and charged with five counts of felony. Given the seriousness of the charge he faced a fine of up to $1.25 million and up to 20 years in prison. The student's family couldn't meet the $100,000 bail that the court had filed for (Are you thinking what I am? If you seriously thought this man to be a potential terrorist why would you let him out on bail?) and the poor soul spent nine months behind bars awaiting trial. Good sense finally prevailed when Chief US District Court Judge Norman C. Ruettger described the business as a 'travesty of justice' and freed the unfortunate student.

> *From the air, the distinctions between residential, commercial, and industrial areas are easily understood while town, county, and state boundaries go unseen.*
>
> – OLIVER GILLHAM, THE LIMITLESS CITY, 2001

Feeling Lonely

In those far-off days when America thought that Cuba and Fidel Castro were a serious threat to world peace it was not an unheard of act for some dissident or otherwise unhappy Cuban to attempt to hijack an aircraft in order to fly to America to find freedom. In one unusual case a man, his wife and their baby hijacked an American aircraft and made it fly to Cuba. For a while it seemed like they would get away with it, at least in so far as they made it to Havana Airport. It was there that things started to go wrong.

The 747 and its occupants were sitting on the ground in Havana while the hijacker negotiated with the authorities from the upper deck of the aircraft. They had been there some time when an enterprising steward decided to open the downstairs galley door and see if there was any way to escape. He took all the seat-belt extensions that he could find, clipped them together and secured the end inside the aircraft. He lowered the other towards the ground and found that it reached to within a few feet. He waved a tablecloth out of the hatch to let any waiting marksmen know there was no threat then climbed down the makeshift rope, dropped to the tarmac and ran off under the aircraft towards the rear.

One by one all the passengers and crew climbed down the seat belts and made their escape. Finally the two flight attendants who had been keeping the hijacker talking were left. One said to him, 'I'm going downstairs to get a drink. Would you like anything?' And left. After a few minutes the final crew member said to the hijacker, 'She's been a while, I'm going to see what's taking her so long.' And left too.

After 20 minutes the hijacker realised that he was holding an empty plane hostage and gave himself up.

The excitement didn't end there. After their ordeal and dramatic escape, the crew were visited by Fidel Castro, who presented each of them with a signed photograph of himself. His largesse didn't extend to the American airline, however. It was refused the fuel to get home until the captain paid for it with his credit card.

FLYING FACTS

Fact or Fiction

FedEx almost went bankrupt as Christmas 1973 approached. Fred Smith convinced his workforce to take a 30 per cent pay cut and took what money was left in the company coffers to Las Vegas and made enough to ride out the storm.

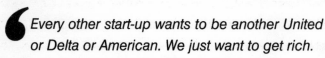

Every other start-up wants to be another United or Delta or American. We just want to get rich.

– ROBERT PRIDDY, CHIEF EXECUTIVE OF VALUJET

Test Case

In the post-9/11 era airline staff are extremely vigilant for any attempted hijacking. The security systems and procedures are under constant review and improvement. But the airlines are still trying to carry huge numbers of passengers to their destinations every day. One captain had to handle a very difficult situation when it was reported to him that a man in his mid-30s of Middle Eastern appearance had boarded the aircraft for a flight from Washington, DC, and had paused to look carefully at the cockpit door.

The captain thought, 'It's probably nothing, but we'd better check out the passenger.' The gate agent was able to print out the passenger's travel itinerary: Atlanta–Washington, DC–Newark–New York. Not a lot of comfort there. They checked his address. It was a rented apartment in Atlanta. No comfort either. The flight was now late for take-off.

The pilot decided they had better do their best to control the situation so asked the head of cabin crew to see if there was a frequent flier sitting in an aisle seat in the first few rows behind the suspicious passenger. Fortunately there was, so he was upgraded into first class and one of the armed sky marshals took the seat to keep an eye on the dodgy-looking character.

At the time there was a regulation that passengers were not allowed out of their seats until half an hour after take-off from Washington. Out of 142 passengers, the suspicious man was the only one who wanted to get up. He tried three times, but in each case was prevented from doing so by the cabin crew. The officer sitting behind him was quietly monitoring his every move. After 30 minutes the seat-belt light had to be turned off and people could move around. The man went to the toilet three times in 15 minutes.

None of this is a crime, but he was sufficiently suspicious in his actions and such is the level of vigilance that airport security met the passenger as he exited the aircraft. He may have been entirely innocent, or he may have been a terrorist testing the security systems before a planned attack.

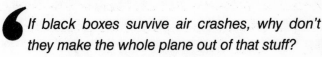

If black boxes survive air crashes, why don't they make the whole plane out of that stuff?

– AMERICAN COMEDIAN GEORGE CARLIN

Eye Opener

Have you ever got on an early morning flight and been amazed just how many people ask for a drink, other than tea and coffee that is? The reasons why they do so are of course many and varied. There are those who just need a drink to get themselves through the whole experience – fear is a dreadful thing. I remember one early morning flight from Glasgow to London where a lady passenger was so fearful that she had taken a couple of Valium, and then once on board she set about the drink. Twenty minutes from landing she had fallen sound asleep and when the aircraft landed in London she was still out for the count and had to be carried off the plane. There are others for whom that early morning drink is the hair of the dog, and then there are those who have a drink problem. Last of all there are those who drink for the simplest of reasons: it's free.

So nothing unusual on the 6.30 a.m. flight from Detroit to Fort Wayne, Indiana, when two men got on and one started drinking. It's only a 25 minute flight but by the time they arrived he'd already become a little excitable. Some passengers disembarked, and more got on for the next leg to Indianapolis. Soon enough they were underway again and the man continued to drink. His behaviour went from rowdy to downright obnoxious, to such an extent that the flight attendant informed the captain.

Once they arrived at Indianapolis the captain decided the man's behaviour was unacceptable and ordered him off the flight. The drunken passenger argued that he needed to carry on to Atlanta, but the captain was having none of it. His sober companion appealed too, but the captain was unmoved and the inebriated man was taken off the flight.

Once they were in the air again and about 25 minutes into the hour and a half flight to Atlanta, the cockpit radio crackled into life.

The conversation went like this:

'Captain, did you kick a passenger off your flight in Indianapolis?'

'Yes, he was drunk and disorderly.'

'Was he with someone?'

'Yes.'

'Is he still on the plane?'

'Yes.'

'That's good. The man you ejected was Sergeant XXX from the Detroit Police Department and the man with him is the prisoner he's escorting.'

The captain immediately asked the flight attendants to upgrade the prisoner to first class. Once they landed in Atlanta, he went back to see the man and thanked him for flying with the airline. The pilot then told him that some people had come to meet him off the flight. 'You know?' asked the man. 'Yes, we know,' replied the captain. The white-collar prisoner was then returned to custody and his case continued. It is not known how the sergeant's return to the office went, or whether he has yet lived the episode down.

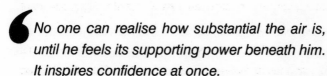

No one can realise how substantial the air is, until he feels its supporting power beneath him. It inspires confidence at once.

– AVIATION PIONEER OTTO LILIENTHAL

Getting Away with It

An event in the 1970s still remains a mystery despite the best efforts of the FBI. It continues to be the only unsolved hijacking case in the US, and seems likely to be kept open until the individual involved can no longer be alive.

On 24 November 1971 a slim man calling himself Dan Cooper flew on a Northwest Orient Airlines Boeing 727 from Portland, Oregon, to Seattle, paying in cash for the one-way ticket. He sat at the back of the plane. Shortly after take-off he showed a stewardess the contents of his bag – red sticks which looked like dynamite and a bundle of wires. He told her it was a bomb and that he wanted $200,000, four parachutes and 'no funny stuff'.

When the plane landed at Seattle-Tacoma International Airport the authorities gave him what he had asked for. He demanded that the aircraft fly towards Mexico via Reno at no more than 10,000 feet. He jumped out of the plane over southwestern Washington State and has never been heard of since. Cooper was careful in his choice of aircraft. If he had chosen a conventional side-opening door and jumped out it would likely have been fatal. Boeing 727s have a rear air stair that made his exit far safer. (Boeing subsequently changed the design of the 727 and added what has been called a 'Cooper Vane' that prevents the air stair being lowered in flight.) Some of the ransom was recovered when a child dug up a bundle of $20 bills on a sandbank of the Columbia River west of Vancouver in 1980. The authorities know no more about Cooper, other than that he drank whisky, smoked Raleigh cigarettes and was familiar with aerodynamics.

The town of Ariel, Washington, close to where it's thought Cooper landed, holds a Dan Cooper ceremony every year to commemorate the incident. In 1981 a film starring Robert Duvall and Treat Williams was made about the affair.

If God had really intended men to fly, he'd make it easier to get to the airport.

– AMERICAN WIT GEORGE WINTERS

Parting Shot

A German tourist acquired a novel memento of his trip when he found a pistol in his suitcase when he arrived home after a trip to Israel. He was advised that the Israeli airport security agents occasionally sneak inoperable firearms into passengers' baggage to test the screening agents. Normally, however, they take them out again before the bags are loaded onto the plane.

'TWA 2341, for noise abatement turn right 45 degrees.'

'Center, we are at 35,000 feet. How much noise can we make up here?'

'Sir, have you ever heard the noise a 747 makes when it hits a 727?'

Bad Shoe Day

Next time you have your bags searched at the security checkpoint, spare a thought for the unfortunate shoe salesman en route from Shanghai to New York. The 27-year-old man was planning to debut his new invention at a trade show in New York, where he was hoping that self-heating shoes would take the world by storm.

However, the FBI, San Francisco police and National Guard troops were scrambled to secure United Airlines Gate 75 and interrogate the man when his prototype size 10 loafers wired with batteries and heating elements were spotted in his bag at a security check.

The authorities quickly realised that he wasn't a threat and allowed him to continue his journey, but just to be sure they blasted the shoes to pieces with a shotgun.

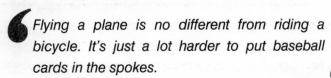

Flying a plane is no different from riding a bicycle. It's just a lot harder to put baseball cards in the spokes.

– CAPTAIN REX KRAMER, IN THE MOVIE AIRPLANE

Escort Service

In August 2002 the passengers on Continental Airlines Flight 61 from Brussels bound for New York were surprised to look out of the windows and see a pair of RAF Sea Harriers flying alongside within feet of the airliner.

Contact had been lost between the cockpit and the airline's Houston, Texas, controllers. Despite repeated attempts on a range of frequencies they could not raise any response from the flight crew.

Fearing the worst, they alerted the UK authorities as the plane was in British airspace. The Sea Harriers were diverted from a training flight between RNAS Yeovilton and Cottesmore to fly alongside the passenger aircraft and establish visually what was going on in the cockpit. When he spied the warplanes within touching distance of the windscreen the pilot very quickly got into contact with ground controllers, and the flight continued without incident to its destination.

In America there are two classes of travel – first class, and with children.

– ROBERT BENCHLEY

Riding Along on a Carousel

Not long after Robert Mugabe came to power in Zimbabwe he was to visit London and was booked on a British Airways 747 from Harare to London. When it came time for him to board he did so at the last minute and was accompanied by a whole bunch of people, including some security men who were to be guarding their leader. These guys were all carrying guns and the BA captain and ground staff in Harare were not happy with this arrangement. As we all know, guns and aircraft don't mix. After a good deal of debate, not to say argument, the security men were relieved of their weapons. This was mostly as a result of the captain refusing to take off unless they did. Their weapons were all put in a bag and secured with the crew bags in the hold.

The rest of the trip passed off uneventfully until they got close to London, when the captain was informed that Heathrow was fog-bound and it was likely that they would have to divert. Given the importance of one of their passengers the aircraft remained in the holding pattern as long as possible before finally having to divert to Edinburgh when shortage of fuel became an issue.

On landing at Edinburgh the passengers disembarked and when the aircraft was clear so did the crew. Because the crew were going to have to be flown back to London on a shuttle flight they had to collect their bags from the normal baggage carousel. All the passengers had picked up their baggage and had left the terminal, including the Zimbabwean president and his entourage. When the crew arrived to pick up their bags everything was all present and correct, except that there was one extra bag. The holdall containing the guns was merrily going around the baggage belt.

> *In the space age, man will be able to go around the world in two hours – one hour for flying and one hour to get to the airport.*
>
> – NEIL MCELROY, LOOK, 1958

The Lost Box

Airlines are often called upon to fly coffins, usually when someone is going to their home country for burial. Sometimes people die when they are abroad and then the body is flown home. Some years ago a family were on holiday in Portugal when the husband sadly died and the coffin was flown to London aboard the same plane as his family. When the widow and her children had cleared Customs and Immigration at Gatwick they were taken to the freight shed, where a hearse had been arranged to pick up the coffin.

When the family arrived at the warehouse the hearse was there, but unfortunately no coffin. All the freight had been brought into the warehouse from the aircraft, but there was absolutely no sign of the coffin. The family were naturally distraught and could not understand how a coffin had just disappeared... nor for that matter could anyone else. Senior managers were dispatched to the freight shed to deal with the situation and promised a thorough investigation. Most important of all they said that they would find the coffin.

Naturally, blame fell on the Portuguese loading staff. They had obviously failed to load the coffin or worse still put it on the wrong flight – but to who knows where? Eventually, after 48 hours, it turned up in Caracas in Venezuela, and the Portuguese were totally innocent. It had been loaded on the aircraft in Lisbon but no one had thought to unload it in London. The coffin had remained on board and gone with the aircraft on its next flight from London to the Venezuelan capital.

Why do Russian aircraft look like bad copies of aircraft built in America and Europe? Because they are!
– ANON.

Great Plane Robbery

Dan Cooper's escapades in the 1970s may have been the inspiration for another airborne stick-up, but the mile-highwayman lacked his predecessor's sangfroid and good preparation. In 2000 a Philippine Airlines Airbus was on a 90-minute flight from Davao to Manila when a hysterical man wearing a blue ski mask and goggles threatened 278 passengers and 12 crew with a grenade and a pistol.

Claiming that his family had left him, his wife had gone off with a policeman and he needed money, he forced the cabin crew to collect cash from the passengers. As they went along the aisles taking money the maniac wildly fired his gun into the aircraft's bulkhead. Against the odds the bullets didn't hit any controls or pierce the aircraft's skin causing depressurisation and a potential major catastrophe.

He wielded the grenade with its pin removed as he confronted Captain Butch Generoso (why do pilots all seem to have such great names?) and ordered him to return to Davao City. When informed that the aircraft lacked the fuel to make it, he instructed the pilot to descend to 6,000 feet and circle. The man then stuffed the bank notes into his pockets and a bag and strapped on a home-made parachute.

The cabin was depressurised and a flight attendant opened a door. Finally, with the aid of a stewardess who was ordered to push him (an instruction she was probably quite happy to follow), he jumped out of the aircraft about 30 miles from Manila. The crew was unable to close the door again so the aircraft had to land with it open.

As a warning to others who may be inspired by this particular form of robbery the postscript makes for sombre reading. Apparently the parachute failed to hold together and a witness on the ground said: 'I saw the parachute separate from the person.' The local chief of police later told reporters, 'The body was embedded in the ground with only the hands protruding.'

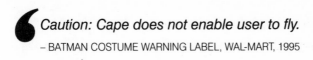

Caution: Cape does not enable user to fly.
– BATMAN COSTUME WARNING LABEL, WAL-MART, 1995

Shaggy Dog Story

A man was sitting in a plane that was about to take off when a man with a dog occupied the empty seats alongside him. The dog sat in the middle, and the first man was looking quizzically at the dog when the second man explained that he and the dog worked for the airline.

The dog's owner, to put the passenger's mind at ease, said, 'Don't mind Rover, he's a sniffer dog, the best there is. I'll show you once we get airborne and I set him to work.' The plane took off and had levelled out when the handler said to the man beside him, 'Watch this.' He told the dog, 'Rover, search.' The dog jumped down, walked along the aisle and sat next to a woman for a few seconds. It then returned to its seat and put one paw on the handler's arm. He said 'Good boy.' He turned to the passenger and said, 'That woman is in possession of marijuana, so I'm making a note of this, and the seat number, for the police who will apprehend her upon arrival.' 'Fantastic!' replied the first man.

Once again he sent the dog to search the aisles. The dog sniffed about, sat down beside a man for a few seconds, returned to its seat and placed both paws on the handler's arm. The airline employee explained, 'That man is carrying cocaine, so again, I'm making a note of this, and the seat number.' 'I like it!' said the first man. Once again he sent the dog to search the aisles. Rover went up and down the plane, and after a while sat down next to someone, but then came racing back, jumped up onto the seat and emptied his bowels all over the place. The first man was surprised and disgusted by this, and asked, 'What the heck is going on?'

The handler nervously replied, 'Err, he's just found a bomb!'

Now I know what a dog feels like watching TV.

– A DC-9 CAPTAIN TRAINEE ATTEMPTING TO CHECK OUT ON THE 'GLASS COCKPIT' A-320

FLYING FACTS

Happy Landings

It's not just on charter flights that people clap when the plane lands; they do it on almost every flight in Russia.

PC Down Under

This story is a double whammy. It highlights the absurdity of the politically correct world in which we now live with airlines panic-stricken that they might do the wrong thing. Qantas has apparently decided to introduce a new policy that affects men travelling alone. The Australian airline, which operates domestic flights in New Zealand, has introduced a policy that prevents unaccompanied children from being seated next to men. The spokesman said: 'The airline believed it was what customers wanted.'

News of the policy leaked out when an Auckland man, Mark Worsley, reported that an air steward approached him after take-off on a Christchurch to Auckland flight and told him to change seats with a woman sitting two rows in front. The steward said it was the airline's policy that only women were allowed to sit next to unaccompanied children. 'At the time I was so gobsmacked that I moved. I was so embarrassed and just stewed on it for the entire flight,' said Mr Worsley, the 37-year-old father of two-year-old twins.

The absurdity of the policy will be tried to the limit when there are full flights and the Qantas stewards are furiously trying to play musical chairs with the passengers. It will turn into an onboard game of solitaire.

To make matters worse the PC madness has spread to Air New Zealand, which confirmed that it had a similar policy to that of Qantas. 'Airlines are temporary guardians of unaccompanied minors so we have preferred seating for them,' she said. When their spokeswoman was asked if the airline considered male passengers to be dangerous to children, she replied: 'That's not what I said.' When it was suggested that that was the implication of the policy, she repeated: 'No, that's not what I said.'

Chapter**THREE**

Do You Know Who I Am?

I don't mind flying. I always pass out before the plane leaves the ground.

– A LONG-LEGGED SUPERMODEL

t was as recently as the 1950s that the first jet airliner flew across the Atlantic on a scheduled flight between London and New York. It was not, for once, an American aircraft or airline but a British Overseas Airways Corporation Comet that inaugurated the service in early October 1958. Before the month was out a Pan American Boeing 707 began services from New York to Paris. Six months before either service began Frank Sinatra released one of his great Capitol albums; its title was Come Fly with Me and Frank was right on the button in terms of appealing both to Americans and British people on the whole romance of travel.

Back in 1958 Sinatra's evocative invitation to 175 million Americans was little more than something they could dream of. For a start, hardly any of them had a passport, let alone the money to travel. For the masses a trip overseas on an aeroplane was pure fantasy. Frank, of course, being both rich and famous, took it all in his stride.

Travel, and in particular air travel, has always had the authentic ring of celebrity about it.

These days almost anyone can travel, indeed it's been said that allowing so many people to fly has spoilt it for those who see it as their divine right. There are many people who have no idea of what it feels like to turn right when they get on board an aircraft. While many are business people the rest of those who fly near the front, or on the upper deck of those long-haul aircraft, are invariably the rich and famous. The public are fascinated by celebrity at the best of times, and ever more so today. But when it comes to the exploits of those who are in Andy Warhol's 'famous for 15 minutes' club we are particularly excited by what they get up to on planes.

Those who live under the intense glare of the media spotlight 24/7 can expect that their behaviour on board aircraft will come in for even more scrutiny. Given that fact then it is perhaps surprising that so few examples of serious celebrity sex have come to our attention.

One notable aspect of celebrity travel is how many of them expect one of two things, either a free or a cheap ticket, and when they have bought the cheapest economy fare, how naturally they expect not to be made actually to sit in economy class. There is not enough room to recount the multitude of stories that check-in staff in particular will tell about the vast numbers of celebrities of all grades who, as they hand over their boarding pass, utter those dreaded words, 'Do you know who I am?' Unfortunately these days it's as often as not people who just have ideas above their station. Businessmen and even those in government have now got in on the act. Recently a British diplomat was flying home from Thailand when he was heard to shout those immortal words, or at least a variation upon them. It landed him in Isleworth Crown Court on a charge of being drunk on board an aircraft. Still, what can you expect when, in a recent survey of 14 year olds, 60 percent of them, when asked, 'What do you want to be when you grow up?', replied, 'Famous.' There will be a time in the not too distant future when everyone will be a celebrity, but – guess what – to most of us the luxury behind the curtain that divides first class from economy will remain a mystery!

PLANE SPEAKING

Student Pilot: *'I'm lost; I'm over a big lake and heading toward the big E.'*

Controller: *'Make several 90 degree turns so I can identify you on radar.'*

Short pause...

Controller: *'OK then. That big lake is the Atlantic Ocean. Suggest you turn to the big W immediately.'*

Best Seat in the House

Celebrities are notorious for their eccentric behaviour and some are well known for their close relationships with animals. And some manage to combine the two...

A very well-known blonde celebrity who was married to an extremely wealthy, elderly Texan man was taking a flight in first class with her secretary and lawyer. It was widely known that she had a tiny dog as her constant companion, but this was nowhere to be seen as she swept on board wearing a white fur coat, fur hat and sunglasses.

The flight attendant thought it was a little unusual when the celebrity asked for her steak to be cut up into very small pieces and regularly wanted cups of water, until he caught a glimpse down the lady's ample cleavage and the mystery of the little dog's whereabouts was solved.

> *In order to invent the airplane you must have at least a thousand years' experience dreaming of angels.*
>
> – CANADIAN POLITICIAN ARNOLD ROCKMAN

A Dog's Gotta Do What a Dog's Gotta Do

The strangely named Paris Hilton (I wonder if she's named after Paris, France or Paris, Texas?) was travelling between Los Angeles and New York with her two small dogs. During the flight she took them into the lavatory, spread paper towels on the floor and let them 'go' if they needed to. Unfortunately during this process the aircraft hit turbulence and the unlocked toilet door sprang open, releasing the two dogs. A quick-acting flight attendant leapt into action and scooped up the two canine escapees as they emerged from the cubicle. As she stood up proudly with one under each arm she looked into the toilet to see that the young heiress had decided that she needed to 'go' too. It is believed that the celebrity is very careful about locking toilet doors now.

The Wright Brothers created the single greatest cultural force since the invention of writing. The airplane became the first World Wide Web, bringing people, languages, ideas, and values together.

– BILL GATES, MICROSOFT CORPORATION

Air Pistol

Notorious punk icon and Sex Pistol's bass player Sid Vicious had a short and dramatic life, the sort which would test even the most loving mother's patience. Not so his doting mum Anne Beverley. She has been accused of supplying the heroin which killed him, which may or may not be true, but it also seems she may have let him down after death.

While the official line is that his ashes were scattered on his girlfriend Nancy Spungen's grave in Philadelphia, witnesses maintain that Beverley dropped the urn at Heathrow, smashing it and sending the contents into the airport's ventilation system.

Smells like teen spirit?

I've never known an industry that can get into people's blood the way aviation does.

– ROBERT SIX, FOUNDER OF CONTINENTAL AIRLINES

The Iron Lady

Many heads of state only travel on government aircraft, but some use commercial flights. For some unknown reason, travelling with a world leader causes great excitement among some of the crew, which was certainly the case on a Lockheed L1011 flight in the 1980s.

In the first class cabin were Margaret Thatcher, Lord King, the then head of British Airways, and various assistants, aides and security personnel. The American flight attendants had been briefed about how to speak to the British Prime Minister and were very nervous. However, everything went well, the Iron Lady belied her image and was charm personified and soon everybody was becoming steadily more relaxed. After a few hours the chief steward even felt bold enough to ask her if he might call her Maggie for the rest of the flight. Apparently she only laughed.

Observing all this from his seat at the rear of the cabin was an MI5 agent. Once the meal had been served and the lights dimmed he quietly approached one of the stewards and asked him if he knew any good bars at their destination; he remembered one with a tree inside it. The steward thought for a while before replying cautiously that the only one he could think of was called Hoola's, but it was a gay establishment. To the steward's surprise the MI5 agent was delighted to join the steward and some friends for the evening in the bar, rather undermining the image of British Secret Service agents created by the Bond films.

FLYING FACTS

Boeing after Boeing

The Boeing 767 entered service in 1982 with United Airlines. Since then almost 1,000 have been built and delivered. The Boeing 757 entered service in 1983 with Eastern Airlines and when production finished in 2004, over 1,050 had been built. If you are flying on a 757 you'll possibly consider yourself to be in good company. The US vice president normally flies in one.

Casino Express

Some people enjoy sufficient wealth to be able to make the airlines operate to suit their schedule, and can even dictate the on board service. In the 1970s a flight attendant had finished her rostered duties and called into the scheduling department to see if she would be released and could go home. Since this was in the days before mobile phones she called from a payphone in the airport terminal. The scheduling people asked her where she was and told her to hold while they checked if there were any more flights for her to work.

After a 10 minute wait they came back on the line and told her to go straight to the gate for a flight to Las Vegas. When she got to the gate she found that she was to provide the cabin service on a specially chartered Boeing 737, which was carrying just four passengers.

When she met her colleague who was to be the other flight attendant it emerged that the passengers had stipulated two stewardesses, one blonde and one brunette, both young and attractive. Both had had similar-length waits on hold when they phoned in to be released while someone from scheduling had raced to look at their pictures to see if they fitted the requirements.

The passengers? Dean Martin, Sammy Davis Jr, Frank Sinatra and Joey Bishop. The Rat Pack had chartered the aircraft to go gambling on a whim.

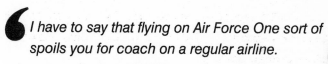

I have to say that flying on Air Force One sort of spoils you for coach on a regular airline.

– PRESIDENT RONALD REAGAN

The Five of Spades

Texas International, a small regional airline that eventually bought Continental Airlines in the early 1980s, was so-named because it flew to Mexico and not, like many residents of the Lone Star State, because it felt Texas was one country and the rest of America was another. The carrier operated scheduled services and also lucrative charter flights to Las Vegas carrying gamblers to the city that has been nicknamed 'the holy land'. These flights were invariably fun affairs, with frequently an all-male passenger complement. The girls who flew these flights had a lot of fun. On one flight where the drink was flowing liberally the banter with a happy crew of three particularly good-looking girls went on right to the time that the aircraft was descending into Las Vegas Airport. As the aircraft was coming in to land the senior flight attendant was making her announcements from behind the curtain at the front of the aircraft.

'Gentlemen, I hope you've enjoyed your flight today with Texas International. I'll ask you to remain seated, with your seat belts firmly fastened, until the captain has bought this li'l ol' aircraft to a complete stop and has turned out the seat-belt sign. I also want to wish you good luck in Vegas and I hope you win lots of money.'

At this everyone on board cheered loudly. 'And if you need a bit of extra luck think of me, and the five of spades.' At this point the flight attendant came out from behind the curtain and stood in the middle of the aisle with her arms aloft and spread in a V, her legs apart. All she was wearing was her black gloves and black shoes. Luckily all the guys followed her earlier instructions and kept their seat belts fastened... but the cheering was even louder.

Our headline ran, 'Virgin screw British Airways'. We'd have preferred 'British Airways screws Virgin', but we had to run with the facts.
– NEWS EDITOR, THE SUN

Flares and Blazers

Many people dream of throwing a drink over someone, but few get to do it to a celebrity during the course of their jobs and get away with it.

Richard Pryor was flying in the first class cabin. A few minutes after take-off the flight attendants noticed the smell of smoke and immediately began to check around the cabin for the source. They soon realised that Mr Pryor had lit a cigarette and dropped it in his lap, igniting his polyester jogging trousers. The quick-thinking stewardess immediately threw a huge jug of iced tea into his lap and averted a disaster.

> *Lady, you want me to answer you if this old airplane is safe to fly? Just how in the world do you think it got to be this old?*
> – ANON.

Doors Ajar

Rock stars behaving like rock stars is what we have come to expect from the kind of people who in all honesty make Spinal Tap seem ordinary. Somehow or another, mixing rock and flying just seems to bring out the worst in our heroes. Of course the fact that some of them may have been indulging themselves prior to flying could be at the root of the problem. One man who had a reputation for behaving badly whenever the opportunity presented itself was Jim Morrison, the lead singer with The Doors. On one occasion he and his companion, Thomas Baker, caused quite a stir on a flight from LA to Phoenix, Arizona. The Federal Bureau of Investigation's report dated 20 November 1969 details the pair's antics, most of which seem very familiar in the light of what present-day rock stars get up to. The report also shows that the sober style of such official documents hasn't changed a bit and still makes the whole episode, if possible, even sillier.

FBI file EP 164-30 details the actions of Thomas F. Baker and James D. Morrison, with Morrison alleged to have been 'responsible for a good portion of the commotion on the flight'. A witness notes that they were both, '... extremely obnoxious from the time they boarded the aircraft'. She goes on to state, '... their actions were very disturbing to everybody in the first class section and it was surprising that these two hippy-appearing individuals were the only boisterous ones as they are two of a group of approximately six individuals who are known as "The Doors", a musical group.'

The report continues, 'Morrison was smoking a cigar while the plane was still on the ground in spite of the fact that the "No Smoking" sign was on. She stated on one occasion Baker went to the toilet and removed all of the bars of hand soap from the compartment and with a handful of the hand soap, walked up and down the aisle asking who wanted to buy some soap and then dumped the entire handful in the lap of his partner, Morrison. She stated Morrison then called the stewardess in an attempt for her to get the soap back. She stated that following the demonstration of the emergency oxygen mask equipment by the stewardess, Baker clearly and loudly for all the persons to hear made the remark, "My girl has one of those and she calls it a diaphragm."'

The witness's statement goes on, 'In her opinion, both had been drinking before they boarded the aircraft and Morrison appeared to be intoxicated. She stated that she heard Baker repeatedly say, "Let me see the comic book." He was directing this remark to his friend, Morrison, and Morrison would then pass the comic book that concealed a bottle of liquor back to Baker to drink. She stated that in addition to that, each of them had two bottles or miniatures of liquor, which is the allowable amount which is served aboard the aircraft, and she noted that Morrison opened one of the bottles and drank it down in what appeared to be one big gulp. She stated that she heard Baker remark to Morrison, "Let's kill them." She stated that in her opinion, this was merely a "popping off" on their part rather than an actual threat to the stewardesses... '

The cabin crew tried to get the situation in hand, and again the scene escalated in a very familiar way. The FBI report carries on its tale: '... after several occasions of talking to Baker and Morrison, the stewardess told them that if they did not straighten out, that she would have to call the captain of the plane to talk to them. She stated that this did not seem to make any difference in their actions or attitudes and the captain of the plane did come back and speak to both Baker and Morrison. The captain informed them that if they did not straighten out, he would turn back to Los Angeles and assured them that the police would be waiting for them on the ground.'

The inevitable end came when the two stars still couldn't quite keep themselves from misbehaving. The report describes the end of the road for the two troublesome musicians: '... this seemed to straighten out the two boys for a short time, but it was not long until they resumed their annoyance and disturbance. She stated when the plane arrived at Phoenix and Baker and Morrison noticed the police at the ramp on gate, Baker jumped up and commented several times, "I didn't do a God-damned thing." She stated the police boarded the plane and after searching Morrison and Baker, they were handcuffed and taken off.'

Perhaps they should have been happy that the man who had been dubbed 'The Lizard King' didn't behave as badly as he did on one occasion while performing on stage. He freed his lizard from the confines of his leather trousers, an act that had him in no end of trouble with the authorities.

FLYING FACTS

Jumbos on Order

In April 1966 Pan Am became the first airline to order the Boeing 747 Jumbo Jet. It entered service with the American carrier in January 1970. The 1,000th 747 was delivered in 1993; almost 1,500 have been built or are on order.

I'm a Celebrity, Let Me in There

Celebrities are well known for behaving as if they are a law unto themselves, but some take matters to extremes when flying. The history of air travel is littered with stories about the regrettable antics of the famous. Here are a few high, or rather low, lights of celebrities behaving badly.

The former Irish Grand National Champion jockey Timmy Murphy caused chaos on board a Virgin Airways flight from Japan to Heathrow when he drunkenly groped a hostess and urinated on an aircraft door. His escapade landed him with a six-month jail sentence.

Ian Brown, ex-front man with rock band the Stone Roses, spent two months in prison after threatening to chop the hand off a stewardess when she offered him duty-free goods. He then hammered on the cockpit door and screamed abuse at the crew as his plane came in to land at Manchester.

Football star Paul Gascoigne's wild mid-air birthday party was reported to have ended in tears when police met the flight returning the England team home from a Far East tour. The full facts have never emerged, but at the time it was alleged that extensive damage was found to have been caused to the aircraft, including smashed television screens and tables in the business class area where the team was sitting.

Jack Nicholson's ex-wife, Rebecca Broussard, was arrested after becoming violent when her drunken demands for more champagne were declined. She allegedly shouted abuse and lashed out at a hostess on the flight from Los Angeles to Heathrow.

Celebrity hairdresser John Frieda, ex-husband of Lulu, assaulted a steward after being told to return to his seat. He pushed a trolley down the aisle into another steward, sending bottles flying. He was fined £1,800 and put on probation for six months.

Coronation Street actress Tracey Shaw blamed pre-menstrual syndrome, complimentary champagne and the pressure of having just stopped smoking for her violent attack on her husband Robert Ashworth in business class on a British Airways flight from the Cayman Islands to the UK. The blazing row culminated in Shaw hitting her husband across the face and bursting into tears.

Rock star and actress Courtney Love was released with a warning by police in London for 'causing harassment, alarm and distress' on a transatlantic flight in 2003. Love, widow of Nirvana star Kurt Cobain, was held on suspicion of disruptive behaviour and endangering the Virgin Atlantic flight from Los Angeles. The former lead singer of rock band Hole was accused of hurling abuse at flight staff during the flight. The crew were said to have tried to calm her down but she refused their requests that she return to her seat and put her seat belt back on. The captain called the airport as Virgin's Flight VS08 was on its approach to Heathrow. Staff on the ground alerted police, who were waiting for her as the plane touched down.

Celebrities can also be the victims of bad behaviour on aircraft. A drunken passenger twice attacked ex-Baywatch star Pamela Anderson during a flight from Florida to California in 2003. Her assailant, Louis Zizza aged 52, was angry at the star because he believed, incorrectly, that she had publicly opposed the war in Iraq.

Actress Lara Flynn Boyle became the centre of attention in the first class cabin of British Airways Flight 282 from Los Angeles to Heathrow in 2005. The star consumed several alcoholic drinks and took some pills before undressing and trying to climb into 'bed' with the stranger sitting next to her. He took the episode with good humour, even joking with the crew that it would make a good story in the papers (it did). Miss Flynn Boyle, who starred in Men in Black 2 and Wayne's World and has had relationships with such famous actors as Bruce Willis, Harrison Ford and Jack Nicholson, continued to flash her breasts at cabin crew and passengers. There were no formal complaints about the star, who also appeared in the TV series Twin Peaks.

Sir Elton John is not immune from throwing the odd hissy fit after a long and tiring trip. When he arrived at Taipei Airport, Taiwan, where he was due to perform a concert a few years ago, he left the aircraft wearing dark glasses and a bright blue tracksuit to face the assembled reporters and photographers. In no mood to force a smile, Sir Elton shouted, 'Rude, vile pigs! Do you know what that means? Rude, vile pigs! That's what all of you are.' It wasn't an ideal start to the final leg of his Far East tour, which he later attributed to the failure of the police to protect him adequately from the media throng.

The Taiwanese media are no strangers to celebrities behaving badly. When he arrived at the airport in 2001 Robbie Williams launched an expletive-laden appraisal of Taiwan. Some reporters objected to his description, to which he replied, 'I didn't insult your country; but I will insult you.' And treated them to a further stream of invective.

In a case that smacked more of air rage than air guitar, REM guitarist Peter Buck was arrested after he was accused of attacking two British Airways staff on a flight from Seattle to London. He allegedly threw yoghurt over them, swore at the captain, knocked a trolley over and tried to steal a knife. He apparently mistook the trolley for a compact disc player, an easy mistake after you've drunk 15 glasses of wine. A Mr Whittaker, REM's tour manager, accompanied him on the flight and he, like Mr Buck, failed to cover himself in glory, although he did take off his shirt and cover his face with ice cream. He tried the old 'Do you know who I am?' approach, apparently telling the captain, 'I am REM and I can make up a story that I was assaulted.' He was later cleared of assault after blaming a sleeping pill and alcohol, which turned him into 'a non-insane automaton'.

Oasis front man Liam Gallagher was banned from Cathay Pacific flights for life after he was apparently 'drunk and disorderly' on a flight from Hong Kong to London in 1998. He hurled food at passengers, refused to stop smoking and threatened the pilot when he tried to calm him down. A fellow passenger labelled him 'arrogant and ignorant grot'. Liam's form continued the following year when he got himself into trouble for allegedly groping a British Airways hostess on a flight from London to Rio de Janeiro.

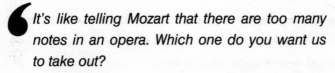

It's like telling Mozart that there are too many notes in an opera. Which one do you want us to take out?

– GORDON BETHUNE, CHAIRMAN OF CONTINENTAL AIRLINES,
COMMENTING ON US GOVERNMENT CRITICISM THAT CARRIERS
SCHEDULE TOO MANY FLIGHTS

Grab a Grand

Back in the late 1980s and early 1990s the owner of a casino in Las Vegas had his own airline that served the stars who regularly came to his hotel. The planes were equipped with velvet seats and four 'staterooms', which had a double bed in each one. Some of the stars made ample use of the staterooms, while others just used the bathrooms in pairs. Perhaps most revealing are some of the antics of those passengers who were just there for the flight.

Apparently Madonna had a special custom-made couch that cost $25,000 and would only be served by male flight attendants. Lauren Bacall, a lady with quite a reputation, would ask younger stewardesses, 'Do you know who I am?' She would apparently demand that she 'get three times the amount of caviar everyone else received'.

Another unnamed ageing star was the worst passenger of all. She was so bad that the flight attendants would mix her a special cocktail made up of Baileys, vodka, Kahlua, milk and... the biggest gobs of spit they could conjure up.

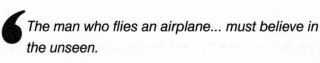

The man who flies an airplane... must believe in the unseen.

– AUTHOR RICHARD BACH

The Cream of Country Music

In 1980, when I was working for British Caledonian Airways, I thought it would be a good idea to get involved with the Country Music Festival that was held at Wembley each year. Sponsoring such an event would give us profile with the fans of the music, who would then naturally rush to book seats to America on board BCAL. The Country Music Festival was a major annual event that was organised by the delightfully named Mervyn Conn. After a number of meetings with Mr Conn at his offices in London we finally agreed a deal that would see BCAL transporting most of the artists, who were flying in from the USA, on our flight from Atlanta. Logistically this was easier said than done as trying to organise 200 musicians to be in Atlanta, many of whom were flying from Nashville and surrounding cities, was a challenge. Actually, it wasn't that over-used euphemism at all – it was a major problem!

Eventually everything was duly organised and my colleague Chris Gilbert drew the short straw and went to Atlanta to oversee things at that end. He was also to fly to London on the same flight as the cream of country music. Everything went pretty well and the flight got off on time. Everything, apart from the fact that a number of the musicians in the smoking section thought that smoking applied not just to cigarettes but also spliffs! God knows what the atmosphere was like on that plane! It was fortunate that in those days the air in the cabin was changed more frequently than it is now. Today it's changed less often in order to save fuel.

The other incident that occurred somewhere over the Atlantic was a fracas on board between Jerry Lee Lewis, otherwise known as the Killer, and his wife, who were travelling in first class. They got into a bit of an argument and the diplomatic skills of the purser and some of the other cabin staff would have done the United Nations proud.

The police met the DC-10 on arrival and no charges were pressed... thank goodness.

Not His Day

The American singer and guitarist Howie Day was arrested at Boston's Logan Airport shortly before Christmas 2005. A few days later he pleaded not guilty to charges of being abusive on board an American Airlines flight from Dallas to Boston. Inevitably he was sitting in first class when he became unruly – allegedly smoking a cigarette in the aircraft toilet, kicking the back of the seat in front of him and being verbally abusive. According to an eyewitness, 'He and a bunch of his people were getting drinks and food from the stewardess and he was kind of charming her, so she was paying him a lot of attention. But it was really disturbing how many drinks they were all allowed. I mean, it was completely out of hand.' Day was arrested by police waiting at the gate when his flight arrived. Day's lawyer admitted the singer was drunk on the plane, and extended an apology for him in court. While he awaited his trial he was banned from flying with American Airlines (we hope he wasn't collecting their frequent flyer miles).

On 26 April 2006 Day was sentenced to one year's probation and ordered to write letters of apology to the crew and passengers and attend an alcohol counselling programme.

This was not the 25-year-old's first run-in with the law. In March 2004, he allegedly locked a woman in the toilet of his tour bus, reportedly because she refused his sexual advances. If that wasn't enough he allegedly broke the mobile phone of another woman who tried to call the police. When questioned by the police over the bus incident Day said, 'That was probably wrong of me, but I felt violated.'

Not a lot of people...
An anagram of British Airways is: This is war by air

PLANE SPEAKING

Controller: *'FAR 1234, confirm your type of aircraft. Are you an Airbus 330 or 340?'*
Pilot: *'A340, of course!'*
Controller: *'Then would you mind switching on the other two engines and give me a 1,000 feet per minute ascent rate, please?'*

Identity Crisis

Tara Palmer-Tomkinson found that being a famous 'It Girl' isn't enough to satisfy airline requirements for formal identification. The star of I'm a Celebrity Get Me Out of Here arrived for a Ryanair flight from Stansted to Blackpool without her passport. Since she lacked proper identification the airline's staff refused to allow her on board the flight.

The embarrassed star was furious with the situation and commented, 'I didn't have anything else they would accept – not even a copy of Hello with my picture in it!' She was forced to drive to Blackpool in order to appear at the hotel opening she was due to attend.

It's a shame for Tara that she didn't have the resources to call upon which another famous person caught without identification did in May 2005. The Prime Minister's wife, Cherie Blair, was travelling to Istanbul, Turkey, in her personal capacity as a barrister. She was horrified to find when she arrived at Heathrow that she had forgotten her passport. There was no getting around customs rules for her, but rather than take a later flight, she was able to have a police motorcyclist make a blue-light run from Downing Street to the airport with the requisite document.

Apparently British Airways delayed the flight until the passport arrived and she was able to carry on with her journey. We put this story here because these days even politician's wives are considered to be celebrities.

It Runs in the Family

Not to be out-done in the forgetfulness stakes, her husband was recently found to be travelling on the Heathrow Express without a valid ticket. Obviously still rather institutionalised from his time as Prime Minister, he discovered that not only did he not have a ticket, he also lacked any cash or cards to buy one with.

It emerged that an aide had given him the money for the ticket the night before, but he'd sadly mislaid it. Eventually his bodyguard offered to pay for it, however (and this is a first to our knowledge) the inspector said there was no need. The operator noted that this was not official policy; 'We welcome all former Prime Ministers on Heathrow Express, but we don't offer them special discounts.' said a spokesman. While on the subject of Heathrow, and the new Terminal 5 in particular, Naomi Campbell was an early victim in 2008 of the teething trouble experienced at the new flagship facility. She was widely reported in the press for her outburst when told her bags had been lost, and got herself banned from BA flights for life on the strength of it. We thought she was having an attack of the 'VIP's' and coming over all hissy if her Gucci luggage wasn't being properly looked after. She's now cleared that one up; she was actually expressing outrage on behalf of all the unfortunate souls whose luggage was also lost at T5. 'I was speaking for all those who were disrespected.' Said the Patron Saint of baggage handling victims.

 All my life, I've never been able to get enough airplanes. This will keep me flying every day.
– ASTRONAUT ROBERT 'HOOT' GIBSON, COMMANDER OF FOUR SPACE SHUTTLE MISSIONS, ON HIS TAKING A JOB AS A SOUTHWEST AIRLINES BOEING 737 FIRST OFFICER, 1996

Floats like a Butterfly

The rich and famous don't always succeed in flouting the rules, as Mohammed Ali found out on one particular flight. After he had boarded the aircraft and sat in his first class seat, the flight attendant asked him to buckle his seat belt in order for the aircraft to push back off the stand. The champ said, 'Superman don't need no seat belt!' The savvy flight attendant replied, 'Superman don't need no airplane, either!' The Greatest buckled up without another word.

Never let an aircraft take you somewhere your brain didn't get to five minutes earlier.

– ANON.

A Fair Sheik?

In 2007 a sheik, from one of the Gulf States, apparently held up a British Airways flight at Milan Airport for nearly three hours because three of his female relatives had been seated next to men they did not know. No business class passengers would agree to swap seats, so the sheik, a member of his country's ruling family, went to the pilot, who had already started the engines, to complain. The pilot ordered the Sheik and his travelling companions – the three women, two men, a cook and a servant – off the plane.

It's unclear whether the sheik was in business class or he was in first class and the women in business class. It's also unclear as to whether they tried to book specific seats before they checked in. I'm absolutely certain that this is not the first time an Arab woman has been sat next to someone she didn't know on an aircraft. I guess the sheik like many other 'celebrities' believes his rank has perceived privileges. Apparently in his case they do not.

> '*Truly superior pilots are those who use their superior judgement to avoid those situations where they might have to use their superior skills.*'
>
> – ANON.

Hello My Darlings

While he probably didn't bother uttering the famous line 'Do you know who I am?' the story of Mohammed Ali is similar to another involving the diminutive British comedian Charlie Drake. Many years ago, when he was, despite his height, a huge star, he was flying from London to a European destination to do some filming. Probably having consumed slightly more of the demon drink than he ought, he apparently began paying a little too much attention to a particularly gorgeous British European Airways hostess. He pushed his luck by asking her whether she would be spending the night at their destination before flying back the next day. When she said she was doing a 'night-stop' as it's called in the airline business, Mr Drake wanted to know the name of her hotel and kept dropping hints about how nice it would be to meet up later that evening. The hostess was the very model of decorum, and dealt with Charlie in a kindly, but never patronising way in offering nothing but polite refusals.

When the aircraft landed and had taxied to the terminal building the captain told the passengers that they could disembark the aircraft. As

Charlie got up and walked towards the exit he said quietly to the lovely hostess, 'What would you say to a little fuck?' Without missing a beat she smiled sweetly and replied, 'Hello little fuck.'

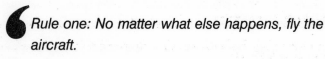

> *Rule one: No matter what else happens, fly the aircraft.*
> – ANON.

Club Class Travel

Some celebrities can cause trouble and make other passengers' lives a misery even when they are not on the same aircraft. A couple of years ago the 233 passengers aboard an Air 2000 flight en route from Gatwick to Faro in Portugal were 35,000 feet or so above France when they were surprised to learn that their plane was going to turn around and return to the UK. The captain was quick to point out it was not a mechanical problem, nor was it putting the passengers lives at risk. Landing back at Manchester Airport the mood turned ugly when the passengers discovered that their five-hour detour had occurred in order to pick up 63 sets of golf clubs belonging to various famous people and professional players who were to compete in the Jimmy Tarbuck Celebrity Golf Classic tournament being held the next day in the Algarve.

The clubs had been due to be transported on an earlier flight but had to be left behind as the aircraft was over-weight. Air 2000 found that it had no other flights able to get the equipment to the destination in time for the start of the tournament, and so the flight control centre had ordered the Faro-bound aircraft and its hapless passengers to return. The passengers were understandably annoyed by the inconvenience, and the mood in the cabin became so ugly that the police were called to restore order. One passenger's behaviour was so aggressive that he was taken off the flight. A case of double bogie?

FLYING FACTS

Supersonic Times

Concorde first flew across the Atlantic in September 1971. Commercial flights with British Airways and Air France began in 1976 and the last commercial flights were in October 2003.

This Is Your Celebrity Speaking

When Independence Air began flying in 2004, the US regional airline had a novel approach to breaking through passenger indifference to the customary safety announcement. They decided to have a variety of celebrities record the briefing and have the flight attendants perform the equipment demonstration in synchronisation with the famous voice. The list of famous (American) voices included Chuck Berry, US soccer star Mia Hamm, comedian Dennis Miller and US political commentators James Carville and Mary Matlin. The results of tests prior to launch were very positive. If the idea ever catches on there's no end to the possible candidates for recording memorable voice-overs; Homer Simpson, Ab Fab's Joanna Lumley, John Humphrys or perhaps Sir Alex Ferguson might all catch the weary traveller's attention.

A cautionary note to any other airlines thinking of using this novel idea. In January 2006 the airline ceased flying. In truth just about every other small carrier that has gone belly up has faced the same problem.

No matter how good the staff are, how much fun they inject into the in-flight experience and no matter how funky their aircraft paint schemes are, success or failure depends on just one thing: how low are your costs and fares in relation to those of your competitors.

> *The modern airplane creates a new geographical dimension. A navigable ocean of air blankets the whole surface of the globe. There are no distant places any longer: the world is small and the world is one.*
>
> – WENDELL WILLKIE, US PRESIDENTIAL CANDIDATE 1940

It's Been Emotional

Ex footballer turned movie hard man Vinnie Jones stayed 'in character' a bit too long when he boarded a Virgin Atlantic flight. The actor, who has played tough-guy roles in a number of films including Lock, Stock and Two Smoking Barrels and Swordfish, admitted assault and using threatening words or behaviour during the May 2003 flight between Heathrow and Tokyo.

Jones slapped a fellow passenger 10 times and threatened to get the crew murdered. It was reported that he suggested that this would cost £3,000, although it was not clarified whether this was each or a package deal. In a statement released after the incident he said he 'regretted it deeply'.

There's little doubt that he did have cause to repent as he was ordered to perform 80 hours community service and fined £1,100. His contract with Bacardi to appear in their TV adverts as the public face of the brand was suspended in the wake of the case. It was also reported that the authorities were lobbied to withdraw his firearms licence in light of his in-flight behaviour.

Prior to embarking on his acting career Jones captained the Welsh national football team and played for Wimbledon, as a member of the famous 'Crazy Gang', Chelsea and Leeds and was player-coach at Queen's Park Rangers. His uncompromising approach to the game was famously captured on camera when he squeezed Paul Gascoigne's testicles to divert his attention.

Not a lot of people...
An anagram of Singapore Airlines is:
Pioneer Asian Girls

Get Me to the Church

As one US television personality planned her marriage in 2004, she maximised the potential for corporate sponsorship. She offered a range of wedding suppliers the chance to have their products plugged on air in return for freebies for her wedding. She took the idea to new heights by listing, on her wedding website, Continental Airlines as the 'official airline of our wedding weekend'. A spokesman for her television show noted that Federal regulations governing on-air product endorsement had not been breached.

PLANE SPEAKING

Lost student pilot: *'Unknown airport with Cessna 150 circling overhead, identify yourself.'*

Take Me to the Pilot

When Bruce Dickinson joined rock band Iron Maiden in late 1981, he played his first gig in Italy after driving 36 hours in a van to get there. He can scarcely have imagined that 20 years later he would be flying to the Mediterranean, and not just as a passenger but piloting a Boeing 737 as a first officer on British charter airline Astreus. After enjoying 12 years with Iron Maiden, Bruce left in 1993, citing the inevitable musical differences. Bruce pursued a solo career and took up flying seriously, gaining his commercial pilot's licence. He did get back with Maiden in 1999 but not before he began flying for an airline. On one occasion, after a flight, he was in uniform in Munich Airport and he was accosted by a German Iron Maiden fan in full battle dress (tour T-shirt, cross, etc.). 'Hello? But I must know... is this the bus to Munich?' The Maiden reunion spawned a number of hits including Wicker Man, which meant that Bruce was the first airline pilot to have a top 10 record on the UK singles chart.

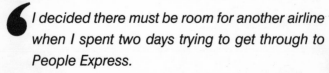

I decided there must be room for another airline when I spent two days trying to get through to People Express.

– SIR RICHARD BRANSON, FOUNDER OF VIRGIN ATLANTIC

'*This is an especially good time for you vacationers who plan to fly, because the Reagan administration, as part of the same policy under which it recently sold Yellowstone National Park to Wayne Newton, has 'deregulated' the airline industry. What this means for you, the consumer, is that the airlines are no longer required to follow any rules whatsoever. They can show snuff movies. They can charge for oxygen. They can hire pilots right out of Vending Machine Refill Person School. They can conserve fuel by ejecting husky passengers over water. They can ram competing planes in mid-air. These innovations have resulted in tremendous cost savings, which have been passed along to you, the consumer, in the form of flights with amazingly low fares, such as $29. Of course, certain restrictions do apply, the main one being that all these flights take you to Newark, and you must pay thousands of dollars if you want to fly back out.*

– DAVE BARRY, IOWA – LAND OF SECURE VACATIONS

'

FLYING FACTS

Death of a Giant

Pan Am, one of the most famous names in aviation history, finally ceased operations in December 1991 after 63 years of flying; the airline had been bankrupt since the previous August.

Beware of Flying Stones

Tales of celebrity excess seem to be a comparatively modern phenomenon. The first people that got into trouble with the airlines and the authorities were, as often as not, pop stars. Possibly that has something to do with the fact that up until the 1960s the chances of people actually flying on planes were very much less. Those celebrities who did so before that time were usually film stars who tended to be a little older, may have been a little better behaved and were also protected by the studio system. Having said that, in the early 1950s Frank Sinatra was accused of hitting a reporter at Los Angeles Airport after he got off a plane and the pressman was apparently bugging him. By the time the Rolling Stones came along in the mid-60s times were changing and they, of course, found it easy to offend people without going anywhere near an aircraft.

This excerpt from Disc and Music Echo of 27 November 1965 records how the Rolling Stones caused a rumpus on a short hop in the Channel Islands:

'The Stones have been banned so often that it gets monotonous now. We have been banned by hotels because of our long hair. Refused meals in restaurants because we have not worn ties. Banned by a television company for being late for a show. And we have even been barred by a major airline, British United Airways. I must tell you about that one because it illustrates the kind of misunderstandings the Rolling Stones have to face all the time. It all blew up one day last August when we were touring the Channel Islands, and were due to fly from Jersey to Guernsey. At Jersey Airport we were climbing up the steps to our plane, when the air hostess said in a stage whisper: "Well boys, have you washed to-day?" That is the sort of comment that really annoys the Stones. But though she could see that they were all angry, she did not let it rest at that. Instead, she added: "When did you last have your hair cut?" That was it. They tore into her quite mercilessly, asking for drinks, coffee and cigarettes, so that she was running up and down the plane, while they criticised her slightest fault – christening her Hilary Hedgehopper. By the time the plane reached Guernsey the hostess was in tears. She had never had to face such abuse in her life, and it was more than she could take. She was sobbing. Naturally, as always happens, the authorities assumed that she was right and we were wrong. The result was inevitable. We were told we could never fly BUA again.'

By 1971 the band had become somewhat infamous for tales of excess, helping to put the drugs into sex and rock 'n' roll. On Monday 29 November 1971, Mick Jagger, his wife Bianca and their daughter Jade; Keith Richards, his partner Anita Pallenberg and their son Marlon; Mick Taylor, his wife Rose and daughter Chloe, the Stones producer Jimmy Miller, and engineer Andy Johns, all flew from Nice to Paris, then Paris to London. They boarded a plane to Los Angeles, but before it took off, there was an incident. According to the Evening

IN-FLIGHT CONFIDENTIAL

News: 'An investigation was ordered after reports from Pan American staff at Heathrow about incidents aboard the plane. Mick Jagger flew in aboard the airliner from Paris with his wife and nine travelling companions. The airliner had been held up by bad weather and the transit time at Heathrow had to be cut short. Mr Jagger and his friends were on their way from a Jumbo jet pier to the airline's VIP suite when it was realised that by the time they got there it would be time to re-board the aircraft. The party were taken back and it was then that the trouble started. According to one official at Heathrow there was a queue of passengers to board the flight but the Jagger party ignored it. The group then went aboard and took seats in the first class compartment. They had first class tickets, but took the wrong seats. Mr Jagger and his friends were asked to move but they refused and according to one airline official they said: "We will sit where we like." A ground hostess insisted that the party took the numbered seats they had been allocated. The girl claimed in her report that she was grabbed by the arm and that foul language, which offended other passengers, was used. Pan American officially confirmed a complaint of foul language. After the captain said that he would not fly the airliner unless Mr Jagger and his friends sat in the proper seats and behaved themselves, they agreed to do this.'

According to Mick the story is a load of nonsense. 'They've made a mountain out of a molehill really. Some people had not turned up to take their seats next to us and we wanted to put one of the children in an empty seat. A receptionist came onto the plane and told us we couldn't use the seat. She was very rude. There was no need to be silly about seating. There was plenty of room and it was not as if we were on a school outing. But she said if we didn't take the child off the seat we couldn't go at all. I said, "Don't be silly," and she said "I'll see that you don't fly Pan Am again." Then she went and spoke to another hostess who said, "They should put them all out at 30,000 feet."'

Probably the airline didn't quite see it that way but after a full investigation they announced a few days later: 'We don't bear a grudge – this is the end of the incident.' Others were not so generous. The Sunday Express said: 'The sooner these boorish heroes of the pop world are cut down to size by airline officials and others the healthier our society will be.'

Perhaps their infamy exacerbated these situations, but it certainly shows that the media's appetite for celebrity antics is not a recent fad.

If God had intended man to fly, he would not have invented Spanish Air Traffic Control.

– LISTER, IN THE BBC TV SERIES RED DWARF

Small is Beautiful

There was a time when the term FedEx was unknown to the world; now it's much like the verb to hoover, in that it has become a generic term for sending small packages. FedEx started as a small package operator in the USA in 1973 and operated from a hub in Memphis, Tennessee. Its unusual concept was to fly every single package into and out of this one hub. So if a shipment was going to New York from Atlanta it still went via Memphis. To begin with many airline people were sceptical of the company's ability to succeed. Most people working in the air-freight business were quick to say, 'It'll never catch on.'

IN-FLIGHT CONFIDENTIAL

In 1976 British Caledonian had begun a service to Houston in Texas from London. There were no problems in filling the aircraft from Houston to London with cargo, on account of the plentiful oil spares traffic, but there was scant cargo in the other direction. Having read about Federal Express I thought the concept was sound and I wrote to its founder and chief executive, Fred Smith, and suggested that there might be some mileage in developing a door-to-door small package service across the Atlantic. I visited Memphis and we began working out the logistics. If people were sceptical of FedEx in America, they laughed out loud at the idea of doing it across the Atlantic.

Undaunted, I persevered and eventually won the backing of the board for such a scheme. The idea was to offer a pick up of a small package in London, fly it to Houston, where the package would be taken into the FedEx system. From there it would be flown to Memphis and then delivered the next day to the customer's door. In theory a Monday pick-up in London would be delivered anywhere in America on Wednesday... and so on.

After much planning and organisation, mostly against the wishes of the traditional cargo people, the service, which we called 'Top Priority', was ready to launch. We decided that we needed an important small package with a bit of kudos attached to it and we came up with the idea of delivering a gold record that had been awarded to the late Buddy Holly. Maria Elena, his widow, lived in Lubbock in Texas and it was duly organised. In order to get some coverage from the press we arranged a breakfast at Gatwick with Tony Blackburn, no less (this was when his celebrity was such that he didn't need to go into the jungle to get the public's attention), to send the package on its way.

Everything went off fine, we got some PR and for the next couple of days life went on as normal.

Somehow or another the gold disc got lost somewhere – it's never been found to this day. It was an omen. We never could get people excited about the concept; door-to-door small packages across the Atlantic as far as the great British public were concerned were never going to catch on.

ChapterFOUR

This Is Your Captain Speaking

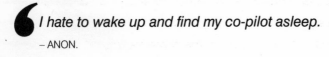 *I hate to wake up and find my co-pilot asleep.*
– ANON.

I f Pontius was the first pilot any of us have ever heard of then how come every one since has been named Speaking: 'Hello from the flight deck, this is your Captain Speaking.'

Why are pilots called 'captain'? More to the point, why are they even called pilots? It all harks back to the days when travel by sea was just about the only way to travel long distances. I often think it would have been great to have had to go on business trips before flying came along – you could be away from the office for years on just one trip!

The airline industry adopted just about every term possible from nautical days. The American airline Pan Am's call sign, 'Clipper', dated from the days when it operated amphibious aircraft for trans-oceanic flights and called them Clipper Ships, after the sailing vessels of the 19th century. Besides pilots and captains, aircraft have galleys, starboard and port wings, the cabin, a hold and stewards, and the paperwork for each flight is referred to as the ship's papers.

Anyway all this boils down to the fact that good old Captain Speaking thinks of himself as clearly a man among men, someone who, like his predecessors on board ship, is a pretty classy chap. And, in fact, when I started in the airline business many of the pilots were ex-RAF Bomber Command types.

Another pilot I knew who flew long-haul insisted that the only way to beat jag lag was to operate on GMT wherever in the world he happened to find himself. This meant that he would go to bed whenever it was night time in London even if it was the middle of the day wherever he was, always assuming he was not flying. He would eat his cereal and toast at breakfast time GMT and so on. This all seemed to be an absolutely wonderful theory until he died in his bed on a Lisbon night stop.

It all speaks to the fact that captains are as often as not an eccentric lot; at least they used to be. These days they are much like policemen in that they seem to be getting younger and younger. Shock horror, they have even allowed women to fly airliners. When I worked at Continental Airlines we had the first all-female captain, co-pilot and engineer flight crew bring a 747 from Newark to London. Prejudice is such that some people would still prefer that Captain Speaking be a man.

The person at the controls does his/her job away from the public's gaze and thus an aura of mystery is maintained. As figures of authority on the aircraft and the ones who have the lives of the passengers in their hands, it's not surprising that pilots enjoy a good deal of adoration, sometimes from other people too. But what really goes on behind the cockpit door? Read on...

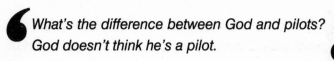

> *What's the difference between God and pilots?*
> *God doesn't think he's a pilot.*
>
> – ANON.

Where Are We?

The famous 'British Reserve' is even noted among the calm, collected community of aircraft captains. During a flight they can hear exchanges on the radio between air traffic control and other aircraft, which can often be highly entertaining, especially if they can laugh at someone else's expense.

A few years ago a British pilot was making contact with the Gander, Newfoundland, air traffic centre towards the end of a transatlantic flight. He was required to report his position and, once they had confirmed it with radar, the Gander centre would direct him into North American airspace. Unfortunately, when they checked the reported position, Gander's radar showed that the aircraft was in fact 40 miles further south. This is obviously a huge error and presented a potential collision risk. At the least it would be reported to the authorities, the airline would be embarrassed and the pilot suspended pending an investigation. So perhaps cause for some pretty heated words from the captain. Not this one. After being advised of his true position there was a pause, and then he replied in measured tones: 'There is less than joy in the cockpit at this time.'

'Flying has torn apart the relationship of space and time: it uses our old clock but with new yardsticks.'

– AVIATION PIONEER CHARLES A. LINDBERGH

Turning Japanese

An American co-pilot who found work as a captain for a Japanese airline was impressed with his new colleagues' attention to correct procedure. When he used the vertical speed control's thumbwheel adjustment with his index finger, the pilot immediately corrected him: 'No, is thumbwheel, please use thumb.'

However, the tables can turn. During an evening approach to Los Angeles there were, as always, many aircraft jostling for a landing position. It was a lovely sunset and a crystal clear sky with almost limitless visibility. The flight crews of the aircraft coming in to land were all listening to air traffic control as they were being positioned. The ground controller wanted to put an American Airlines 737 into line behind a Japanese Airlines 747, after which he would leave the AA aircraft to follow the JAL visually; this would allow the controller to concentrate on other more pressing matters.

The discussion went like this:

Controller: *'AA, do you see the JAL 747, position 2 o'clock?'*

AA pilot: *'Negative.'*

All the other aircraft for a hundred miles can see the JAL Jumbo lumbering along.

Controller: *'AA, do you have visual on JAL 747, now at 1 o'clock?'*

AA pilot: *'Negative.'*

The air traffic controller is showing signs of frustration that the AA pilot can't see the huge plane in front of him.

Controller: 'AA, *surely you can now look out of the window and see JAL 747 at 12 o'clock?*'

AA pilot: '*No, I still can't see those damn Japs!*'

The other pilots listening in wince at this, but another voice interrupts:

JAL pilot: '*Look into the sun, Yankee dog...* '

' *Once you have learned to fly your plane, it is far less fatiguing to fly than it is to drive a car. You don't have to watch every second for cats, dogs, children, lights, road signs, ladies with baby carriages and citizens who drive out in the middle of the block against the lights... Nobody who has not been up in the sky on a glorious morning can possibly imagine the way a pilot feels in free heaven.*

– WILLIAM T. PIPER, PRESIDENT OF PIPER AIRCRAFT CORPORATION '

Radar Love?

Flights arriving from the east into London's Heathrow Airport are as often as not routed via the beacon at Biggin Hill, where sometimes they are required to enter the holding pattern prior to proceeding towards Epsom and from there to final approach for landing. One day a Japanese Airlines 747 was inbound to Heathrow and instead of routing the Jumbo from Heathrow to Epsom the controller gave the JAL flight a different course than normal.

'Japanese Airlines Flight 34, please proceed on a heading of two nine zero and enter the holding pattern at Bovingdon.'

'Roger, proceeding to Bovingdon,' came the swift reply.

After a while, and after handling a number of other inbound aircraft, the controller had not heard back from Flight 34 as to its position or whether or not it had entered the Bovingdon hold.

'Japanese Airlines Flight 34, please report your position. Are you in the Bovingdon holding pattern?'

'Heathrow control, we are having a problem locating the Bovingdon beacon.'

Before the control could make his response an unknown American pilot cut in.

'Really? You had no God-damn trouble finding Pearl Harbor though did you?'

 To most people, the sky is the limit. To those who love aviation, the sky is home.

– ANON.

Tongue-Tied

Despite English being the worldwide language of aviation, air traffic controllers still have to deal with some difficult customers as they endeavour to keep all the aircraft apart and going in the right directions. A language barrier can still exist.

An American pilot who had just landed at Chicago O'Hare Airport had been given directions into the terminal. This is notoriously complicated at O'Hare, where the layout and different names of all the taxiways on the huge airport can be very confusing. For safety's sake, therefore, the pilots have to repeat back the directions they've just been given. Most scribble it all down and read it back off their notes.

Behind the American aircraft was an Aero Mexico plane, which had just landed. Ground control gave it its directions – another long list of taxiway names. After a pause the Aero Mexico pilot replied. 'Roger' (or rather 'Royer' as G is difficult to pronounce for Spanish speakers). There was a pause while ground control waited for the read-back of the list of taxiways. Nothing. So ground control gave the list again. Another pause. Aero Mexico replied 'Royer'. Now somewhat frustrated with this departure from protocol, the ground controller came back on the radio;

'Aero Mexico: Roger WHAT?'

After a moment's contemplation the Aero Mexico pilot responded, 'Roger, errrr, Dodger?'

'*Every flyer who ventures across oceans to distant lands is a potential explorer; in his or her breast burns the same fire that urged the adventurers of old to set forth in their sailing ships for foreign lands. Riding through the air on silver wings instead of sailing the seas with white wings, he must steer his own course, for the air is uncharted, and he must therefore explore for himself the strange eddies and currents of the ever-changing sky in its many moods.*'

– JEAN BATTEN, ALONE IN THE SKY, 1979

FLYING FACTS

Big Wheels

The Boeing 777 entered service with United Airlines in May 1995. There are almost 850 either delivered or ordered by over 40 different airlines. If you're flying on one remember to impress the person next to you with the information that it has the largest undercarriage of any commercial airliner currently in service.

Tongue-Tied II

Mexican pilots have a bit of a reputation at Chicago O'Hare Airport. In another incident an Aero Mexico Boeing 727 was taxiing out to the runway for a flight to Mexico City. This flight was at the very limit of the range of a 727 when it was fully loaded with passengers and cargo and so it needed a full tank of fuel. Given that it was at maximum take-off weight the 727 needed every inch of runway to effect a safe departure.

Air traffic control instructed the pilot to taxi to the end of the runway and 'position and hold'. This translates as 'get to the runway and wait for clearance for take-off'. However, the Aero Mexico pilot replied, 'Roger, position and go'. He immediately brought the throttles up and started his take-off roll.

Air traffic control came back on the air saying, 'No, no, no! Stop! Stop!' The Aero Mexico aircraft came to an abrupt halt a short way down the runway. Air traffic control then said, 'Aero Mexico, position and hold.' To which came the reply, 'Roger, position and go.' Again, the pilot throttled up and started his take-off roll.

Again air traffic control yelled stop and the pilot obeyed. Again

ATC advised him to 'Position and hold'. Yet again, he replied, 'Roger, position and go,' and started to thunder down the runway for take-off. Clearly fed up with all this, ATC decided that it was safer to let him go and get rid of him. But all the stopping and starting had put the aircraft quite a way down the runway, which was already only just long enough to be safe. The Aero Mexico aircraft rolled and rolled and finally the nose lifted off, followed by a huge cloud of dust as its rear wheels went off the tarmac and onto the verge of the runway.

As it disappeared airborne in the cloud of debris, the watching air traffic controller radioed the pilot, 'Aero Mexico, are you going to make it?' To which he replied, 'I think soooo... '

' *WhhheeeEEEEEEEEEEEEEEE! The scream of jet engines rises to a crescendo on the runways of the world. Every second, somewhere or other, a plane touches down, with a puff of smoke from scorched tyre rubber, or rises in the air, leaving a smear of black fumes dissolving in its wake. From space, the earth might look to a fanciful eye like a huge carousel, with planes instead of horses spinning round its circumference, up and down, up and down. Whhheeeeeeeeeee!* '

– AUTHOR DAVID LODGE

Tongue-Tied III

If you are reading this book while on board a Mexican airline we apologise for perhaps worrying you unnecessarily and we should like to point out that we are not picking on Mexicans and neither should you be alarmed.

In another incident an exasperated air traffic controller instructed a Mexicana pilot to 'Hold short' of two taxiways as he was navigating through the airport. This was to allow another aircraft to cross in front. The Mexicana pilot replied 'Roger' to both instructions, but went straight through both positions. Rather irate at this, ATC radioed to the pilot, 'Mexicana, you went straight through both taxiways I told you to hold at. Now stop saying "Roger" and start doing what you're told!' The Mexicana pilot's response? 'Roger.'

PLANE SPEAKING

Controller: *'Air Force 53, it appears your engine has... oh... disregard, I see you've already ejected.'*

Next in Line

Sometimes aircraft operating in their home airport are given a bit of priority by air traffic control over those other aircraft from foreign countries. At least that's what the crew of a Lufthansa 737 in Frankfurt expected when they began to taxi out towards the runway and were told to follow a Pan Am aircraft. They disregarded this instruction and nipped in front of the Pan Am aircraft. The radio conversation went like this. Pan Am's call sign is 'Clipper'.

ATC: *'Lufthansa, I told you to follow the Clipper.'*

Lufthansa: *'I didn't see the Clipper.'*

ATC: *'Lufthansa, turn right, right, right and right again.'*

After a minute, during which the Lufthansa jet executed the manoeuvre and had therefore gone 'around the block' to a point behind the Pan Am aircraft...

ATC: *'Now do you see the Clipper?'*

Pilots track their lives by the number of hours in the air, as if any other kind of time isn't worth noting.

– AUTHOR MICHAEL PARFIT

Fear of Flying

Pilots, of course, are not mere mortals like the rest of us. They are spared that strange phenomenon that some passengers experience, that feeling of stark terror when in the act of hurtling through the air in a tiny metal tube at vast altitude and being kept there by mysterious forces until a controlled crash reunites them with the ground.

Although they seem to thrive on it, they do have some worries. They worry about making a mistake. Some recite Shepard's Prayer (astronaut Alan Shepard's prayer): 'Oh Lord, please don't let me screw up.' Amen.

During training would-be captains are weeded out if they exhibit signs of discomfort with flying. I know of one trainee who was removed from a course when he began to throw up when going flying was even mentioned. The reason for being dropped from the course was recorded as 'MOA', a neat acronym for Manifestation of Apprehension, or being scared sick.

While they are concerned about making an error, pilots don't really worry about making a big mistake such as running out of fuel or getting totally lost; they're too professional and well trained. What they really fear is making a small mistake which makes them look really silly to other pilots.

After a perfect night flight, an immaculate landing and going through all his post-flight checks, one captain left his aircraft and walked down the jetway into the airport terminal. As he approached the airport building he noticed that it was very brightly lit. 'Hmm,' he thought, 'there must be a movie being filmed in here.'

As he turned the corner he scanned the concourse for celebrities. Then his heart sank. He'd left the aircraft's enormous landing lights on and they were blazing away into the terminal building. He very quickly ran back and turned them off. It wasn't just embarrassment; perhaps the thought of using jump leads on a Jumbo jet was too awful to contemplate.

Crew Behaving Badly

Air crew can sometimes get high spirited when they are on a layover in a nice, hot, part of the world and they are lucky enough to be staying in a lovely hotel with a great swimming pool. High spirits inevitably reach new levels when drink is involved. On one occasion some members (in both senses of the word) of a crew had ended up skinny dipping in the pool.

Egged on by some of the girls, one of the flight deck crew got out of the pool and was doing a variation on the dance of the seven veils using a similar number of towels. He finally, and some have said rather proudly, got down to the last towel and was parading along the edge of the swimming pool, which had what appeared to be a glass wall beside it. Unfortunately the glass wall was a one-way glass out of which the diners in the hotel's restaurant could see but through which those outside could not see in.

> *It may be questioned whether civil aviation in England is to be regarded as one of those industries which is unable to stand on its own two feet, and is yet so essential to the national welfare that it must be kept alive at all costs.*
>
> – MAJOR-GENERAL SIR FREDERICK SYKES, FIRST DIRECTOR OF
> BRITISH CIVIL AVIATION, 1919

Knock, Knock...

The theory of flight for most pilots is that it is hours and hours of sheer boredom punctuated by the odd, and I mean very odd, moment of blind panic. The boring part on long-haul flights mainly takes place during the cruise phase of the flight, that period when the aircraft is controlled by automatic pilot. One day the captain of an African airline was in this phase of a flight when the call of nature sounded loud and clear and he left the cockpit to use the lavatory. Unusually all the first class toilets were engaged, and rather then head back to one of the economy loos – for some reason passengers never like to see a pilot walking about the aircraft – he stood around waiting.

Given that he was gone for rather a long time the co-pilot decided he was hungry and instead of calling for one of the cabin staff to bring him a sandwich he thought he would nip out and get one for himself. Naturally this is totally against normal procedures, but he reasoned that the plane was on autopilot and either he or the captain would be back in no time at all. Unfortunately he had failed to factor into this equation one vital piece of information: the aircraft was fitted with an anti-hijack cockpit door, the kind that can only be opened from the inside.

Both pilots having left the flight deck, the door shut and when they arrived back at the cockpit door they could not open it. It is testimony to the resilience of the door that after several minutes of furtive shoving and pulling it remained unmoved. To the increasing alarm of the first class passengers who were looking on in disbelief, the two hapless crew took a fire axe to the door. Finally they managed to break down the door and carried on with the flight as though nothing had happened. There are no reports as to how they explained the broken door once they landed back at their base. It is thought that a great many passengers found religion that day.

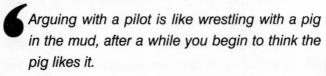

Arguing with a pilot is like wrestling with a pig in the mud, after a while you begin to think the pig likes it.

– SEEN ON A GENERAL DYNAMICS BULLETIN BOARD

Pilots Really are Getting Younger

It's true. In October 2007, at the age of 19, Ed Gardner, who wasn't old enough to drive a bus, and in most countries he would have been too young to hire a car, got his commercial pilots license. A day later he started work with Stansted-based charter airline, Titan Airways, flying a Boeing 737. By December Mr Gardner had reached the ripe old age of 20 and is thought to be the youngest passenger pilot in the UK.

According to Titan Airways Fleet Manager "It is good getting youngsters into the company – we need some new blood." OK…

> *Flying is an act of conquest, of defeating the most basic and powerful forces of nature. It unites the violent rage and brute power of jet engines with the infinitesimal tolerances of the cockpit. Airlines take their measurements from the ton to the milligram, from the mile to the millimetre, endowing any careless move – an engine setting, a flap position, a training failure – with the power to wipe out hundreds of lives.*
> – WALL STREET JOURNAL COLUMNIST THOMAS PETZINGER, JR.

Up at the Sharp End

It's every schoolboy's (and some bigger boys') dream to visit the cockpit and watch those intrepid flyer boys at work. One such passenger was 29 years old in 2002 when he decided to visit the pilot on a United Airlines flight from Miami to Buenos Aires.

Sadly he wasn't invited. He ran through the first class cabin and attempted to barge the door open several times before being set upon by a number of crew members and passengers. As they wrestled with him he managed to kick off a section of the reinforced cockpit door at floor level and crawl partially through it. The Uruguayan's excursion was ended when the flight crew hit him over the head with the blunt end of an axe to subdue him before tying him up with their belts. He was then tranquillised by a doctor who was travelling on the flight. The first class passengers who had leapt into action left the aircraft with their clothes spattered with blood. It is not known whether the man reported back for duty at his place of work in Montevideo. He won't be recounting his tale either, as, 'He doesn't remember what happened', according to a spokesman for the Argentine Air Force.

Both optimists and pessimists contribute to society. The optimist invents the aeroplane, the pessimist the parachute.

– GEORGE BERNARD SHAW

Hard Landing

The pilot responsible for this hard landing didn't have to face the passengers, but the flight attendant made sure that he was held to account when she made the following arrival announcement: 'Ladies and gentlemen, as you are all now painfully aware, our captain has landed in Seattle. From all of us at the airline we'd like to thank you for flying with us today and please be very careful as you open the overhead bins as you may be killed by falling luggage that shifted during our so called "touchdown".'

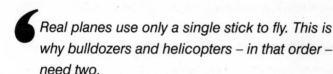

Real planes use only a single stick to fly. This is why bulldozers and helicopters – in that order – need two.

– PAUL SLATTERY

Sleepy, Night, Nights

It sounds like a scene in the spoof movie Airplane but it's true; both pilots were sound asleep as their plane should have been descending and preparing to land at Hawaii's Big Island.

Go! Airlines flight 1002 carried on cruising at 21,000 feet in early 2008 as it came overhead Hilo Airport, prompting frantic attempts by air traffic controllers to contact the flight crew. The plane was 15 miles beyond its destination by the time the snoozing pair were raised.

The Captain Scott Oltman and First Officer Dillon Shipley were suspended for 60 and 45 days respectively by the FAA for reckless operation of an aircraft after their ill-timed nap in February. Both were fired by the airline.

The possibility that carbon monoxide had leaked into the cockpit causing the crew to lose consciousness was investigated and no evidence was found. Still, a bit odd for both to pass out at 9 a.m. Most importantly, the plane was safely landed after its short detour.

PLANE SPEAKING

Tower: *'Delta 351, you have traffic at 10 o'clock, 6 miles!'*
Delta 351: *'Give us another clue! We have digital watches!'*

Whose Height Is It Anyway?

Generally speaking, the higher you fly the less fuel you consume, and so it's important that the crew try and 'negotiate' the best flight level with the air traffic controllers. On one occasion a captain was very keen to maintain a flight level of 36,000 feet and so he was disappointed to get a call from the Egyptian air traffic control to descend to flight level 34 – 34,000 feet.

Somewhat frustrated, the captain asked: 'Why do we have to descend?' 'Conflicting traffic,' came the answer, which meant there was another aircraft flying at that level.

'Well, ask him to move,' responded the captain. 'No,' said ATC.

'Well what aircraft is it?' answered the captain.

'It's the aircraft that's going to kill you unless you descend to 34,000 feet,' responded the Egyptian controller.

There's no answer to that except, 'Descending now'.

'*High-performance jet fighter, fully armed with missiles, guns. ECM equipment, fresh paint (stars and bars painted over), single seat, 97% reliability rate, will out-climb, out-turn F-16, out-run F-14, low fuel burn (relatively), all-digital avionics, radar, terrain following, INS, GPS, Tacan, used only for testing and sales promotion. Now in storage. Contact Northrop Corp. Will trade for MiG-25 and home address of Air Force acquisition officer.*

– ADVERT FOUND IN PACIFIC FLYER MAGAZINE, SHORTLY AFTER
US AIR FORCE'S F-20 FIGHTER PROGRAMME WAS CANCELLED '

Hot Pants

After take-off from John F. Kennedy Airport in New York, the pilot began making the customary announcement over the PA. This captain was even more laconic, more laid back than most. 'Ladies and gentlemen, this is your captain speaking. Welcome to Flight Number 293 non-stop to Los Angeles. The weather ahead is good and therefore we should have a smooth and uneventful flight. Now sit back and relax OH MY GOD!'

The announcement abruptly stopped and in the cabin of the aircraft you could have heard a pin drop. Even the flight attendants seemed momentarily to freeze. There followed a very tense period of silence, one that seemed to go on for an awfully long time. Hardly any of the passengers spoke and most just gripped the armrests of their seats. Some probably prayed, others did other things. Suddenly the intercom came back to life and the laconic captain was back.

'Ladies and gentlemen, I am so sorry if I gave you cause for alarm a few moments ago. While I was talking to you, the flight attendant accidentally spilled a cup of hot coffee in my lap. You should see the front of my pants!' chuckled the pilot.

Not to be out-done a passenger in economy class shouted out, 'That's nothing. You should see the back of mine!'

> *If you are a woman, and are coming to the flying field seeking stimulation, excitement and flattery, you had better stay away until flying is a little bit safer. If you are thinking that flying will develop character; will teach you to be orderly, well balanced; will give you an increasingly wider outlook; discipline you, and destroy vanity and pride; enable you to control yourself more and more under all conditions; to think less of yourself and your personal problems, and more of sublimity and everlasting peace that dwell serene in the heavens – if you seek these latter qualities, and think on them exclusively, why – FLY!*
>
> – MARGERY BROWN, FLYING MAGAZINE, 1929

Equal Opportunities

As an airliner pushed back from the gate, a flight attendant gave the passengers the usual information regarding seat belts, etc. Finally, she said, 'Now sit back and enjoy your trip while your captain, Judith Campbell, and crew take you safely to your destination.'

A passenger sitting in the eighth row thought to himself, 'Did I hear her right? Is the captain a woman?' When the attendants came by with the drink cart, he said, 'Did I understand you right? Is the captain a woman?' 'Yes,' said the attendant, 'in fact, this entire crew is female.' 'My God,' said the gentleman, 'I'd better have two scotch and sodas. I don't know what to think of all those women up there in the cockpit.' 'That's another thing,' said the attendant, 'We no longer call it the cockpit. Now it's the box office.'

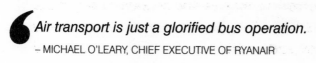 *Air transport is just a glorified bus operation.*
– MICHAEL O'LEARY, CHIEF EXECUTIVE OF RYANAIR

A Very Brief History of Time

In America some airports operate both civil and military flights. One side of the field is for the USAF and civilian aircraft use the other side, with the control tower in the middle.

On one particular day the tower received a call from an aircraft asking, 'What time is it?' The tower responded, 'Who is calling?' The aircraft replied, 'What difference does it make?' The tower replied, 'It makes a lot of difference.

If it is an American Airlines flight, it is 3 o'clock. If it is an Air Force plane, it is 1500 hours. If it is a Navy aircraft, it is 6 bells. If it is an Army aircraft, the big hand is on the 12 and the little hand is on the 3. If it is a Marine Corps aircraft, it's Thursday afternoon.'

Brief Encounter

The controllers at busy Frankfurt Airport are renowned to be a short-tempered lot. They not only expect pilots to know their parking location but how to get there without any assistance. So it was with some amusement that the crew of a Pan Am 747 listened to the following exchange between Frankfurt ground and a British Airways 747 (radio call Speedbird 206) after landing.

Speedbird 206: *'Good morning Frankfurt. Speedbird 206 clear to active.'*

Ground: *'Good Morning. Taxi to your gate.'*

The British Airways 747 pulled onto the main taxiway and stopped.

Ground: *'Speedbird, do you know where you are going?'*

Speedbird 206: *'Stand by, ground. I'm looking up the gate location now.'*

Ground (impatiently): *'Speedbird 206, have you never flown to Frankfurt before?'*

Speedbird 206 (coolly): *'Yes, in 1944. But I didn't stop.'*

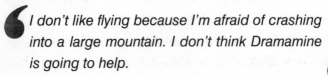

I don't like flying because I'm afraid of crashing into a large mountain. I don't think Dramamine is going to help.

– KAFFIE, IN THE 1992 MOVIE A FEW GOOD MEN

Don't Panic

This was heard on the air many years ago, the cut-glass accent of the pilot reinforcing the notion that British pilots never, ever panic:

Pilot: *'Heathrow Centre, British Airways Speedbird Flight 723.'*

HC: *'British Airways Speedbird Flight 723, Heathrow Centre, go ahead.'*

Pilot: *'Heathrow Centre, British Airways Speedbird Flight 723 has a message for you.'*

HC: *'British Airways Speedbird Flight 723, Heathrow Centre is ready to copy message.'*

Pilot: *'Heathrow Centre, British Airways Speedbird Flight 723, message is as follows: Mayday, Mayday, Mayday.'*

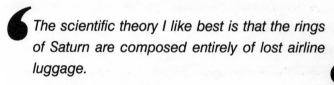

The scientific theory I like best is that the rings of Saturn are composed entirely of lost airline luggage.

– COMEDIAN MARK RUSSELL

Don't Mention the War

To avoid misunderstandings, English is used worldwide for all aviation communications. Not everybody thinks that this is a good idea... this was overheard on the radio at Munich Airport:

Lufthansa (in German): *'Ground, what is our start clearance time?'*

Ground (in English): *'If you want an answer you must speak English.'*

Lufthansa (in English): *'I am a German, flying a German airplane, in Germany. Why must I speak English?'*

Unknown voice from another aircraft (in a British accent): *'Because you lost the bloody war!'*

Avoiding Action

A 'go around' is an aborted landing; during approach if there's a problem the pilot climbs and circles around to try landing again...

Pilot Trainee: *'Tower, please speak slowly, I am a baby in English and lonely in the cockpit.'*

Tower: *'Aircraft on final approach, go around, there's an aircraft on the runway!'*

Pilot Trainee: *'Roger.'*

Pilot continues approach...

Tower: *'Aircraft, I said GO AROUND!'*

Pilot Trainee: *'Roger.'*

The trainee doesn't react, but lands the aircraft on the very end of the runway. He continues moving forward to where a twin-engine aircraft is standing in the middle of the runway, goes around the twin and continues to the taxiway.

Did the Earth Move for You?

For months after California's Northridge earthquake of 1994, aftershocks rocked the San Fernando Valley and Van Nuys Airport. One morning about three weeks after the initial quake there was a particularly sharp aftershock. Moments later on Van Nuys' ground control frequency: 'Uh, four-three-kilo would like to file a pilot report for moderate turbulence on the east taxiway... '

FLYING FACTS

Gambling into the Air

McCarran Airport is the only airport in the world with more than a thousand slot machines throughout the airport terminals.

Little and Large

A tiny single-engine four-seat Cherokee 180 was told by the tower to hold short of the active runway while a 200-seat DC-8 landed. The airliner rolled to the turn-off on the runway, turned around, and taxied back past the Cherokee.

The captain of the DC-8 came on the radio and said: *'What a cute little plane. Did you make it all by yourself?'*

The Cherokee pilot replied: *'I made it out of DC-8 parts. Another landing like yours and I'll have enough parts for another one.'*

' *A military aircraft had gear problems on landing, and as the plane was skidding down the tarmac the tower controller asked if they needed assistance. From the plane came a laconic Southern voice: 'Dunno – we ain't done crashin' yet.'*

– ANON.

Telling Tales

The crew of a US airliner made a wrong turn during taxi and came nose to nose with another aircraft. The female ground controller was furious and practically screamed down the radio: 'Flight 436, where are you going? I told you to turn right on "Charlie" taxiway; you turned right on "Delta". Stop right there.'

She was so cross that she continued to give the embarrassed American crew a verbal lashing and shouted: 'You've screwed everything up. It'll take forever to sort this out. You stay right there and don't move until I tell you to. You can expect progressive taxi instructions in about half an hour and I want you to go exactly where I tell you, when I tell you, and how I tell you. You got that?' There was an embarrassed hush on the airwaves for a few seconds before an unknown male pilot broke the silence and asked: 'Wasn't I married to you once?'

Chocks Away

While taxiing out in sequence behind a Lufthansa airliner at Frankfurt, a C-130 Hercules crew noticed an orange 'Remove before flight' streamer hanging out of the Lufthansa nose wheel well. This indicated that their nose landing gear locking pin was still installed, and after take-off would prevent the undercarriage from retracting.

Wanting to alert their fellow airmen to the problem, but not wanting to cause too much embarrassment by going through the air traffic controller, the 130 crew simply radioed the Lufthansa aircraft on the control tower frequency: 'Lufthansa aircraft, Herky 23.' No reply.

They repeated the transmission and again there was no reply. Instead, the Lufthansa pilot called the tower and asked the tower to tell the Herky crew that, 'The professional pilots of Lufthansa do not engage in unprofessional conversations over the radio.'

The C-130 pilot quickly replied, 'Frankfurt tower, can you please relay to the professional pilots of the Lufthansa aircraft that their nose gear pin is still installed?'

The Wright brothers flew through the smoke screen of impossibility.

– DOROTHEA BRANDE, ASSOCIATE EDITOR AMERICAN REVIEW

Sick Aircraft Syndrome

While English is the official language of aviation, much to the annoyance of the French in particular, some crew members whose native tongue is not English only have a limited grasp of the language. Some foreign language speakers' grip is so tenuous that it seems to be confined to communications with air traffic controllers and to short announcements to passengers – often it sounds like they have been learned by rote. When things don't go according to plan they can find themselves in the deep end of the language pool without the ability even to tread water. In China in the 1980s a DC-3 was loaded with tourist passengers. It had started up and was about to taxi. Suddenly the engines were shut down. The captain left the cockpit and emerged through the door to address the passengers: 'This plane ill! We take other plane!'

They left the aircraft and all walked over to another DC-3 parked nearby. After a few minutes, the engines started, but immediately shut down again. Again the captain emerged from the cockpit, and announced: 'This plane more ill! We take first plane!'

Beech Baron: *'Uh, ATC, verify you want me to taxi in front of the 747.'*

ATC: *'Yeah, it's OK. He's not hungry.'*

Playing a Blinder

During a brief stopover at Heathrow Airport an elderly blind lady passenger preferred to stay on board the aircraft. However, she was concerned that her guide dog should have the opportunity for some exercise, and asked the pilot if he might be so kind as to take him for a walk to stretch his legs. The pilot was only too happy to oblige. The thoughts of the passengers waiting to board the aircraft when they saw the captain stroll through the terminal with a guide dog are not recorded.

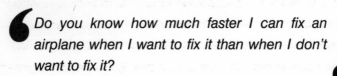

'*Do you know how much faster I can fix an airplane when I want to fix it than when I don't want to fix it?*

– GORDON BETHUNE, CEO OF CONTINENTAL AIRLINES

Anti-Social Hours

Airline crew members are sometimes required to be 'on call' as part of their duties. This means that when not scheduled for specific duty they can be called in at short notice by the crewing department to fly. Being called in for duty is understandably unpopular and it has been known for some to try dodging the assignment.

Airlines take a dim view of this, but being unable to be contacted is regarded as a lesser offence than refusing or missing an assigned trip. One captain gets an 'A' for his creativity in avoiding an assignment. When crew scheduling woke him up at 3.00 a.m. to assign him to a 5.00 a.m. departure, he passed the phone to his wife and said in a voice loud enough for them to hear on the other end, 'Here, darling, I think it's someone calling for your husband.'

There's Always One

Airline aircraft share the skies with a great variety of other machines, from small, slow single-engine planes to supersonic military jets. While the air traffic controllers try to keep them all apart and moving, all pilots tend to think they're pretty special.

The SR-71 Blackbird is a US Air Force reconnaissance jet, which flies at extreme speed and altitude. The pilot of one was no better than any other flier when he saw the chance to show off to his fellow airmen. Blackbird pilot Brian Shul and his co-pilot were screaming across southern California 13 miles up. They were monitoring various radio transmissions from other aircraft as they entered Los Angeles Center's airspace. Although the civilian air traffic controllers didn't have responsibility for Brian's aircraft, they did monitor the Blackbird's movement across their radar scope.

Brian heard a Cessna pilot ask for a read-out of its ground speed. '90 knots,' Center replied.

Moments later a twin-engine Beech pilot required the same. '120 knots,' Center answered.

They weren't the only ones proud of their speed that day, as almost instantly an F-18 jet fighter pilot smugly transmitted, 'Ah, Center, Dusty

52 requests ground speed read-out.' There was a slight pause. '525 knots, Dusty.'

Brian couldn't resist, and a moment later radioed Los Angeles air traffic control. 'Center, Aspen 20, you got a groundspeed read-out for us?' There was a longer pause. 'Aspen, I show 1,742 knots.'
No further inquiries were heard on the frequency.

 Once you get hooked on the airline business, it's worse than dope.

– ED ACKER, WHILE CHAIRMAN OF AIR FLORIDA

Head in the Clouds

The pilot of a commuter plane was flying over Seattle when an electrical malfunction disabled all of the aircraft's communication and navigation equipment. In low cloud and poor visibility the pilot could not determine his position and course to get to the airport. He saw a building, flew towards it and began circling. He drew a handwritten sign and held it up in the cockpit window. The sign said simply, 'Where am I' in large letters.

People watching the aircraft from inside the building scurried about, and were seen to be discussing among themselves before responding by drawing a large sign which they displayed at the window. The sign said, 'You are in a plane.' At this the pilot smiled, glanced at his map, determined his course and shortly thereafter arrived safely at Seattle-Tacoma Airport. While completing their shutdown checks the co-pilot asked the captain how the sign 'You are in a plane' had helped him determine their position. The captain explained that the information on the sign had been technically correct but of no real use. It was therefore easy to deduce that the individuals worked for Microsoft on their help line and so, having got a pinpoint fix, everything else was easy.

I Can See Clearly Now

The following is from a British Airways Operations Department notice:

'There appears to be some confusion over the new pilot role titles. This notice will hopefully clear up any misunderstandings.

'The titles P1, P2 and Co-Pilot will now cease to have any meaning, within the BA Operations Manual. They are to be replaced by Handling Pilot, Non-Handling Pilot, Non-Handling Landing Pilot, Handling Non-Landing Pilot and Non-Handling Non-Landing Pilot.

'The Landing Pilot is initially the Handling Pilot and will handle the take-off and landing except in role reversal when he is the Non-Handling Pilot for taxi until the Handling Non-Landing Pilot hands the handling to the Landing Pilot at 80 knots.

'The Non-Landing (Non-Handling, since the Landing Pilot is handling) Pilot reads the checklist to the Handling Pilot until after the Before Descent Checklist completion. Then the Handling Landing Pilot hands the handling to the Non-Handling Non-Landing Pilot who then becomes the Handling Non-Landing Pilot.

'The Landing Pilot is the Non-Handling Pilot until the "Decision Altitude" call, when the Handling Non-Landing Pilot hands the handling to the Non-Handling Landing Pilot, unless the latter calls "Go Around", in which case the Handling Non-Landing Pilot continues handling and the Non-Handling Landing Pilot continues non-handling until the next call of "Land" or "Go Around", as appropriate.

'In view of the recent confusion over these rules, it was deemed necessary to restate them clearly.' That's cleared that up, then.

> *Landing on the ship during the daytime is like sex, it's either good or it's great. Landing on the ship at night is like a trip to the dentist, you may get away with no pain, but you just don't feel comfortable.*
>
> – LIEUTENANT-COMMANDER THOMAS QUINN, US NAVY,
>
> DISCUSSING AIRCRAFT-CARRIER OPERATIONS

Television Reception

Many flight crews work on the same flight week in, week out, and the routine of the flight and hotel becomes as familiar as going into the office in a 'normal' job. Sometimes they even stay in the same room in the same hotel each week.

One flight attendant was working each week on a flight to Honolulu from the continental United States. He was disappointed to find when he .checked into the layover hotel that the television wasn't working properly. When he checked out for the flight home he filled in a form notifying the hotel staff that the TV was out of order. The next week he returned to the hotel, and was given the same room. He tried to switch on the TV, but to his dismay found that it had not been repaired. When he checked out he again filled in another request for maintenance on the faulty TV. The following week he was again working the Honolulu service, checked into the usual hotel, and was given the same room again. He was astonished to find that the television was still not working, and in his frustration he threw the offending item out of the hotel window. This time when he checked out he filled in a complaint form... that there was no television in the room.

PLANE SPEAKING

An Air Force aircraft was attempting a night landing at an auxiliary field.

Pilot: *'Requesting landing instruction.'*

Controller: *'Aircraft requesting landing instruction, say again call-sign.'*

Pilot: *'Guess who?'*

At this point the airfield runway lights went off.

Controller: *'Guess where.'*

Souvenir Video

The approach to the islands of Hawaii is famously beautiful; the sparkling blue seas surrounding emerald-green, white-sand-fringed islands are special even to flight crews who see this sight regularly. The best view is, of course, out of the cockpit windscreen, which is normally only seen by the flight crew.

During one US airline's flight from Dallas to Honolulu the captain and co-pilot were about to begin descending in preparation for landing when one of the flight attendants came into the cockpit with a camcorder. She asked if, even though it was against regulations, the co-pilot might take some footage of the islands as they came in to land. The co-pilot agreed and took the camera.

He began filming, taking some gorgeous images of the Hawaiian archipelago, while the captain began the descent. As the co-pilot panned around he brought the viewfinder to bear on the captain, who, the co-pilot was surprised to find, was standing up on his seat with his trousers round his ankles and bending over giving the cameraman the 'full moon'. The co-pilot focused on the arresting sight for about 10 seconds before shutting the camera down, convulsed with laughter.

During their overnight layover in Honolulu the crew went out together for some drinks. The pilot and co-pilot were bursting to hear from the flight attendant about what she thought of the film, but she didn't mention it. They assumed she couldn't have looked at it yet.

The next day they were preparing for take-off to fly back home, and the co-pilot called the flight attendant up to the cockpit. Suppressing his laughter he asked her if she'd like them to take some more footage during the climb out from Honolulu, perhaps get some shots of the other side of the islands... 'Oh no,' she said, 'that wasn't my camera; that was a passenger's.'

> *Freddie Laker*
> *May be at peace with his Maker.*
> *But he is persona non grata*
> *With IATA.*
> – HRH THE DUKE OF EDINBURGH

A Light in the Darkness

Another peril faced by weary airline employees when they stay night after night in hotels is the problem of locating the bathroom in a strange room in the dark when woken up by a call of nature. One experienced captain prided himself on his cool thinking and used to explain to new colleagues that he always left the light on in the bathroom, then shut the door, before retiring. This meant that when awoken by a full bladder he just had to look for the light shining under the door to find the bathroom. Simple.

His master-plan suffered a slight setback one night when he got up to 'go', saw the light and opened the door, only to find himself in the hotel corridor. Naked. With his bedroom door locked behind him. Waking up quickly to his plight he raced down the corridor to the room he knew the co-pilot was in. He hammered on the door, whispering loudly, 'Quick, let me in!'

The voice from the other side of the door replied, 'I don't think soooo...'

The frantic captain urged, 'Come on, it's me!'

'I can see that,' said the co-pilot, looking through the spy-hole in the door.

Eventually the co-pilot agreed to throw a towel out for the captain to cover himself with. Predictably it was a hand towel. With the brief camouflage strategically positioned the captain was forced to go to hotel security to ask them to unlock his room. After a few minutes of delay as security asked him for identification, he convinced them that he was legitimate and finally got back into his room, still bursting for a pee and never to rely on his bathroom locator technique again.

> *'How do you like your coffee, captain – cream & sugar?' We are at 30 west, the halfway point between the European and North American continents, and the stewardess in charge of the forward galley is looking after her aircrew during a pause in serving the passengers' meals.*
>
> *Mach 2. On autopilot, 11 miles high, moving at 23 miles a minute. Nearly twice as high as Mount Everest, faster than a rifle bullet leaving its barrel. The side windows are hot to the touch, from friction of the passing air. Despite the speed we can talk without raising our voices.*
>
> *'Milk, please, and no sugar.'*

– BRIAN CALVERT, FLYING CONCORDE, 1982

FLYING FACTS

Regular Travellers

Somehow it seems impossible to imagine a life without frequent flyer programmes but it wasn't until May 1982 that American Airlines launched the first-ever scheme. Not to be out-done United Airlines launched theirs a week later.

Jumbo Jet Gliding Trip

Eric Moody had wanted to fly for as long as he could remember. There was never any doubt in his mind as he grew up; he was going to be a pilot. When he first applied to BOAC for training at 18 he was devastated to be refused on medical grounds due to a deviated nasal septum. Undaunted, he underwent an operation to chisel it straight under local anaesthetic and reapplied. This time he was successful – the doctor performing the medical examination was so impressed by what he had been through to get his nose up to scratch that he immediately passed Eric fit.

Training went smoothly, with two years spent based at Hamble qualifying to fly passenger aircraft. Eric's first solo flight wasn't too auspicious; he got lost and only by spotting the plume of smoke from a train was he able to discover his location by flying so low he could read the words on the railway station sign – Seaton Junction. He followed the track to Exeter airfield where he passed the test.

Nothing he experienced during the 1970s and early '80s in his career flying VC10s, then qualifying as a Boeing 747 captain in 1980, could prepare him for what happened on Thursday 24 June 1982.

Captain Eric Moody, Senior First Officer Roger Greaves and Senior Aircraft Engineer Barry Townley-Freeman left Kuala Lumpur for Perth, Australia, with 247 passengers on board their British Airways Boeing 747 loaded with 91,000kg of fuel and expecting an unremarkable flight. The weather forecast was benign, air conditions smooth and a relatively easy five hours of night flying was in prospect.

Having taken off and levelled out to cruise at 37,000 feet, they turned the autopilot on and ate a meal. Eric scanned the area ahead with the weather radar and found nothing to report other than returns from the sea's surface. He decided to stretch his legs and say hello to some passengers and left the cockpit. He hadn't gone far into the passenger cabin before he was called back to the flight deck. As he entered it he was surprised to see puffs of what looked like smoke coming from the floor vents and noticed the acrid smell associated with burning electrical circuits.

He walked into the flight deck to see the windscreen ablaze with an astonishingly intense display of St Elmo's fire. The patron saint of seamen, St Elmo's name has been given to the phenomenon of dancing lightning that races around the masts of ships and aircraft windscreens in certain atmospheric conditions. Eric quickly retook his seat and checked the weather radar. Again, nothing significant was picked up.

First Officer Greaves then pointed out of the side window; the engine intakes were glowing brightly. At the same moment the windscreen display of St Elmo's fire changed in character to resemble tracer bullets. The few seconds that it took to take in these conditions distracted the crew from the pressing issue of the apparent smoke entering the cabin. Before they could return their attention to that, Engineer Barry Townley-Freeman called out, 'Engine failure number 4!'

Eric called for a fire drill and his two colleagues began to perform it. Within a few moments Barry called out the incredible sequence of indications his instruments displayed: 'Engine failure number 2... number 3... They've all gone!' Later the crew attributed their ability to remain rational in the face of the crisis partly on the fact that it built up gradually, rather than their being plunged straight into the problem.

Eric had practised a four-engine failure only months before during routine simulator training, but had never expected to face one in real life. Such is the incredible level of reliability in modern aircraft that plenty of pilots fly for their whole careers without experiencing even one engine failing. Four engines shutting down was almost unthinkable. Eric put the disbelief from his mind and concentrated on making sense of the situation. The instruments all appeared still to be working and the autopilot remained in control, but the airspeed was decreasing rapidly. They put out a Mayday call.

Eric used the autopilot to fly the aircraft while he and the rest of the crew concentrated on handling the situation. They checked all possible causes of the problem – electrical, fuel, ice build-up – using checklists to ensure that they missed nothing. They started the drill for attempting to relight the engines. All this time they had been descending, until at 26,000 feet the cabin pressure warning horn sounded, indicating that cabin pressurisation had been lost and the artificially high cabin pressure was dropping from the usual 10,000 feet level to that of the real altitude of the aircraft. The lack of oxygen would quickly cause unconsciousness for the crew and passengers and the aircraft's oxygen masks dropped from the overhead panels.

As the crew put their masks on, Roger's fell to pieces in his hands, rendering it useless. Eric was therefore faced with a choice: maintain precious altitude, and therefore time, but see his co-pilot pass out from anoxia; or descend to a lower altitude, losing height and time, where Roger would be able to function. He began an emergency descent. At this point the navigation systems had failed and there was no way of fixing their exact position, but he knew that the area's safe height (i.e. higher than all the mountains in the region) was 10,500 feet, so he decided to descend to 12,000 feet then level off.

By the time they reached 20,000 feet Roger had managed to reassemble his oxygen mask and got it working – no mean feat of concentration and dexterity in the circumstances – and they were able to slow their rate of descent since the risk to Roger had passed. They continually tried to relight the engines without success. The unburned fuel in the engines was, however, igniting behind them so they appeared to the passengers to be on fire. By now the passengers would be in their oxygen masks and Eric decided it was time to put them in the picture. He made an announcement:

'Good evening, ladies and gentlemen. This is your captain speaking. We have a small problem. All four engines have stopped. We are doing our damnedest to get them going again. I trust that you are not in too much distress.'

Eric began to consider the prospect of trying to bring the aircraft down safely with minimal control on the sea at night. Judging height over water is notoriously difficult even for experienced seaplane pilots, which is why they never operate at night. As he was preparing himself for what seemed the inevitable, cries from Roger and Barry revealed that number 4 engine had restarted. An interminable 90 seconds later all four had got going. They were at 12,000 feet as they cut short their celebrations and began to climb again, but at 15,000 feet the St Elmo's fire started again. As they set the controls to level off below the lightning, number 2 engine began to surge so violently that they thought the aircraft would fall apart. Reluctantly they shut it down.

So concerned was Eric for the condition of the engines that he elected to leave their throttle controls alone and control the aircraft using speed-brakes, flaps and undercarriage as they approached Jakarta Airport. They were cleared to land and began to descend towards the airport, but had trouble making out the landing lights. They radioed ahead asking for them to be turned up and finally spotted them through a side window. As they started to line up for landing the lights vanished again; the crew realised that the front windscreen glass had been sandblasted opaque. Eric brought the aircraft in for a gentle touchdown using the aircraft's instruments while sitting on the arm of his seat to squint out of a small clear patch in the windscreen and looking out of the side window at the runway edge lights.

After they had brought the aircraft to a halt the jubilant applause which broke out in the cabin lasted for minutes. The crew disembarked to a heroes' reception and went off to recover from their ordeal. After the aircraft was examined it emerged that they had unwittingly flown through the dust and ash plume above the erupting volcano Mount Galunggung. There was no information available to them prior to the event that this cloud of particles existed.

The post-incident report detailed the enormous amounts of dust and ash that had entered the engines and choked them, entered the cabin (the 'smoke') and how the particles had stripped the paint from the wings, scratched the windscreen opaque and ground away the edges from engine components.

The fact that this story has a happy ending is testimony to the skill and courage of the crew, and to the professionalism of the airline and industry, which trains and equips its pilots to handle even unthinkable situations. They never stopped trying to get the engines restarted, even after so many attempts when it must have seemed futile (later, Barry said that if the aircraft had landed in the sea, he would still have been trying to restart the engines even as they filled with water!) managed each problem as it arose and kept thinking clearly despite the combination of issues demanding simultaneous attention.

The incident captured the public imagination and made a hero out of Captain Eric Moody, who became a celebrity in the aftermath and is still called upon to speak on aviation matters years after having retired and decades after the event that defined his flying career. Once, when asked what it was like to land an aircraft with no forward vision in the dark, he replied, 'It was a bit like negotiating one's way up a badger's arse.'

PLANE SPEAKING

Transmission as a DC-10 rolls out long after a fast landing:

San Jose Tower: *'American 751 heavy, turn right at the end if able. If not able, take the Guadalupe exit off Highway 101 back to the airport.'*

> *I've got the greatest job in the world. Northwest sends me to New York 10 times a month to have dinner. I've just got to take 187 people with me whenever I go.*
>
> – COLIN SOUCY, NORTHWEST AIRLINES PILOT

Top Tips for the Budget-Conscious Traveller

Airline crews are given allowances out of which they can buy their food and essentials when they are staying in a hotel on a layover. Budget-conscious aircrew can always be relied upon to know where the cheapest breakfast and the best bars with the cheapest beers are to be found, almost anywhere in the world; the aircrew with the best tips are invariably the flight engineers.

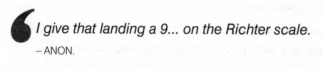 *I give that landing a 9... on the Richter scale.*
– ANON.

Why I Want to be a Pilot

Many children on their first flight dream of one day being in command of an aircraft. Few, however, offer such rational reasoning for their career ambitions as this one, when asked by his teacher to write down what job he hoped to do when he grew up:

'When I grow up I want to be a pilot because it's a fun job and easy to do. That's why there are so many pilots flying around these days.

'Pilots don't need much school. They just have to learn to read numbers so they can read their instruments.

'I guess they should be able to read a road map, too.

'Pilots should be brave so they won't get scared if it's foggy and they can't see, or if a wing or motor falls off.

'Pilots have to have good eyes to see through the clouds, and they can't be afraid of thunder or lightning because they are much closer to them than we are.

'The salary pilots make is another thing I like. They make more money than they know what to do with. This is because most people think that flying a plane is dangerous, except pilots don't because they know how easy it is.

'I hope I don't get airsick because I get carsick and if I get airsick, I couldn't be a pilot and then I would have to go to work.'

Purported to have been written by a fifth-grade student at Jefferson School, Beaufort, South Carolina. It was first published in the South Carolina Aviation News.

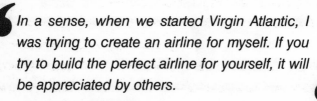

In a sense, when we started Virgin Atlantic, I was trying to create an airline for myself. If you try to build the perfect airline for yourself, it will be appreciated by others.

– SIR RICHARD BRANSON

Two Wrongs

Have you ever wondered what type of chap, for it is usually a chap, is up there flying you safely to your destination? Brave and fearless, intelligent and well organised, all in all a very sensible kind of a guy. Think again. One night after a particularly good night out in New York one of the flight deck crew returned to his hotel and picked up his key at reception. On reaching his room and opening the door he was horrified to find it totally empty; all his clothes, bags and everything had gone.

He immediately phoned down to reception and insisted the police be called to investigate the theft of his property. After they had agreed, he was sitting on the bed looking around when it dawned on him: this was not his room! Worse than that, it wasn't even his hotel. He quietly left the room and staggered back to the correct hotel, which to be fair was next door and therefore justified his simple mistake.

The Irish have long enjoyed, if that's the right word, being the butt of many a joke but in 2006 a pilot flying for the Irish airline Ryanair landed at the wrong airport in Northern Ireland. Flight 9884 was en route from Liverpool to Derry in Northern Ireland, but somehow contrived to land at Ballykelly Camp Army airfield, five miles from Derry. According to an airline spokesman, 'Never in our 20-year history has an incident like this happened.' This is comforting, I suppose.

After the passengers were deplaned, which had to be delayed until the steps were driven from Derry to Ballykelly by Ryanair staff, buses took the passengers to their original destination. There appears to be no truth in the rumour that the pilot, who was immediately grounded pending an investigation, has applied for a job – on the buses.

 I really don't know one plane from the other. To me they are just marginal costs with wings.

– ALFRED KAHN, 1977

PLANE SPEAKING

ATC: *'Alitalia 345 continue taxi holding position 26 South via Tango. Check for workers along taxiway.'*

AZA: *'Alitalia 345 Taxi 26 South via Tango. Workers checked – all are working.'*

Out of Fuel on the Zambezi

It's not just on flights that crews get to have fun. Of course the best fun is had on those long layovers in exotic destinations where the crews are usually put into the best hotels and while they are away get the chance to sunbathe, sightsee, or do whatever to amuse themselves. In some places there is less to do than in others, and sometimes the crews have been to a place so frequently that they need to find something different. Such was the case for a crew who had a layover in Zambia.

Some of the crew decided to borrow a boat from one of the ex-pats that they knew and to use it for a day trip on the river. Six stewardesses and two flight engineers set off on the trip up the Zambezi. After an hour or so of pottering around, and having travelled a fair distance upriver from where they had started, the boat's engine spluttered to a stop. 'No problem,' was what probably went through the girls' minds, 'we have two engineers with us.' But it was a problem; it turned out they had run out of fuel. Amid much laughter, some of it nervous, the senior flight engineer pulled rank and sent the junior off in search of fuel. Of course it was the senior man's responsibility to stay with the girls.

Some time after dark a rescue boat appeared... luckily, the junior engineer was safely on board. Locals were astonished that anyone would venture to walk miles – unarmed – through relatively virgin jungle. The motivation, according to the junior engineer, was that he didn't want to leave the other engineer too long with all the girls.

The average pilot, despite the sometimes swaggering exterior, is very much capable of such feelings as love, affection, intimacy and caring. These feelings just don't involve anyone else.

– ANON.

At Your Service

On a layover (have you ever wondered why they are called that?) in the Far East a member of the flight deck crew decided to take advantage of the hotel's massage service. He was enjoying the attentions of a lovely Filipino girl when it became obvious that something was 'stirring'. The girl looked at the intrepid flyer and said, 'Ahhh... you want a wank.' Naturally, being a former RAF officer and a gentleman, he hesitated for a few moments before in a slightly embarrassed voice, he said: 'OK then... yes please.'

'OK,' she said, 'I come back in 10 minutes.'

When you are served a meal aboard an aircraft, the aircraft will encounter turbulence.

– GUNTER'S FIRST LAW OF AIR TRAVEL

What! No Beer?

Another risky aspect of long-haul flying for aircrew is the potential for being stuck in places in times of crisis. It used to be a greater hazard than it is today with the infrequent flights of former times to some of the world's lesser cities. But frankly, even now, if the fighting is very bad, then no plane is going to be allowed to land, however frequently the flights are scheduled.

I once went to Lagos on a day trip and ended up staying weeks after there was a coup and no flights operated in or out of the capital's airport.

In another trouble spot things were even more serious for the crew. After an aircrew arrived in the Yemen, serious fighting broke out. It raged around the airport, and in the streets of the capital, Sanaa. The aircrew were confined to their hotel, unable to get in or out, a situation that applied to everyone including the hotel staff. In London the airline was making every effort to secure some way of getting them evacuated. From the hotel windows Scud missiles could be seen and at times the situation got quite tense. But not as tense as when the hotel announced that all the beer was gone and the engineer would have to switch to drinking spirits!

When things quietened down some of the local lads came by the hotel selling 'genuine Scud missile remnants'. However, on closer inspection they turned out to be bits of an old can of tomatoes.

 The strength of the turbulence is directly proportional to the temperature of your coffee.
– GUNTER'S SECOND LAW OF AIR TRAVEL

Puppet on a String

One idiosyncratic Boeing 727 pilot based in Chicago became well known among fellow flight crew members for his unusual way of communicating. Whenever he wanted to make it known to a colleague that he wanted something done differently, he would slip a sock puppet onto his hand and announce that, 'Herman says you shouldn't do it that way.' At the end of one flight, while the aircraft was taxiing to the gate, the co-pilot began to pack up his belongings. This led to displeasure from his captain, who donned his puppet and said, 'Herman says you shouldn't be packing your bag while I'm taxiing the airplane.'

After deplaning and loading the next load of passengers the same crew reconvened on the flight deck. They had got a bit tired of Herman's hectoring. When the engineer boarded eating an ice cream, the captain pulled the puppet on and observed, 'Herman likes ice cream.' Herman got a mouthful of it for his trouble.

He didn't learn his lesson, though. Once the puppet was cleaned up the crew began pre-flight checks. During these the captain didn't like the way the first officer was working, and good old Herman was put on before the pilot advised, 'Herman says you shouldn't do that.' The co-pilot had finally had enough of Herman. He replied, 'Herman, you need some air,' opened the window, grabbed the puppet and threw it out. Herman did not appear on a flight deck again.

Not a lot of people...
An anagram of United Airlines is: Insure in Detail

Chapter**FIVE**

Here For Your Safety

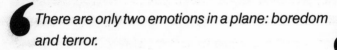

There are only two emotions in a plane: boredom and terror.

– ORSON WELLES

I n Britain we call them stewards and stewardesses or air hostesses (but for some reason not air hosts), which seems infinitely more logical than the American idea of calling them 'flight attendants'. Surely on some flights attentive is what they are not! Of course stewards and stewardesses is more nautical terminology. In a continuation of the nautical theme they are also known by the collective noun, cabin crew – a name that perfectly suits that band of fearless men and women who are 'primarily here for your safety'.

Whatever they are called, the cabin staff have a difficult job. They are expected to deal with a plane-load of bored, sometimes drunk, demanding people who think that for the few pounds they have paid for their ticket they are entitled to five-star service and unlimited hospitality. Most passengers are polite and reasonable, but not all, and the airlines' representatives in the cabin have to handle anything thrown at them in a very confined environment.

Given that the job has a lot of downsides, why is that so many people want to do it? Clearly in the good old days it had something to do with the fact that it really was a glamorous job – especially when long-haul flights kept crews away sometimes for weeks at a time. Perhaps what attracted a number of women, and not a few men, to the job was the idea of doing something different. Back in the 1960s airlines had no difficulty in recruiting the very best people to the job, often demanding that they spoke at least one other language and paying them more money the more languages they could speak. By the 1970s the allowances, the perks of the job and lots of time off still made the career somewhat exclusive.

By the 1980s all this had changed, with it being far less of a career than a short-term job for many of the people who join the ranks of the trolley dollies or the tarts on the carts.

From their roots as on board nurses the cadre of cabin crews have come a long way, although they must sometimes wonder these days if they're really in charge of a kindergarten or at best a school outing. From knife fights in first class to naked hide and seek in the dark, they've seen it all, and manage to keep on smiling.

From Nurse to Stewardess

Today's flight attendant has evolved from an idea by Ellen Church, a trained nurse, who in 1930 persuaded Boeing Air Transport (later to become United Airlines) to hire eight nurses to act as the first stewardesses.

Some airlines had already started using 'cabin boys', who loaded luggage and assisted passengers. Church argued that women in general, and uniformed nurses in particular, would not only present a more comforting presence but would also be able to deal with any ailment that a passenger suffered in flight.

The trial was a success and stewardesses quickly became a fixture in aircraft cabins. The passengers appreciated having someone on duty to provide drinks, sandwiches, a whiff of smelling salts in the case of a faint and chewing gum to alleviate earache. They also checked in the passengers, kept watch for fuel leaks and loaded the luggage.

The requirements for the job were very strict; they had to be trained nurses, be under five feet four inches in height and weigh less than 118 pounds, be aged between 20 and 26 years and be single. A training manual of the times dictated that, 'A rigid military salute will be rendered to the captain and co-pilot as they go aboard the plane and deplane before the passengers. Check with the pilots regarding their personal baggage and place it on board promptly.'

'*United hired gentlemen with the expectation of training them to become pilots, Northwest hired pilots hoping to train them to become gentlemen. To date, despite their best efforts, neither carrier can be considered successful.*'

– AMERICAN POLITICIAN ED THOMPSON

Glory Days of the Stewardess

The spirit of the times in the swinging '60s saw a revolution in the image of the stewardess. From dowdy nurse she metamorphosed into a sex goddess and marketing tool. Airlines shamelessly flaunted their charms as uniforms changed into micro-mini skirts and hot pants. Some wore lapel badges reading 'Pure, Sober and Available', all in an attempt to lure male business passengers.

Braniff took things to a new level when it used renowned designer Pucci to come up with a minidress for its stewardesses. The airline ran an advertisement at the time asking, 'Does your wife know you're flying with us?' It then ran another advert, which caused even more feminist outrage, showcasing the versatile outfit (it was brilliantly designed, using comfortable fabrics rather than the stiff, scratchy materials seen hitherto, and its various components allowed it to convert from rainwear to a minidress), which was loaded with innuendo.

National Airlines capitalised on the sexual undertone of its service with the slogan 'I'm xxx, Fly Me' under a picture of a stewardess (immortalised by 10cc in their hit I'm Mandy Fly Me). American Airlines and Delta got in on the act, too. Pacific Southwest Airlines was not to be left behind in the race to sexualise the cabin service, with its eye-catching uniforms and unashamedly flirtatious approach.

Things became a little more sober during the '70s and '80s as airlines moved away from the emphasis on wooing male business travellers in favour of a more family-friendly image, emphasising quality, service and comfort over short hemlines as the move from sexy stewardess to asexual flight attendant occurred (Oh, how we long for the good ol' days).

Just Desserts

Flight attendants work very hard in an effort to help their passengers enjoy their flight. But some very definitely go that extra mile.

On a flight between Cincinnati and Seattle, the 12 first class passengers were being served dinner by a stewardess who was handling the luxury cabin for the first time. Unlike her previous experience in economy, the first class service was rather elaborate. She wanted to ensure that the passengers got to savour every drink, appetiser, main course, dessert and coffee; in fact she wanted no morsel of the meal to be missed. Unfortunately she was so unhurried in her service that they hadn't got through all the courses by the time they had to land. Undaunted, as the passengers departed the aircraft she presented each of them an airsick bag containing their dessert – and of course a smile.

The most dangerous thing about flying is the risk of starving to death.

– DICK DEPEW, TEST PILOT

Don't Mess with the Flight Attendants

Passenger rudeness is an unfortunate hazard of the cabin staff's job. Invariably they manage to keep smiling and politely handle the situation. However, sometimes things go too far and get out of hand. Passengers beware.

On a late-night flight in America a passenger wanted to contact a business associate and demanded use of the aircraft's communications equipment. The flight attendant refused since the system was restricted to aircraft crew communications by Federal Aviation Administration regulation. The man continued with his demands and the more he demanded, the more she resisted. It wasn't long before he became very abusive and aggressive.

It got to the point where other passengers were finding the situation unpleasant and a lady seated next to the man joined in the debate. She was very firmly on the side of the flight attendant and pointed out that if federal regulations forbade him using the communications system then he had no right to be so rude.

Somewhat chastened but still ready to fight his corner, the man asked her who she was. She replied that she was a special investigator for the Internal Revenue Service and she'd like to know his name and address. Understandably the man apologised, came over very quiet and was no more trouble for the rest of the flight.

After he had disembarked the flight attendant and her off-duty colleague who had just impersonated an IRS officer could barely walk off the aircraft for laughing.

> *Americans have an abiding belief in their ability to control reality by purely material means... airline insurance replaces the fear of death with the comforting prospect of cash.*
>
> – CECIL BEATON

The Fastest Man in the Air

The excitement, or perhaps the boredom, of air travel can cause people to do the strangest things. Add some alcohol, high spirits and a group of friends eager to impress each other, and you have a recipe for men behaving badly.

A few hours into a flight a stewardess was brewing coffee when she saw a naked man emerge at the opposite end of the cabin and streak down the aisle. His plan was presumably to go through the galley and back down the other aisle. However, as he turned the corner the attendant looked him up and down and said, 'Ahh, look, it's so small.' The crestfallen man stopped dead in his tracks and was swiftly strapped into a seat in the back row with seat-belt extensions. The crew threw a blanket over his nudity and left him there until they arrived at Los Angeles, where he was arrested.

FLYING FACTS

Golden Oldies

If you're on a Boeing 737, and there's a good chance that you are as at any one time there are over a thousand in the air, you might be surprised to know that the first one was ordered by Lufthansa in February 1965. The first 737 flew in 1967 and entered service with the German airline in February 1968. To be fair there are many new versions of the basic design flying with the world's airlines. Over 5,000 have been delivered and the oldest is the 10th off the production line, which still flies in America with Air California.

A Woman in Uniform

Flight attendants are famously immaculate in their dress and personal appearance and airlines take great pains to ensure that they project the right image for their companies. However, like the rest of us, they can sometimes be very forgetful.

Shortly after take-off on a flight to Chicago one of the cabin crew suddenly realised that she'd left her luggage on the jetway in the rush to load the passengers and prepare the aircraft for take-off. She had nothing other than the clothes she was wearing. One of her colleagues reassured her and told her she could borrow some toiletries and some clothes to go out for the evening before they flew back to base the next day. So no problem.

The crew went out for dinner and more than a few drinks and the forgetful flight attendant decided to sleep in the same room as her friend. The trouble started when she got up the next morning to go back to her own room to dress in her uniform and discovered she had lost her room key. Worse, she couldn't remember her room number.

At the hotel's reception she explained the situation, but they would not tell her the room number, nor would they let her into the room unless she could prove it was hers. Since she had no identification, they were unmoved. By now it was getting close to the time that the crew would have to leave for the airport and she was getting frantic, standing in a hotel lobby in borrowed jeans and a T-shirt while her uniform was locked in her room.

Finally the crew bus arrived and she had no choice but to get on board and drive to the airport. It was then that inspiration struck. She went straight to the lost property office, charmed the staff and walked out wearing a mismatched and only just fitting outfit of a black skirt, white blouse and slightly too big shoes. She worked the flight back home and was reunited with her luggage.

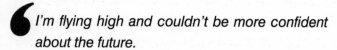

I'm flying high and couldn't be more confident about the future.

– SIR FREDDIE LAKER, 3 DAYS BEFORE THE COLLAPSE OF LAKER AIRWAYS

Boats and Planes

Being late for work is more serious for a flight attendant than in many professions as they might quite literally miss the plane. One stewardess gets full marks for determination to make her flight.

She had been enjoying a few hours out on the water off San Diego in her kayak before reporting for duty in the late afternoon for her flight. Unfortunately the tide and currents were stronger than she had expected and she found herself unable to return to land anywhere near where she had parked her car. After a lot of increasingly frantic paddling she ended up a long way down the coast. She hauled her boat back along the beach and arrived back at her car exhausted, bleeding from where she'd tripped up on some rocks, wearing a swimsuit and covered in sand.

Still determined to report for duty she put the kayak on the roof of her car and drove straight to the airport. Time was tight and she had no way of securing the boat to her car and she was concerned that the kayak would be stolen. After a quick wash and change she persuaded the flight crew to help her stow the kayak in the aircraft. Towards the end of their three-day duty the captain and co-pilot began to find sharing the cockpit with a wet, sandy kayak somewhat less amusing.

> *The world is divided into two kinds of people: normal, intelligent, sensitive people with some breadth of imagination, and people who aren't the least bit afraid of flying.*
> – LAYNE RIDLEY, AUTHOR OF WHITE KNUCKLES: GETTING OVER THE FEAR OF FLYING, 1987

Drawing on Experience

The question of how to keep passengers amused and happy on a long and tedious flight is one that constantly – well sometimes – occupies flight attendants. One hit upon the idea of handing out paper and coloured pencils and asking the passengers to do some drawing. She has found that most passengers are just happy drunks and will be kept amused for hours coming up with a masterpiece, which will be displayed and judged by the other passengers in a competition for the best artist on the aircraft.

The flight attendant has been doing this for so long that she's won employee recognition awards for it and Crayola have sent her huge amounts of free drawing materials in sponsorship. Some of the works of art have been displayed in airports, one of the best being by a Disney animator who was on one of her flights. The moral of the story? Treat passengers like children.

Branson 'dirty tricks' claim unfounded.
– HEADLINE OF AN ARTICLE IN THE BRITISH AIRWAYS
NEWSLETTER BA NEWS, 1992. THE ARTICLE BECAME THE
CENTRE OF THE LARGEST LIBEL PAYMENT IN BRITISH LEGAL
HISTORY

The Whole World Loves an Anorak

As a passenger, how do you please your flight attendants? Most people just do what comes naturally, they smile and are polite and pleasant – and that's all the cabin crew would ask.

But one man has taken his appreciation of the airline staff's hard work to entirely new levels. Mr Ogg, who has been flying regularly for 30 years, has spent the time compiling a database of the flight attendants with whom he has flown. He checks whether he has flown with them previously and reviews his prior rating of their service. On several occasions when he has been particularly impressed he has sent the airline a letter of commendation and a certificate to recognise their performance. During the 3.2 million miles he has flown to date he has encountered many cases of exemplary service and been pleased to dispatch many certificates.

Not content with that, Mr Ogg always makes sure he carries four dozen muffins with him when he travels. One dozen for the skycaps, a dozen for the check-in staff, a dozen for the ground crew and the final 12 for the flight crew. Mr Ogg generally enjoys very, very good service.

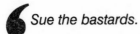

Sue the bastards.

– SIR FREDDIE LAKER'S ADVICE TO SIR RICHARD BRANSON

REGARDING BRITISH AIRWAYS' DIRTY TRICKS CAMPAIGN

AGAINST VIRGIN ATLANTIC

Rare Service

Over the years Britain has helped many nations to establish their own national airlines. It's not just the British – many years ago Aer Lingus helped run Zambia Airways, but that's a whole different story. When it was government-owned, British Airways also provided staff training to many fledgling airlines. Sometimes, though, cultural issues were underestimated when they were concentrating on how to deliver luxury airborne service.

After many months of work and training the inaugural flight by Nigerian Airways left London to fly to Kano and on to Lagos. The cabin crew of the Nigerian aircraft, who were supervised by BA staff, were operating a flight for the first time. As befits such an event, the first class cabin was full of dignitaries, including the heads of major companies whom the new airline was hoping to impress and secure their long-term business.

All went well on the flight to Kano, the food and drink was immaculately presented and everyone was highly impressed with the professionalism of the flight attendants. At Kano there was a partial crew change, with some cabin crew leaving and being replaced by fresh staff for the next leg of the flight to Lagos.

Unfortunately, the airline had not accounted for the deep ethnic divisions and rivalry that existed in Nigeria. People from the same cultural background had staffed the flight from London to Kano and all had been harmonious; sadly, some of the crew who got on at Kano were from another tribal group.

Trouble broke out shortly after take-off when, with great flourish and skill, one of the stewards began carving from a large joint of roast beef on a trolley. The roast was taken down the aisle in the first class cabin and each passenger's meal was carved and served to them. During the service the man doing the carving was approached by one of the new crew who had boarded at Kano. Unfortunately the newly arrived attendant was from a different ethnic group and such was the animosity the steward with the carving knife felt towards him that, without hesitation, he plunged the carving knife into the man's chest.

As the struggling pair fell to the floor a large amount of blood was shed, some of which sprayed over the chief executive of a major international company; displaying admirable self control, he commented, 'Oh dear, I wanted mine well done.'

FLYING FACTS

Security in the 1970s

You'll probably be surprised to know that the first airport to screen passengers was New Orleans International way back in 1970 when skyjacking in America seemed to be a pretty popular pastime.

Hide and Seek

Airlines operate to very tight margins and aircraft that are sitting on the ground and not flying are costing money, not making money.

The schedulers who plan the deployment of an airline's planes set out to have the maximum number of hours flown by each and every aircraft. Sometimes, in the midst of an operational problem, aircraft are required to position empty to another airport. Flights like these are the equivalent of a Sunday afternoon drive in the country, but with none of the attendant pleasures.

One such flight was to bring an aircraft back from Singapore to London – the equivalent of a month of Sunday drives. On board were four flight deck crew and 16 cabin staff. Initially they revelled in the novelty of operating a flight without passengers. They watched the film, ate and drank and tried out every seat in the cabin without the inconvenience of people to serve. It's a long flight, though, and after a few hours boredom set in.

To cheer things up the captain suggested a game of hide and seek. He set the aircraft on autopilot and the first officer remained in the cockpit in case of emergency while the rest of the crew split up into two teams. Each team had a 'base' at one end of the aircraft cabin. The idea was that team members had to try to sneak up to and touch the opposite team's base to win.

To add to the fun, they turned off all the cabin lights so it was pitch dark. For further spice they then all stripped stark naked with hefty forfeits to be levied if players were found with any clothing on. There was a fairly even mix of men to women, so the chance that the person brushed up against in the dark was of the opposite sex was about 50/50. However, the excitement was heightened by the fact that four of the male stewards were gay.

The semi-hysterical atmosphere was tipped into chaos when the first officer, a bit fed up with sitting on his own in the cockpit while everyone else had a good time, flicked on the cabin lights for a second or so every so often. Suggestions that the game be adopted on all flights, with the passengers taking part, did not impress the airline's management.

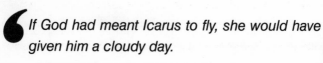

If God had meant Icarus to fly, she would have given him a cloudy day.
– LEON M. WISE

Man in the Mask

The route between London and Paris is popular among many cabin crew. It's a very short flight – around 45 minutes – and usually after a short time on the ground the aircraft flies back to London. A flight attendant rostered on one of these duties can expect to be away from home for something like four or five hours – if all goes according to schedule.

On one particular service between London and Paris the aircraft landed safely and the passengers disembarked. However, during pre-flight checks before the return leg, a mechanical fault was discovered. The problem could not be repaired and replacement parts would not be available until the following day. The aircraft was to have operated the airline's final flight from Paris to London for the day, so all of the passengers would either have to be found seats on other airlines' flights or be put up in a hotel for the night until the aircraft could be repaired and fly them out in the morning.

Some seats were free on alternative services and a few lucky passengers were rebooked. The airline's staff began to make hotel reservations and handle the situation as they normally would. All perfectly routine, other than for one of the female flight attendants, who was becoming increasingly agitated. She kept insisting that she simply had to be back in London that evening. In fact, a night spent in Paris was totally out of the question. She practically demanded that there must be a seat on a flight for her that evening.

No matter how many times she was told that all available seats had gone to passengers, that it was perfectly normal to wait a night in a hotel, that she'd be home in the morning, she remained insistent and was getting hysterical. But no matter how many times she was asked, she wouldn't say why it was so important. Finally, in frustration, the manager of the Paris ground staff contacted head office so the problem could be discussed with the overall duty manager.

Fortunately the manager had previously worked for many years as a cabin steward and knew the upset flight attendant quite well. He spoke to her on the telephone and explained that it was simply impossible to get her home that night. Once she realised that there really was no way to get back, she finally decided that she should divulge the reason for her distress. She'd left her husband at home. In the under-stairs cupboard. Trussed up like a chicken in leather bondage gear. And a hood.

The duty manager contacted the police and accompanied them to the stewardess's house, where they broke down the front door and, to the huge entertainment of the officers involved, released a very embarrassed, and highly relieved, man from his prison.

> *The three worst things to hear in the cockpit:*
> *The second officer says, 'Oh shit!'*
> *The first officer says, 'I have an idea!'*
> *The captain says, 'Hey, watch this!'*
> – ANON.

Passing in the Air

Everything involving humans can and does happen in aircraft cabins: death occasionally, birth rarely, even conception from time to time. Most deaths are very peaceful and brought on from stress caused by the combination of low pressure, low oxygen and hours of sitting still. The elderly are the most vulnerable and flights to Australia are renowned for experiencing fatalities among older passengers who rarely fly, going to see their children who have moved 'down under'. Often they have a couple of brandies after the meal, even though they don't drink normally, then they miss their medication since their pills are in their luggage in the hold, then slip away. The flight attendants simply move them as quietly as possible to a crew seat, strap them in and put a blanket over them.

> *There are four ways to fly: the right way, the wrong way, the company way and the captain's way. Only one counts.*
> – ANON.

Are You Sitting Comfortably?

The ritual of the pre-flight announcements and safety demonstration is familiar to all airline passengers, to many frequent fliers wearily so. In the unlikely event of an emergency the information given is vital to the safety of the aircraft's occupants, but despite this a great many passengers ignore the announcements of the cabin crew. Airlines wrestle with this problem and have come up with a variety of ways to engage their customers' interest.

One US airline's approach is a novel one. Rather than prescribe the spiel to be presented, they have taken their light-hearted approach to business to new heights by encouraging their flight attendants to ad-lib and use comedy. The following is a taste of the fare on offer:

'Above your head you will find a series of buttons. Three of these buttons turn on the overhead lights. There is also a button to call the flight attendant. Pushing this button will not turn on the flight attendant.

'We would also like to remind you that federal law prohibits tampering with the smoke detectors or video cameras in the lavatories.'

One attendant marked the airline's inaugural service between Philadelphia and Pittsburgh by presenting the safety information Elvis style, to the tune of All Shook Up:

In your seat pocket there's a safety card,

Take it out and read it, it's not very hard.

Make sure your luggage is under your seat.

Slide it up, uh, with your feet.

Oh, oh, oh. Yeah, yeah.

He treated the passengers to an exit announcement to the tune of The Beverly Hillbillies.

IN-FLIGHT CONFIDENTIAL

The airline does not have assigned seating, just boarding passes marked A, B or C; as a gate agent announced to the bleary passengers on the early morning flight in Pittsburgh as boarding commenced, 'If you have D on your pass, you're here with me all day.'

Another flight attendant had clearly had enough when coming out with the following announcement, which could broadly be called a safety briefing:

'Welcome aboard this flight. To operate your seat belt, insert the metal tab into the buckle, and pull it tight. It works just like every other seat belt, and if you don't know how to operate one you probably shouldn't be out in public unsupervised.

'In the event of a sudden loss of cabin pressure, oxygen masks will descend from the ceiling. Stop screaming, grab the mask, and pull it over your face. If you have a small child travelling with you, secure your mask before assisting with theirs. If you are travelling with two or more small children, decide now which one you love most. Help that one first, and then work your way down.

Weather at our destination is 50 degrees with some broken clouds, but they'll try to have them fixed before we arrive. Thank you, and remember, nobody loves you, or your money, more than we do.

 The bulk of mankind is as well equipped for flying as thinking.

– JONATHAN SWIFT, WRITER, 1667-1745

Russian Roulette

There have been plenty of incidents involving unruly passengers, but not many about out-of-control flight attendants. Think twice, though, before complaining about the service on the Russian national airline. A passenger on an Aeroflot flight complained that the cabin crew serving him were drunk and he would like to be attended by someone sober and capable. His request earned him a severe beating by two stewards. Somewhat reassuringly, the entire crew was suspended after the flight landed.

Which is now a more hopeful statement than Swift intended it to be.

– WILL DURANT, PHILOSOPHER

No Smoke Without Fire

Fire on board an aircraft is, of course, extremely serious and the crew of an easyJet flight from Glasgow to Amsterdam in June 2002 leapt into action when smoke was seen coming from a rear toilet cubicle.

The 134 passengers watched in terror as the crew battled the blaze with fire extinguishers and the aircraft diverted to Newcastle Airport, where nine fire engines and eight ambulances met the aircraft.

The crew's delight at averting disaster turned to embarrassment when it was discovered that the 'smoke' was in fact nothing more than vapour from discarded bags of dry ice, used to keep food cold, which had been dumped in the toilet's bin by the aircraft crew.

> *The air is annoyingly potted with a multitude of minor vertical disturbances, which sicken the passengers and keep us captives of our seat belts. We sweat in the cockpit, though much of the time we fly with the side windows open. The airplanes smell of hot oil and simmering aluminum, disinfectant, faeces, leather, and puke... the stewardesses, short-tempered and reeking of vomit, come forward as often as they can for what is a breath of comparatively fresh air.*
>
> – AUTHOR ERNEST K. GANN, DESCRIBING AIRLINE FLYING IN THE 1930s

Let's Hear it for the (New) Girl...

Aircrew are notorious for playing tricks on new girls, particularly on long-haul flights where they have more hours to while away. One old favourite on transatlantic flights that take a northerly routing over Greenland on a clear day is to get the girl into the flight deck for a bit of polar bear spotting.

'You can spot them by their black noses,' would be the helpful tip from one of the pilots; all this, of course, from well over 30,000 feet. It is surprising how many girls spotted them from almost six miles high. Another wheeze perpetrated by the flight deck on the young and innocent hostesses was to invite them to come to the flight deck just as the sun was coming up in order to see the phenomenon of the – dawn horn.

A male pilot is a confused soul who talks about women when he's flying, and about flying when he's with a woman.
— ANON.

Ladies and Gentlemen...

Here are a few of the flight and cabin crew announcements to passengers which stray from the official company line that have been recorded over the years:

'There may be 50 ways to leave your lover, but there are only four ways out of this airplane.'

'As you exit the plane, make sure that you gather all your belongings. Anything left behind will be evenly distributed among the flight attendants. Please do not leave children or spouses.'

'We've reached our cruising altitude now, and I'm turning off the seat-belt sign. I'm switching to autopilot too, so I can come back there and visit with all of you for the rest of the flight.'

'Should the cabin lose pressure, oxygen masks will drop from the overhead area. Please place the bag over your own mouth and nose before assisting children or adults behaving like children.'

Airline PA: 'Ladies and gentlemen, welcome to Glasgow, we hope you enjoyed your flight and thank you for flying easyJet. If you didn't enjoy your flight, thank you for flying Ryanair.'

After a hard landing: 'That was quite a bump and I know what y'all are thinking. I'm here to tell you it wasn't the airline's fault, and it wasn't the pilot's fault, it wasn't the flight attendant's fault. It was the asphalt!'

And another: 'We ask you to please remain in your seat as Captain Kangaroo bounces us to the terminal.'

And another: 'Ladies and gentlemen, please remain in your seats until Captain Crash and the crew have brought the aircraft to a screeching halt at the gate. Once the tire smoke has cleared and the warning bells have been silenced, we'll open the door and you can pick your way through the wreckage to the terminal.'

'We'd like to thank you folks for flying with us today. Next time you get the insane urge to go blasting through the skies in a pressurised metal tube, we hope you'll think of us here at US Airways.'

'Your seat cushions can be used for flotation, and in the event of an emergency water landing, please take them with our compliments.'

From a pilot's welcome message: 'We are pleased to have some of the best flight attendants in the industry. Unfortunately, none of them are on this flight.'

On an Air NZ flight with a very 'senior' flight attendant crew, the pilot said, 'Ladies and gentlemen, we've reached cruising altitude and will be turning down the cabin lights. This is for your comfort and to enhance the appearance of your flight attendants.'

After a long wait at the gate for departure: 'I'm sorry for the delay, but the machine that smashes your baggage and pulls the handles off is broken, so the ground crew is having to do it by hand.'

'Please be careful opening the overhead bins because "shift happens".'

'Ladies and gentlemen. Our pilots FLY much better than they DRIVE so please remain seated until the captain finishes taxiing and brings the aircraft to a complete stop at the terminal.'

Taxiing down the tarmac, the DC-10 abruptly stopped, turned around and returned to the gate. After an hour-long wait, it finally took off. A concerned passenger asked the flight attendant, 'What, exactly, was the problem?' 'The pilot was bothered by a noise he heard in the engine,' explained the flight attendant. 'It took us a while to find a new pilot.'

After making his announcement, the pilot of an airliner turned to the co-pilot and said, 'Right now I could really go for a cup of coffee and a blow job.' In the back galley, the head flight attendant was shocked to hear this comment come over the PA to the entire cabin. As she ran to the cockpit to tell the pilot he had a 'hot mike' an elderly female passenger was overheard to say to her, 'Have some dignity, dearie. Don't run to him, walk.'

After the routine extinguishing of cabin lights prior to departure, a Northwest pilot remarked: 'Folks, as soon as we have the electric bill paid we can turn the lights back on.'

'Please be sure to take all your belongings. If you're going to leave anything, please make sure it's something we'd like to have.'

'Last one off the plane cleans it!'

'Ladies and gentlemen, if you wish to smoke, the smoking section on this airplane is on the wing and if you can light 'em, you can smoke 'em.'

On an American Airlines 727 preparing for take-off from San Diego to Chicago, the captain came on the intercom and encouraged the passengers: 'Well, folks, just sit back, tighten up your seat belts, dig your fingernails into the armrests and we'll see if we can get this turkey into the air.'

When asked by a passenger if they served nuts... 'Yes, Sir, we don't discriminate.'

'Please remain seated until the plane is parked at the gate. At no time in history has a passenger beaten a plane to a gate, so please don't even try.'

'In case of a water landing, your suede boots are toast.'

'In the event that our flight should unexpectedly become a cruise, you will find that your seat cushion may be used as a flotation device, and as you kick and paddle your way to the nearest beach you can rest assured that your flight crew will be following close behind you, bringing the peanuts and alcohol.'

Air Canada pilot explaining how they'd made up time after a late start: 'We drove 'er like we stole 'er.'

Half-Baked Alaska

A quick-typing laptop user (who should have had it switched off) managed to transcribe this announcement made by a flight attendant on a flight from Seattle:

'Hello and welcome to Alaska Airlines Flight 438 to San Francisco. If you're going to San Francisco, relax – you're in the right place. If you're not going to San Francisco, you're about to have a really long evening. We'd like to tell you now about some important safety features of this aircraft.

'The most important safety features we have aboard this plane are... the flight attendants. Please look at one now.

'There are five exits aboard this plane: two at the front, two over the wings, and one out the plane's rear end. If you're seated in one of the exit rows, please do not store your bags by your feet. That would be a really bad idea. Please take a moment and look around and find the nearest exit. Count the rows of seats between you and the exit. In the event that the need arises to find one, trust me, you'll be glad you did. We have pretty blinking lights on the floor that will blink in the direction of the exits. White ones along the normal rows, and pretty red ones at the exit rows.

'In the seat pocket in front of you is a pamphlet about the safety features of this plane. I usually use it as a fan when I'm having my own personal summer. It makes a very good fan. It also has pretty pictures. Please take it out and play with it now.

'Please take a moment now to make sure your seat belts are fastened low and tight about your waist. To fasten the belt, insert the metal tab into the buckle. To release, it's a pully thing – not a pushy thing like your car because you're in an aircraft – HELLO!

'There is no smoking permitted in the cabin on this flight. There is also no smoking in the lavatories. If we see smoke coming from the lavatories, we will assume you are on fire and put you out. This is a free service we provide. There are two smoking sections on this flight, one outside each wing exit. We do have a movie in the smoking sections tonight... hold on; let me check what it is. Oh here it is; the movie tonight is Gone with the Wind.

'In a moment we will be turning off the cabin lights, and it's going to get really dark, really fast. If you're afraid of the dark, now would be a good time to reach up and press the yellow button. The yellow button turns on your reading light. Please don't press the orange button unless you absolutely have to. The orange button is your seat ejection button.

'We're glad to have you with us on this flight. Thank you for choosing Alaska Airlines, and giving us your business and money. If there's anything we can do to make you more comfortable, please don't hesitate to ask.'

> *Since 1978 the record pretty well shows that no start-up airline... has really been successful, so the odds of JetBlue having long-term success are remote. I'm not going to say it can't happen because stranger things have happened, but I personally believe P.T. Barnum was, in that respect, correct.*
>
> – GORDON BETHUNE, CEO OF CONTINENTAL AIRLINES

Where Do Planes Come From?

A mother and her son were flying Southwest Airlines from Kansas City to Chicago. The little boy, who had been looking out the window, turned to his mother and asked, 'If big dogs have baby dogs and big cats have baby cats, why don't big planes have baby planes?'

His mother, who couldn't think of an answer, told her son to ask the stewardess. So the boy asked the stewardess, 'If big dogs have baby dogs and big cats have baby cats, why don't big planes have baby planes?'

'Did your mother tell you to ask me?' The boy admitted that this was the case. 'Well, then,' the stewardess replied, 'tell your mother that there are no baby planes because Southwest always pulls out on time. Your mother can explain THAT to you.'

Be Careful What You Wish For

Soon after boarding a flight, a white woman in her 50s was seated next to a black man and was sufficiently disturbed by this to press the flight attendant call button. The attendant asked her what she needed. The lady replied that she objected to sitting next to 'someone from such a repugnant group' and demanded another seat. The flight attendant kept her composure and explained that the aircraft was very full but asked her to be patient while she checked whether there were any other seats available on the flight.

After a few minutes the flight attendant came back and said, 'Just as I thought, there are no other available seats in economy class. I have spoken to the captain and he informed me that business class is full, but there is one empty seat in first class. It is not usual for our company to permit someone from economy class to sit in first class. However, given the circumstances, the captain feels that it would be scandalous to make someone sit next to someone so disgusting.'

As the satisfied smile came over the white woman's face, the flight attendant turned to the black man and said, 'Therefore, sir, if you'd like to take your hand luggage I'll show you to your new seat in first class.' The passengers sitting around the scene had been shocked into silence by what they had heard previously but now broke into spontaneous applause as the gentleman walked along the aircraft aisle with the flight attendant.

> *'Insurer: 'It was pilot error.'*
> *Pilot: 'It was design error.'*
> *Insurer: 'I disagree. The pilot is at fault for*
> *trusting the designer.'*
> – ANON.

PLANE SPEAKING

O'Hare Approach Control: *'United 239 heavy, your traffic is a Fokker, one o'clock, three miles, eastbound.'*

United 239: *'Approach, I've always wanted to say this... I've got that Fokker in sight.'*

Watch Out

Duty-free sales on board aircraft are not the money-spinners that they used to be – either for the airlines or the cabin crew. Many airlines operated lucrative incentive schemes to get their cabin staff selling more duty-free. With changes in the law the discounts against high street prices are not what they used to be and with airports, and there's no better example than those of BAA, being turned into glorified shopping malls many passengers are shopped out by the time they've got on board. The other potential losers in all this are the cabin crew, and not just because they've lost out on commission. There was a time when some unscrupulous stewards and stewardesses developed a nice little scam. Flying long-haul as some of them did to the Far East there were many opportunities to purchase fake watches of almost every 'brand'. There were some who then would take these onboard and discreetly swap them for the real thing that was in the duty-free cart. There are undoubtedly people who have found out that they have been duped when they took their watch to a reputable jeweller, either for a new battery or a repair, but there may be others who have no idea what has happened to them.

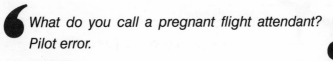

What do you call a pregnant flight attendant? Pilot error.

– ANON.

On the Job Training

An airline captain was breaking in a new stewardess. The route they were flying had a stopover at their destination. Upon arrival, the captain showed the stewardess the best places for airline personnel to eat, shop and stay overnight. The next morning as the pilot was preparing the crew for the day's route, he noticed the new stewardess was missing. He knew which room she was in at the hotel and called her up wondering what had happened to her. She answered the phone, sobbing, and said she couldn't get out of her room.

'You can't get out of your room?' the captain asked. 'Why not?'

The stewardess replied: 'There are only three doors in here,' she cried, 'One is the bathroom, one is the wardrobe, and one has a sign on the handle that says "Do Not Disturb!"'

' *The three most common phrases in airline cockpits were 'Was that for us?' 'What'd he say?' and 'Oh shit!' Since computers are now involved in flying, a new one has been added: 'What's it doing now?'*

– ANON.

,

Deadheads

The sight of some uniformed flight crew sitting in the passenger cabin is not uncommon. Most airlines need pilots to cover a flight at an airport other than the one at which they're based and need to transfer them to the required airport. When crew members travel like this as passengers, it is known in the industry as 'deadheading'. In some cases, owing to weather, mechanical problems or crew flight-time legalities, crews are called out at very short notice to catch a flight. Normally they sit quietly in their uniforms not causing any alarm among the fare-paying passengers, but not always.

A few years ago, while taxiing out for take-off, an airliner suddenly came to a stop. With the aircraft still on the taxiway, the flight attendant in the back lowered the aft stairway. Behind the plane, a van with flashing lights came to a screeching halt and out jumped three deadheading pilots. They grabbed their bags and ran to the plane.

After they ran up the stairs onto the aircraft the one in front continued running up the aisle to the cockpit shouting, 'I can't believe the stewardess got the plane this far. I didn't think she'd even be able to start the engines!'

'*Everything in the company manual – policy, warnings, instructions, the works can be summed up to read, 'Captain, it's your baby.'*
– ANON.

The Definitive Layover Party

Crew high jinks, when on an overnight layover between scheduled duties, are the stuff of legend, but one crew took rest and relaxation to new heights. This is an edited version of a letter that appeared in an airline's staff newsletter in the mid-90s.

'Sir, In your icy, indeed hostile, telephone call of yesterday, you requested a report about the alleged proceedings involving my crew at the overnight port. As the reports from the local authorities and the head of the local diplomatic service were undoubtedly a complete fabrication, I take the opportunity to put the truth of the matter on file.

'Management's kind offer to "buy a round of drinks" was taken on board by the crew who decided to upgrade the event to its correct status, so appropriate quantities of libation and food were purchased, with festivities being held in my hotel suite.

'An enjoyable evening ensued but insufficient supplies had been obtained, so several members of the crew left in order to make further purchases at a local bar. In a truly magnanimous gesture, 10 bar girls from that establishment helped carry the beer back to the hotel. To demonstrate our appreciation of their generous assistance, we served them some cool drink. They then offered to show us some local culture, and, in order not to offend, we allowed them to dance some exotic dances.

'The banging on the walls of my room had, by now, quite honestly, become invasive, and it was disturbing the dancers, so we arranged an amusing little deterrent. Second Officer Smith's impersonation of the police officer was excellent! In full uniform, with an aluminium rubbish bin upside down on his head, he goose-stepped to each room and harangued the occupants with a very witty diatribe about disturbing hotel guests. I personally heard nothing of his alleged threats of life in Alcatraz or the gulags, claimed by the sister of the Minister of Police whose room was, unluckily, next door.

'I have no doubt that this woman was the sneak who called security and hotel management and I absolutely refute that the shout "Look out, here come the Indians! Circle the wagons!" was made. The simple coincidence of security arriving just as we stood the double bed on its side across the door to make the dance floor bigger is obvious.

'The major damage to the room occurred when a group of gate crashers, whom we could not know were hotel security, forced their way in just as most of us happened to be leaning against the bed watching the dancing.

'The reports on subsequent events in the foyer of the hotel are an equally vicious distortion of the facts. I was explaining what had taken place to the general manager of the hotel and noting that other guests were fabricating stories of noise, drinking and singing at the celebration, when First Officer Jones (ex-SAS) and several other keep-fit enthusiasts, in keeping with their almost monastic pursuit of health, organised the race up the curtains which hang along the foyer wall. It says nothing for the workmanship of some of these nations that the fittings were torn from the wall before most of the crew were even halfway up.

IN-FLIGHT CONFIDENTIAL

'At this stage, in an amazing display of international posturing, the governor of the city, who was attending a cocktail party in the foyer, cast some denigrating remarks about our culture. Although he misunderstood our gestures of greeting, Female Flight Attendant Brown rescued the situation with her depth of knowledge of local culture.

'Her performance as the fertility dancing maiden in the foyer's "Pool of Remembrance" was nothing short of breathtaking. Normally this dance is performed wearing just a sarong skirt, so FA Brown's extra step to nature was a bold advance.

'Unfortunately, during one intricate step, FA Brown slipped and fell beneath the fountain, so we were lucky that S/O Smith, who had the great presence of mind to strip to avoid getting his uniform wet, leapt in to help. That the tiles of the pool were slippery is beyond dispute, as it took nearly 10 minutes of threshing about before S/O Smith could actually complete his rescue. Such concern was there for these two exemplary crew members' safety, that the rest of the crew were forced to assist, and I deny that this massed altruistic rescue attempt could be construed as a "water polo" game. This thoroughly slanderous accusation was first put to me by the chief of the Riot Squad, whose storm troopers had apparently been called by some over-zealous fascists at the cocktail party.

'Order had nearly been restored when the fire started.

'I prefer F/O Jones's version of events that the curtains had caught fire from being against a light fitting, and that he dropped his cigarette lighter while trying to escape the flames. Had host management fulfilled their responsibilities and used fire-retardant material instead of velvet, the fire would not have spread to the rest of the hotel.

'The responsible attitude shown by my crew in assisting the bar staff to carry out drinks from the cocktail party is to be commended, not condemned, and the attempt by male members of the crew to extinguish pockets of fire using natural means has been totally misrepresented in some quarters. I cannot overstate how strongly I resent the assertions made in the chief fire officer's report.

'I made an official protest about these matters when the Ambassador visited us at the police station the next morning. However, not only did he not attempt to refute the preposterous allegations made against me and my crew, but also by failing to secure our release immediately, caused the subsequent aircraft delay.

'I did not know that royalty was expected to be aboard our aircraft, but I am sure that her 12-hour visit to that country was very much appreciated by local dignitaries and probably HRH herself.

'Finally, I note that it is many years since the airline has been mentioned in so many newspapers. (Some people in the company would die for coverage like that.) The main newspaper at the slip port coincidentally mentioned our name 75 times on its front page alone, although some of the coupled epithets can only be described as the worst journalistic excesses of the gutter press.

'I trust that now I have outlined the correct version of events, we may allow ourselves a discreet smile as to the lack of social sophistication of some of these developing nations and put all this behind us. As far as I am concerned, the crew carried on our finest traditions.

'Regards, Captain xxxxx

'P.S. I checked among the language-qualified members of the crew, but no one was up to speed on Latin. Can you recommend anyone in the International Department who could translate the phrase "Persona Non Grata"?'

> *Everyone already knows that the definition of 'good' landing is one you can walk away from. But very few know the definition of a 'great' landing. It's one after which you can use the aircraft another time.*
>
> — ANON.

Singapore Girls

It is no coincidence that Singapore Airlines is famous for its elegant flight attendants. Since it became independent from Malaysia-Singapore Airlines in 1972 it has cultivated a staff of stewardesses (they are still not referred to as 'flight attendants') who represent every virtue the company would like to project.

The hundreds of candidates for every job are put through a rigorous selection process, which begins with checking their height – which must be over five feet two inches – and age – which must be under 26. Next is an English pronunciation test and then an interview. Those who pass round one are evaluated wearing swimsuits, for a swimming test, and examined for scars, blemishes and the quality of their complexions. The survivors then enter stage three, in which they mingle with their competitors at a tea party and are assessed for their social skills. Finally, they address an audience for two minutes on a topic they are given, testing their self-confidence and poise.

The few candidates who survive all that then go on to a four-month training programme at the SIA Training Centre next to Changi Airport. Here they are turned into the polite, elegant, immaculately attired and made-up visions for which the airline is famous and which are central to its image. They are drilled in etiquette (including how to address members of governments and royalty), manners and deportment, even how to pick up something gracefully from the floor with a straight back. They are educated in fine food and wine, some even qualifying as sommeliers.

In grooming classes they receive comprehensive training in hair care and make-up skills, individually tailored to each girl's hair and complexion. Different day and night make-up styles are practised and shades of lipstick, nail and toenail varnish are selected (they must always all match). Weight maintenance is also crucial; if a few pounds are gained the stewardess is given three months to slim down or may be grounded. They also receive plenty of practice in emergency response, using exit slides and swimming with an injured colleague in choppy seas. Finally they are drilled in how to handle rude and abusive passengers without becoming even slightly ruffled.

Once they have completed all that they are qualified to don the slinky dress that is the airline's trademark uniform, and continue the tradition that gave rise to the airline's advertising slogans, 'This Girl's in Love with You' and 'Singapore Girl, You're a Great Way to Fly'.

Virgin Air

Air China takes a great deal of care when it hires new flight attendants; one of the credentials required for all applicants is apparently virginity. The airline's staff interview the prospective cabin crew's teachers to determine how much time the 19-year-old school leaver applicant spent with the opposite sex (male or female). If they fraternised too much, they are out of the reckoning.

Once they are in the job they are free to marry and start a family, but the chances of their husband or wife originating in a passenger seat are remote. According to Hao Yu-Ping, director of the carrier's flight attendant training centre, personnel with little experience of dating are harder workers and tend not to get entangled romantically with passengers.

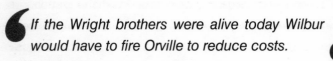

If the Wright brothers were alive today Wilbur would have to fire Orville to reduce costs.

– HERB KELLEHER, SOUTHWEST AIRLINES

Changing Places

Flight attendants are trained to remain polite to the passengers even in the face of extreme provocation, and 99.9 per cent of the time they manage to pull it off and present the right face of the airline to the public. Every so often, however, they are pushed too far and can't resist giving the passengers what they deserve.

On a flight from India to Frankfurt there were a lot of wealthy Indian passengers in first class who were used to having servants around to assist in those everyday tasks that the rest of us take in our stride.

One lady passenger misjudged the airline employees' duties when she called a male flight attendant over to her seat. She handed him her baby and said, 'Please could you change him?'

The flight attendant stared back at her in disbelief as she repeated the question. Realising that she meant the baby's nappy, but outraged by the request, he decided to take her at face value. He walked back down the cabin with the baby until he found a black couple travelling with their children. One was only a few months old. They obligingly let him borrow their baby, which he took back to the Indian woman and presented to her with a smile and said, 'Here you go, I changed your baby for you!' The passenger was predictably furious, but she took care of her baby's nappies for the rest of the flight.

Everything is accomplished through teamwork until something goes wrong, then one pilot gets all the blame.

– ANON.

Nauseating Tales

Flight attendants don't relish airsickness any more than the passengers who suffer from it, but it is an unfortunate fact of life for them. The crew of an American Eagle flight between Nashville and Knoxville, Tennessee, on a small commuter aircraft knew that, even though it was a short flight, the weather conditions were going to cause a lot of turbulence.

The nature of things is such that one passenger being sick usually triggers off others, so once it starts it unfortunately tends to spread. Knowing what was likely to face them and deciding they might as well have some fun with it, the pilot and flight attendant decided to have a bet on how many passengers would throw up during the outbound and return flights. The flight attendant won; there were seven on the way out, four on the way back. More surprising, even to the jaded, seen-it-all flight attendant, was the fact that a 10-year-old boy managed to fill five bags. The crew are considering a wager on volume as well as numbers next time turbulence is expected.

Bad Hair Day

Sometimes the flight attendant is simply having a bad day and can't resist a snappy comment to a passenger, whether they really deserve it or not. One lady boarded a flight in a dishevelled state, looking like she'd had a hard night and without having spent much time on her appearance that morning, and sank into her seat. The flight attendant chirpily greeted her with, 'Hello, where are you going today?' 'LA,' the passenger groaned. 'Oh my, all the way to Los Angeles without a hairbrush...'

 Aerobatics: it's like having sex and being in a car wreck at the same time.
— ANON.

Rubbish

Part of a flight attendant's many duties is to clean up the cabin. You wouldn't perhaps believe it after seeing the debris strewn across the aircraft when it lands after a long flight, which ground-based cleaners deal with, but the cabin crew do a lot of clearing up. Some report that in addition to all the food service packaging that they have to collect there is often passenger's own waste, which has been dropped on the floor by some inconsiderate customers.

Perhaps she'd just had enough one day when an American flight attendant was pushing a rubbish cart down the aisle. A passenger leaned over and said, 'Excuse me, are you trash?' The flight attendant replied, 'I used to be when I was younger, but I've cleaned up my act now.' Whether this answered the question is not clear.

> *As of 1992, in fact – though the picture would have improved since then – the money that had been made since the dawn of aviation by all of this country's airline companies was zero. Absolutely zero.*
>
> – WARREN BUFFETT, BILLIONAIRE INVESTOR

Ooh La La

A man was rather disappointed when one of his colleagues left the office he worked in for a new career as a flight attendant; he was secretly in love with her and was afraid they'd never meet again. However, during her training with the airline she kept in touch with her old workmates and his prayers were answered when they all agreed to go out together for a reunion one evening.

Things could not have gone better and he found himself late on in the evening enjoying a slow dance with his secret amour. His legs were reduced to jelly when for the three or four minutes the song lasted she whispered sweet nothings in French into his ear. Utterly seduced by the sexy mutterings he was smitten and they went on to start a relationship.

After a few weeks together he asked her what she'd said to him that night on the dance floor. Slightly embarrassed, she admitted that it was the pre-flight safety demonstration announcement used on flights to Paris.

Aviation has created many millionaires, primarily from the ranks of multi-millionaires.

– ANON.

Help the Aged

A young and inexperienced flight attendant was busy looking after the passengers when she noticed one who might be in need of special care. A lady in her early 90s was travelling alone at the back of the aircraft.

The flight attendant asked if there was anything she could do for the passenger. The old lady said yes, there was; she would like to visit the lavatory, but would need some help. Slightly unsure what would be required but eager to help, the flight attendant assisted her down the aisle and into the toilet cubicle.

She helped the passenger remove her clothing and get settled, then excused herself and shut the door. After a few minutes she asked if the passenger was ready and went back into the toilet. Still slightly embarrassed by the operation the young flight attendant briskly pulled up the passenger's underwear and trousers, tucked her blouse in and stood back ready to escort her back to her seat. The old lady was very hunched over, almost bent double and breathing quite heavily. Concerned for her welfare, the flight attendant bent down and asked her, 'Ma'am, are you OK?' 'I'm fine,' gasped the old lady. 'But you just tucked my boobs into my pants.'

 Screw the share price, this is a fare war.
– MICHAEL O'LEARY, CHIEF EXECUTIVE OF RYANAIR

Room at the Back

Toilets and nudity do occur on planes, but not so often together, and even less regularly causing a delay in take-off. As they prepared the cabin for departure on a full flight from Los Angeles to Orlando, Florida, a flight attendant noticed that one seat in the economy cabin of the Boeing 767 was empty. Since she knew there was a full passenger load and that all had boarded, the empty seat could only mean that the passenger was in the toilet. The aircraft could not leave until all the passengers were safely belted into their seats, so she went to the lavatories at the rear of the aircraft and started knocking on doors.

There was no reply from any of the cubicles, so she began to try the doors. One was locked. She knocked and called, but the occupant remained silent. Several flight attendants were now involved and they started to try and coax the passenger out in several languages, but without success. The attendants used their key to unlock the door from the outside, but each time they did it the passenger in the WC immediately locked it again.

Finally they managed to get the door unlocked and keep it that way, but couldn't open it as the passenger was bracing her body against it. Frustrated by her intransigence they called a mechanic, who boarded the aircraft and managed to remove the door from its hinges and take it away. The crew were astonished to find the occupant was a middle-aged lady, who had removed all of her clothes. It emerged that she was terrified of flying and had resorted to her naked lavatory siege in response.

The aircraft was already delayed by an hour and, anxious to get things moving, but reluctant to make the poor passenger streak down the cabin, the flight attendants shrouded her in a blanket and put her on a food service trolley to wheel her down the aisle and out of the aircraft.

Airplane travel is nature's way of making you look like your passport photo.

– VICE PRESIDENT AL GORE

Undercover Story

Just when they think they've seen it all and nothing the travelling public can come up with will surprise them, veteran flight attendants are generally faced with a situation they've never seen before.

During a late-night flight a male passenger in his 80s came up to an attractive flight attendant working in the galley of the aircraft and asked her if he might buy her underwear for £200. He explained that he had a collection of underwear from ladies in a variety of professions – teacher, lawyer, doctor, soldier – but didn't yet have an example from a member of an airline cabin crew. The flight attendant was a little taken aback and refused, explaining that the set she was wearing was really rather unglamorous.

One of her colleagues, a gay male, heard about the extraordinary conversation and remarked, 'Shit, I'll sell him mine for £20!' The passenger was a choosy sort and declined the transaction.

 This is a nasty, rotten business.
– ROBERT L. CRANDALL, CEO AND PRESIDENT OF AMERICAN AIRLINES

Lost In Translation

From the in-flight information on Aeroflot's service to the Far East...
'Attention please passengers travelling to Japan. According to new requirements of the Japanese Air Authorities, the conditions of immigration control upon arrival will be changed. Since November 2001 all foreigners will have to leave their fingerprints and be shot while passing immigration control.'

PLANE SPEAKING

British Airways flight asks for push-back clearance from terminal.
Control Tower replies: *'And where is the world's most experienced airline going today without filing a flight plan?'*

How to Get Ahead

Dreaming of joining the glamorous world of airline cabin staff but just a mite under size? Itching to swan down the first class aisle doling out champagne but a fraction off the right stature? Keen to see the world but a little on the petite side? Help is at hand (or rather at head). After being approached by a woman who was marginally too short to qualify for an airline's minimum height requirements to land her 'dream job' of becoming a flight attendant, a Spanish surgeon has had a moment of inspiration.

Dr Luis de la Cruz has hit upon the wheeze of, rather than invasive and debilitating leg extension surgery, and more permanent than wearing Sarko-style Cuban heels, to add an inch or two by performing a 'head implant'. Yup, under local anaesthetic he just slips a silicon implant under the scalp and, hey presto, you're taller. 'The patient is very happy with the result and is now an air stewardess,' he reports.

He's subsequently performed the operation on 17 people, adding up to two inches to their height, at a cost of about £4,000 a time. However, people with thin faces beware – he says you shouldn't go for it as you'll look odd. In contrast to the pack of Mekons he's already done it on, we're sure. So if the flight attendant serving your next meal looks a bit like she's fresh from a Tefal advert, you'll know why.

The future in aviation is the next 30 seconds. Long-term planning is an hour and a half.

– ANON.

Immigration Competition

During the 1950s many people decided to leave Jamaica and the Caribbean to come to the UK and start a new life. BOAC flew many Boeing 707s full of immigrants on their one-way trip to London and the crews tried to make the journey as enjoyable as possible for their new countrymen and women. In that era many members of cabin crew had previously served as stewards on cruise ships and had plenty of experience in entertaining people cooped up on long journeys.

This being long before the days of political correctness or feminism, one steward was in the habit of organising a competition among the female passengers for the biggest bust. The prize was a BOAC pen. The passengers on many flights enthusiastically engaged in these events, but eventually the fun had to end when one lady complained. She was convinced that she had a bigger chest than the winner and felt the pen had been wrongly awarded.

The stewards were very sympathetic to the situation of many newly arrived immigrants. They had often been very poorly prepared for the move by the authorities in their homeland and boarded the aircraft wearing shorts and T-shirts. The temperature in London when they arrived came as an almighty shock and the crews regularly handed out the in-flight blankets to stop them from freezing.

Chapter**SIX**

Coffee, Tea, Or...

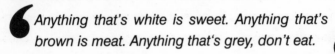

Anything that's white is sweet. Anything that's brown is meat. Anything that's grey, don't eat.

– STEPHEN SONDHEIM

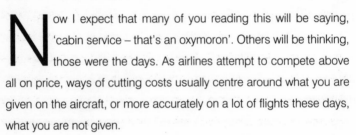

Now I expect that many of you reading this will be saying, 'cabin service – that's an oxymoron'. Others will be thinking, those were the days. As airlines attempt to compete above all on price, ways of cutting costs usually centre around what you are given on the aircraft, or more accurately on a lot of flights these days, what you are not given.

However, from the silver cutlery and linen napkins up at the sharp end, to the plastic boxes and bendy forks way back in steerage, the main event of a flight is usually the mouth-watering ordeal of the food and drink service. The technique for opening the silver foil top of a carton of orange juice while holding your elbows tightly into your sides, bracing your knees against the seat in front (which is still reclined) and not having the drink explode over you and your neighbour is something often practised but seldom perfected.

The provision of refreshment is a hot topic in the airline industry; some airlines don't, some do it brilliantly, others do it appallingly. But among those which continue with the ritual of handing out the trays of, at best, edible treats, it continues to be one of the main ways in which passengers judge their favourite airline. We're accustomed to expecting to be flown efficiently and quietly to where we're going, more or less on schedule, safely and competently. The great excitement of the trip comes in cling film, is reheated in the aircraft galley and is delivered to us by a flight attendant. It's costly (for the airline), heavy (so, again, costly in terms of fuel consumption), is difficult to handle for the staff and often ghastly to eat, but how else are they supposed to amuse the punters?

To give you an example of the kind of thought that goes into airline catering, especially in first class, let me tell you what happened when I joined Continental Airlines. We were to compete on the Houston to London route with British Caledonian, who had arguably the best service of any airline flying across the Atlantic; it was going to be tough. When I went to Houston, not long after I joined the American carrier, for a presentation on the food service I had one of those moments at which you don't know whether to laugh or cry. After seeing what they had proposed for the meal service, which didn't look at all bad, we got around to discussing the wine. When I say discussing what I mean is that the president of the company told me what wine we were to be serving in first class; it was to be Texan wine – white wine if you really want to know. Never heard of it? Neither had I. Having lived in Texas for several years I assumed he was either joking or referring to Lone Star beer. It was not either of those two options; he really meant it. It took me a while but in the end I persuaded him that we should perhaps not buck tradition and it would be more conducive to selling seats if we stuck to a Meursault or at a pinch a Zinfandel.

Lower your tray table, peel back the foil and see what treats are in store for your delectation.

Not a lot of people...
An anagram of Lufthansa is: Fatal Huns

Plain Nuts

Complaints about airline food are 10 a penny. But accusations of discrimination among snack foods are a little more unusual. Southwest Airlines received a letter from the 'Corn Nut Producers of America' appealing to them to reconsider the sidelining of the 'beloved yet overlooked corn nut in preference to the peanut. The airline reassured the organisation in its response, noting that, 'Southwest does not practice snack snobbery.' Pointing out their record of serving toasted cheddar cheese crackers, raisins, pretzels and strawberry fruit bars over the years, they did have to confess, 'However, we are quite fond of our peanuts.'

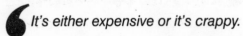 *It's either expensive or it's crappy.*
– JETBLUE AIRWAYS' SPOKESMAN CONSIDERS AIRLINE FOOD

X-Rated

Keeping passengers amused on long, boring flights is a challenge for every airline. The in-flight movie is the main source of entertainment, and on aircraft without individual screens the choice of films is the subject of great care by the airline. Since it will be shown on a large screen in front of all passengers the carriers go to great lengths not to show a movie with inappropriate content. Even then most films have to be edited to ensure nothing too racy is shown. Despite all this caution, El Al fell foul of some passengers' sensibilities when they showed a watered-down version of R rated Changing Lanes starring Ben Affleck and Samuel L. Jackson on a flight from Tel Aviv to Zurich in September 2002.

The film, described as a family drama, was being shown when some of the passengers, who belonged to the ultra-Orthodox Hareidi community, objected to the content. They announced that they were unwilling to expose their children to it and covered one of the screens. This brought shouts of protest from other passengers who were enjoying the film and escalated into pushing matches as control of the screen was contested. A flight attendant broke down in tears trying to restore order. Eventually the film was not shown. One passenger noted afterwards that the anti-movie passengers were lucky they were travelling on El Al, as another airline might well have had them arrested upon landing for their behaviour.

 Most executives don't have the stomach for this stuff.

– ROBERT W. BAKER, AMERICAN AIRLINES

Weight and Balance

Modern fliers are very familiar with 'no frills' airlines and well accustomed to service that is a long way from the linen tablecloths and bone china used on other, more luxurious, carriers. While the passengers on a UK budget flight were not expecting silver service, they were a bit surprised when the Boeing 737 had to be stripped of its food, drink and in-flight magazines in order to be lightened sufficiently for safe take-off.

The aircraft was declared 'too full' and was delayed for an hour while the expendable weight was jettisoned. At least that solved the problem; it is not unheard of for some African airlines to solve the issue of over-booking passengers by organising a race around the aircraft and allowing the fastest passengers back on board the aircraft, shutting the door when all seats are full.

The service was flying from Luton to Madrid, far less than the 3,600 miles a Boeing 737-700 aircraft can travel, but still it was determined that the plane couldn't safely take off with its 149 seats full and its load of baggage, food and reading material on board.

'It's a very rare occurrence,' said a spokeswoman. If an unusually large number of passengers arrive with excess baggage, then the maximum take-off weight can be exceeded. 'We don't know about it until check-in closes,' said the spokeswoman. 'Instead of offloading passengers, it's standard procedure to offload catering.'

The hungry passengers were on board when the call was made and the food removed, so had no way of buying some provisions to sustain them for the flight. Their enforced fast may be beneficial in the long term for aviation, however. Airline pilots' weight and balance calculations are based on an estimated weight of 93kg (14st 9lb) for each male passenger and 75kg (11st 7lb) for each female. Given the increasing size and weight of people in the Western world it can't be long before these average weight figures become out of date and passengers' actual weight needs to be measured with scales at the check-in desk, and fares charged accordingly.

 To me, an airplane is a great place to diet.
– WOLFGANG PUCK, RESTAURANT OWNER AND GOURMET

Catering for All Tastes

Airline food ranges from the dire to the very good and the variety of food served on board aircraft is astonishing. The logistical challenge of preparing, transporting, heating and serving a tasty meal within the weight and space restrictions of an aeroplane has taxed generations of airlines.

Despite some operators now cutting out all food service to keep prices down, most still provide meals and do strive to produce food that does the carrier credit.

If you are curious about what's being served on, say, Ariana Afghan Airlines, what breakfast looks like on Druk Air or whether Ukraine International's grub is up to scratch then www.airlinemeals.net is the website for you. The site contains an extensive archive of photographs showing meals from thousands of flights from last week to the 1960s.

Airlinemeals.net welcomes new material, so next time you're flying why not take a snap of the food on your tray table and send it in. It all goes to prove that you really can find anything on the internet.

‘ *The quality of food is in inverse proportion to a dining room's altitude, especially a top bank and hotel buildings (airplanes are an extreme example).* ’

– BRYAN MILLER, NEW YORK TIMES RESTAURANT CRITIC

A Bug's Life (or Death)

Ever flown to Grenada, India, Kiribati, Madagascar, Trinidad and Tobago, or Uruguay? If so you may remember the crew coming down the aisles spraying an aerosol can shortly before landing. It was a pesticide. The routine spraying of cabins, often right over passengers' heads, termed 'disinfection' in the airline industry, is required on all incoming flights to those countries.

It usually involves the spraying of a pressurised solution containing a two per cent concentration of phenothrin. The treatment should be preceded by an announcement, although there is little the passengers can do to escape it. The aerosol may have ill effects on infants, asthmatics and pregnant women, and flight attendant unions have concerns about the repeated exposure for their members and argue that mechanical insect prevention systems would be just as effective and less risky.

An alternative method is required by six other countries. Australia, Barbados, Fiji, Jamaica, New Zealand and Panama require the spraying of every surface in the cabin with a solution that contains two per cent permethrin. This is done before the crew and passengers board the aircraft.

The Northwest Coalition for Alternatives to Pesticides (or NCAP to you and me) notes that pesticides could cause greater harm on aircraft since up to 50 per cent of the air in the cabins is recycled. 'Pesticides break down slowly in the enclosed, poorly ventilated aircraft,' warns the NCAP. Airlines are not required to inform passengers at ticket purchase of flight sprays, and there is also no control over how much pesticide is applied on the aircraft. The Association of Flight Attendants reported in 2001 that one airline used 50-60 per cent more pesticide than the maximum recommended by the World Health Organisation.

Between 2000 and 2001, one cabin crew union received complaints of pesticide-related illness on more than 200 flights. Many complaints cite damp surfaces and pesticide odours in crew rest compartments. Crews and passengers have reported sinus problems, swollen and itchy eyes, coughs, difficulty breathing, hoarseness, skin rashes/hives that vary in intensity, severe headaches and fatigue, and heightened sensitivity to other chemicals. However, to be fair, some of these symptoms could have their causes based in altogether different activities. Some crew members have medical documentation of reactions consistent with nerve gas exposure, such as blood, optic nerve, and nervous system abnormalities.

Fortunately alternative methods to control insects on aircraft have already been developed. Since the 1980s, the US Department of Agriculture has successfully used curtains made of overlapping strips of plastic to keep Japanese beetles off aircraft destined for the Western states during the summer. Chemically treated mosquito netting and blowers in jetways may also be used as alternatives.

'*The more I fly, the more I'm convinced that the true wonder of modern aviation is the transformation of tasteless particles into something known as airplane food.*'

– BOB BLUMMER, AUTHOR OF THE SURREAL GOURMET

PLANE SPEAKING

Tower: *'Eastern 702, cleared for take-off, contact Departure on 124.7.'*

Eastern 702: *'Tower, Eastern 702 switching to Departure. By the way, after we lifted off we saw some kind of dead animal on the far end of the runway.'*

Tower: *'Continental 635, cleared for take-off, contact Departure on 124.7. Did you copy that report from Eastern?'*

Continental 635: *'Continental 635, cleared for take-off, roger; and yes, we copied Eastern and we've already notified our caterers.'*

And the Winner Is...

A friend of mine was on a flight one day when, shortly after the meal service, one of the crew got onto the aircraft PA and said:

'Ladies and gentlemen we will shortly be passing through the cabin offering you the chance to win a superb watch. If you look on page 14 of your duty-free brochure you will see the watch that we are proposing to raffle. It's available in either a ladies' or gents' size and the winner will be able to pick which one they would like as their prize. Tickets are £1 each or three for £2.'

The watch was priced at just under £100 and, with a couple of hundred people on the plane, the chances of winning were not that good. Nevertheless, as the crew began coming through the plane many people took them up, and after about half an hour a winner was announced. This was not some new way of the airline making money but a lucrative little scam by the cabin staff to boost their earnings.

Chapter**SEVEN**

A New Passenger Manifesto

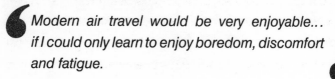

' *Modern air travel would be very enjoyable...
if I could only learn to enjoy boredom, discomfort
and fatigue.*
– ANON.

'

M any years ago I worked for an airline at which the operations director was keen on saying, with total conviction, 'This would be a great airline, with superb on-time performance, clean planes, and high operational standards if it wasn't for all the passengers.' He, like many people who work in the industry, saw the passengers as a necessary fact of business that got in the way of lots of boys playing with very expensive toys.

Early in 2006 there was a situation where Ryanair, whose chief executive, Michael O'Leary once said, 'Air transport is just a glorified bus operation', had to cancel a flight from Germany to Prestwick Airport in Scotland. There was outrage, with television news and the popular press taking Ryanair to task as scores of poor pensioners were interviewed about their plight, having been stranded for several days. Many were demanding the European Union do something about their appalling treatment. Putting aside, for the moment, the fact that as a nation we generally demand less EU intervention until it is something that gets up our national nose, it does raise an interesting point.

At the heart of the debate is an airline industry that used to be highly regulated having metamorphosed into one with far looser rules. If we are to have the lower fares that we all demand, then it is inevitable that standards will slip. The nature of air travel is such that the expectations of passengers far outweigh the reality of what any airline can deliver. Most of us have an image of sophisticated international travel that is reinforced by TV travel programmes and articles in the press that are either presented or written by pampered travel journalists who are rarely put through the same rigours as people who pay their own way. And of course those politicos in Brussels who are regulars on the cheap flights to and from EU headquarters (while claiming full fare allowances) are the first to point out that there must be free market forces, open skies and the ability for airlines to compete whenever and wherever they want. As for most things in life there never is only an upside. Air travel is no different from any other product; there never will be champagne at beer prices.

However they are regulated or run, the airlines exist to transport people from A to B. As with any company providing a service to the public there is a wealth of experience generated by the astonishing antics of customers. However, the pressures, cramped conditions, boredom and access to alcohol unique to flying conspire to create some extraordinary situations. From the corpse in the galley to the giant lizard in first class, all human life is there.

> *I think it is a pity to lose the romantic side of flying and simply to accept it as a common means of transport, although that end is what we have all ostensibly been striving to attain.*
>
> – AMY JOHNSON, SKY ROADS OF THE WORLD, 1939

Delayed Departure

The death of a passenger is always inconvenient to the smooth running of a flight, but sometimes the way that the event is handled can ease the burden. On a flight from Honolulu to Los Angeles the cabin crew noticed that a very large passenger in first class was not looking at all well. In fact, the stewardess suspected he might even have died. With some help from a couple of other flight attendants he was moved to the galley area.

The captain was, of course, advised that the passenger was unwell, and he made an announcement and asked if there was a doctor on board the flight. Fortunately there was. Unfortunately he confirmed the crew's fears; the man was dead. By now the captain had come back to the galley to see what was going on. The doctor told him the bad news, to which the captain replied that, if the passenger was dead then regulations required them to turn around and go back to Honolulu. He went on to mention that if only the passenger had died 20 minutes later then the flight would be over the half-way point in its route and therefore could carry on to Los Angeles.

The doctor suddenly felt a pulse. This became steadily fainter until, after just over 20 minutes, he declared the passenger deceased. The cadaver spent the remainder of the flight propped up in the forward galley with the crew working around him. In order to stop any other passengers walking past and seeing his body the crew declared the forward toilets out of order.

The aircraft landed safely in LA and the body was taken off after all the passengers had deplaned. Timing is everything.

> *I ask people who don't fly, 'How can you not fly when you live in a time in history when you can fly?'*
>
> – WILLIAM LANGIEWISCHE, AUTHOR

FLYING FACTS

They're Everywhere

A Boeing 737 takes off from an airport somewhere in the world every 30 seconds.

Class Envy

Although animals are normally carried in the pressurised cargo hold, rare or valuable specimens can sometimes travel in the main passenger cabin. On one flight this led to difficult passenger satisfaction issues.

A gila monster and a chimpanzee were being transported with their handlers on a flight in the passenger cabin. The gila monster was in the first class section, the chimp in economy. For some reason the passenger next to the gila monster took exception to sitting in close proximity to a very large lizard and demanded to be moved. Even stranger, no one else in first class was prepared to swap with him.

After a lengthy and heated debate the gila monster was sent down into the cargo hold.

Meanwhile the chimpanzee was going 'ape' in the economy cabin, which was causing a good deal of alarm among the passengers. In an effort to settle it, the handler brought the monkey up to his colleague in first class, whereupon the chimp quietened immediately. Since the passenger who objected to the gila monster didn't mind spending the flight next to a monkey, the chimp was duly installed in first class and enjoyed the rest of the flight. The gila monster's comments on his treatment were not recorded.

'Bums on seats' was how Captain Eddie Rickenbacker of Eastern Airlines liked to describe the airline business.

– ANON.

A Breath of (High Altitude) Fresh Air

Two British women joined the ranks of the awfully behaved in the air in mid 2008 when they went on a drunken spree aboard an XL Airways Boeing 737. The charter flight from Kos to Manchester was forced to make an emergency landing in Germany where the pair were removed by armed police to the delight of their fellow passengers.

The two women were returning from holiday and were already drunk when they boarded. They were refused further service because of their condition, but decided to continue drinking from a bottle of vodka they'd bought at the airport. When the cabin crew asked them to desist, a mini riot broke out as the two women attacked crew members with the vodka bottle and had to be wrestled to the floor and put in restraints. At one point one of the inebriated pair tried to open an emergency exit, screaming 'I want some fresh air'.

Panicked passengers were screaming in fear as the melee between the flight attendants and the pair continued, and one witness described it as '... a hell of a scene. The crew were brilliant, wrestling them to the ground and slapping plastic handcuffs on them. We all thought we'd had our chips.'

After two hours at Frankfurt Airport the flight continued to Manchester. Both protagonists have now been repatriated to the UK, but expect to face charges of interference in air traffic and attempted assault; they will also be expected to repay the thousands of pounds of costs associated with the emergency landing. Hopefully a sobering experience.

 The airplane has unveiled for us the true face of the earth.

– ANTOINE DE SAINT-EXUPERY, WIND, SAND, AND STARS, 1939

There's a Mouse Loose

Smaller aircraft do not have cargo holds to carry animals in, so they have to be put among the luggage at the back of the cabin with everything else.

On a commuter flight leaving Seattle, four crates of white mice destined for Washington State University were loaded along with the passengers and baggage. During the flight some turbulence was experienced which caused the cargo to shift and one of the crates broke open, releasing its load of mice onto the cabin floor. The passengers were 14 female students returning to the university from a holiday. Amid the ensuing chaos, the pilot didn't even try to get the passengers seated for landing.

> *First Europe, and then the globe, will be linked by flight, and nations so knit together that they will grow to be next-door neighbours... What railways have done for nations, airways will do for the world.*
> – CLAUDE GRAHAME-WHITE, AVIATION PIONEER, 1914

On the Spur of the Moment

Passengers' attire is the source of much insight into the character and background of the travellers. Airline crews see businessmen in suits, women in saris, people in shell suits, fliers in shorts and T-shirts and others in blazers and panama hats. However, sometimes a passenger arrives wearing something seriously unsuitable.

On a flight leaving Dallas a man sat down in first class wearing his finest Texan outfit including huge Stetson hat, cowboy boots and spurs. He proceeded to indulge in the beverage cart and hence had to visit the lavatory. Coincident with his rather unsteady trip down the aisle was an episode of turbulence, which made him even wobblier on his feet. The flight attendant, concerned for his safety, asked him to return to his seat.

Unfazed by the trifling matter he rebuffed her request with the suitably macho response, 'Don't worry little lady, I can handle it.' And continued into the WC. The turbulence worsened during his visit, causing him to lose his footing mid-stream and fall backwards through the unlocked door and land flat out in the aisle. Clearly there was no stopping what he'd started; as he lay there he continued to urinate in an arc over himself and the floor. Once the situation was back under control and cleaned up he went back to his seat, a little chastened.

The aircraft reached its destination and the cabin crew expected the man to be first in line to leave the aircraft after his embarrassing performance. But not a bit of it, he stayed put in his seat while all of the other passengers disembarked. Eventually he was the only passenger left so one of the flight attendants approached him and asked him if he'd like to get off the aircraft now. 'I can't,' he replied, 'my spurs are stuck under the seat.' The spurs refused the entire crew's efforts to release them, so the man had to sit tight until a mechanic came on board, partially dismantled the seat and finally allowed him to get away. The passenger stuck to horses for transport in the future.

> *All they have to do is look down at the traffic and suddenly they don't feel like (flying is) that expensive a way to travel after all.*
>
> – JIM HERRON, AUTHOR

First Class Ass

A businessman made a name for himself in the First class cabin of a flight from New York to Buenos Aires in 1995 by not only becoming drunk and unruly, but by taking matters way beyond the 'norm' for those who specialise in that peculiar form of behaviour that has become known as air rage. Mr X, as we shall call him, ended up destroying the food service on the entire flight thanks to his extraordinary antics. The court papers of the Eastern District of the State of New York begin the sordid tale:

'Prior to the flight taking off, the passenger began to drink alcoholic beverages (that's booze to the rest of us); he continued to drink alcoholic beverages during the course of the flight. Initially, these beverages were served to him by members of the flight crew, as required by flight regulations.' However, he eventually started getting up and serving alcoholic beverages to himself – obviously his manners were a little lacking in that he appears not to have offered other passengers a drink. 'At this point, members of the flight crew told the passenger that it was against regulations for him to serve himself alcoholic beverages. He continued to serve alcoholic beverages to himself. Flight crew members then advised him that he would not be permitted to drink any more alcoholic beverages. Mr X then approached a male flight attendant and demanded that the flight attendant serve him additional alcoholic beverages. When the male flight attendant refused, Mr X threatened the male flight attendant, indicating that he was going to "bust (his) ass".'

It was at this point that things got way out of hand, even by the standards of drunkenness on board an aircraft. 'At one point in the flight, Mr X approached a female flight attendant and demanded that she provide him with more alcoholic beverages. When she refused, he pushed her by placing both hands on her chest, causing her to fall into one of the seats on the plane. A male flight attendant then entered the first class section and saw Mr X with his pants and underwear down defecating on a service cart used by the flight crew. Mr X then used linen napkins as toilet paper and wiped his hands on various service counters and service implements used by the crew. The captain of the aircraft was notified of Mr X's behaviour. In response, the captain suspended all food and beverage service on the flight due to the possibility of an infectious condition.'

What possessed this passenger to act as he did will remain a mystery (probably to him too, once he sobered up), but serves to illustrate the horrendous behaviour of some passengers (so often in first class...) that the cabin crew have to deal with.

Model Passengers

The old airline adage about 'bums on seats' has been taken to a new level by Exeter, UK based airline Flybe. Like all their peers they're keen to get as many seats on their flights filled as possible, however the pressures exerted by their deal with Norwich Airport has led to some extraordinary tactics.

In order to fill the passenger quota required under the contract, and to avoid losing £280,000 if they failed, in 2008 the airline took the unorthodox step of advertising in the local press for actors to come and take a flight between Norwich and Dublin to make up the numbers. The ruse may have back fired as the airport's managing director has questioned whether they will permit the payment having become aware of the question over whether some passengers are bona fide.

As well as looking for 'extras' for the flights, the airline kept staff on stand by ready to fill seats. Flybe has said it decided not to use actors after it placed the ad, however Suzanne Moore, a passenger boarding a Flybe aircraft at Norwich said she was a model and had been paid to fly. And we thought it was only Heathrow that people had to be paid to use.

> *I sincerely hope you have a penchant for Thai ladyboys and that your colleagues find out. It is my fervent wish that from now to the end of time your itches are unreachable. And that someone writes something obscene in weedkiller on your front lawn.*
>
> – JEREMY CLARKSON TO A PILOT AFTER HIS FLIGHT
> WAS DELAYED

Pick the Bones out of That

A woman was stopped at Munich Airport last week while en route from Brazil to Naples when the baggage handlers noted some unusual content in her luggage. Imagine the scanner operator's face, well accustomed to clothes, shoes, toiletries etc, when they found the image of a human skeleton coming up on the screen! The 62-year-old lady explained that she was taking the remains of her brother to Italy in order to bury them in accordance with his wishes. He'd died 11 years previously and she'd only just got around to it.

Where he had been in the meantime is a mystery, however once it had been established that she wasn't actually breaking any German laws she was (or, they were) allowed to continue with the journey. What happened when she reached Naples is also unknown, but given Naples' problems with the illegal dumping of pollutants from all over Italy, the authorities may not have been that pleased to see what she was planning to deposit!

Into Thin Air

Many passengers are so familiar with the ritual of the safety demonstration before a flight that they ignore it. Flying is statistically so safe that they feel they will not need to know where the exits are or how to put on a life jacket. The need to don an oxygen mask seems a very remote possibility.

However, these are fitted to aircraft for the very good reason that, if the cabin pressurisation system should fail at high altitude, the consequences can be catastrophic without the ability to breathe supplementary oxygen. There have been a number of aircraft accidents caused by the crew losing consciousness when cabin pressure has dropped.

On a Boeing 757 aircraft flying from New York to Salt Lake City one of the passengers began complaining of feeling unwell about an hour after take-off. Since it was New Year's Day the crew suspected that he might have a hangover. The man swore that he hadn't drunk much the previous night but also said that he hadn't eaten that morning. The flight attendant got him some food, but he still said he wasn't feeling at all good. She informed the flight crew in case they had to divert the flight because of the sick man.

After about a quarter of an hour the warning horn went off in the cockpit, alerting the crew to a drop in cabin pressure. The captain immediately deployed the oxygen masks and performed an emergency descent to 7,000 feet and diverted to Cincinnati where the plane safely landed. It later emerged that the sick passenger had been suffering from the early effects of altitude before the aircraft's safety systems detected the low pressure.

 What separates flight attendants from the lowest form of life on earth? The cockpit door.
– ANON.

Not a lot of people...
An anagram of Delta Airlines is: Ideal Latrines

Pls No Txt

Frustrated that you have to turn your mobile phone off before take-off? Are you absolutely gagging to tell your friends what a great, or not, flight you've just had? You're not alone, judging from the frantic thumb movements of many disembarking passengers hunched over mobiles at either end of a flight.

Most passengers realise the dangers of mobile phones interfering with the aircraft's instrumentation and controls and comply with crew requests to switch their equipment off. But of course there is always one. In January 2006 a man on a flight between Beijing and

Shenyang in northeastern China wouldn't take 'no' for an answer. His determination to continue sending text messages led to the flight being delayed by one hour. So intent on remaining in contact with his SMS correspondent was he that he ignored the repeated and increasingly earnest requests of the cabin crew to desist.

Finally one of his fellow passengers joined in the debate, angry at the delay to departure the man's activities were causing. The situation deteriorated when, having exchanged words, the two passengers got into a fight.

The Chinese use mobile phones, and text messages in particular, very extensively. In 2005 the 388 million subscribers in the country sent 305 billion text messages, an average of 843 million every day. But none of them should be sent on an aircraft, as the hapless passenger was finally made to realise.

 The exhilaration of flying is too keen, the pleasure too great, for it to be neglected as a sport.
– ORVILLE WRIGHT

AA All The Way

One of the perks of working for an airline is that sometimes you get to fly in first class. Some airlines have more lenient policies about which staff are eligible for this rather nice bonus. Some airlines offer it to their staff only when 'on duty', while others restrict it to senior personnel. Whatever the qualifying status, nearly all airlines insist that staff are smartly attired. Some require their staff to wear a jacket and tie – so it's not too difficult deciding who the non-revenue passengers are on a flight, particularly if it's long-haul. How many regular first class passengers dress in a shirt and tie?

I was once sitting in first class waiting for the doors to close so that I could fly home on my transatlantic flight to London. Shortly before we were due to leave, a beautiful girl came onboard. I knew she was going to be seated next to me, as it was the only spare seat in the first class cabin. 'Oh good, this will make the flight more entertaining', I thought.

'Hello,' she said as she sat down, 'I was late for my flight and I've been switched to this one.' With that the gorgeous American began getting herself comfortable, placing her copy of Vogue in the seatback pocket in front of her. The hostess had already put her Louis Vuitton bag in the overhead locker. With that the doors closed and we took off shortly afterwards. About 20 minutes after we took off one of the flight attendants brought me the glass of Meursault I had ordered before take-off and asked the lady next to me what she would like.

'I'll have a still water, no ice.' As the hostess walked away Miss Gorgeous added, 'I don't drink, I'm in AA.' And for the next four hours she lectured me on the perils of drink and how she was lucky to have been saved. The moral of this story: be careful what you wish for.

> **'** *I was engaged in what I believe to be the most thrilling industry in the world – aviation. My heart still leaps when I see a tiny two-seater plane soaring gracefully through the sky. Our great airlines awe me. Yet I know they were not produced in a day or a decade.* **'**
>
> – WILLIAM A. 'PAT' PATTERSON, CEO OF UNITED AIRLINES

Identity Crisis

Airline staff regularly have to deal with irate passengers. Delays and disruption are a fact of life for the traveller and often lead to frustration.

Some passengers can become rude and abusive when faced with such problems. The airline staff usually remain polite and professional despite the ill-tempered customers whom they have to face, but it's a rare gate attendant who handles such a situation with as much aplomb as this one.

A very crowded flight from Brisbane was cancelled after the Boeing 767 due to operate it was withdrawn from service because of mechanical trouble. One beleaguered member of staff was trying to handle the entire flight of inconvenienced passengers; the line stretched out beyond the gate area. Most waited patiently as she worked to rebook them one by one on alternative services and get them to their destinations as quickly as possible. There was a flight leaving shortly with some space on it and she was busy booking people on it.

Suddenly an aggressive passenger pushed to the front of the queue and banged his ticket down on the counter. Ignoring the startled look on the face of the passenger who was being served he said, 'I have to be on the next flight. And it has to be first class.'

The attendant replied that she was sorry, but there was a queue of people whom she was serving and if he would like to take his place in line she would be very happy to help him when his turn came. Ignoring her advice, the irate passenger said very loudly, 'Do you have any idea who I am?' The agent immediately got onto the microphone for the PA and announced to the entire terminal, 'Ladies and gentlemen, may I have your attention please? We have a passenger here at gate

14 who does not know who he is. If anyone can identify him please come to gate 14. Thank you.'

Everyone in the gate area for the flight and those seated at the neighbouring gates started laughing, which got the man even more angry. Red in the face he leant over the counter, got very close to her and said, 'F**k you!' The customer service agent looked him in the eye, smiled sweetly and said quietly, 'I'm sorry sir, but you'll have to get in line for that too.'

Hot Ticket

A cautionary tale is contained in a letter from a Las Vegas man who wrote to Southwest Airlines in December 1991 requesting a ticket refund. The man explained that his ticket from Phoenix to Las Vegas had been destroyed when his rental car caught fire. He helpfully attached the incident report from the rental car company to substantiate his story.

It detailed the cause of the fire. The man had been filling the car up with petrol. Rather than grip the pump in his hand, he propped the lever open with his disposable lighter. When the fuel tank was full and the pump automatically clicked off, the lever flicked the lighter. Bang. No more car, no more ticket. Southwest refunded him the ticket price.

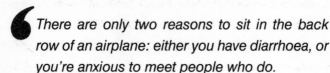

There are only two reasons to sit in the back row of an airplane: either you have diarrhoea, or you're anxious to meet people who do.

– HENRY KISSINGER

Flyers' Remorse

No one can remember what a young boy named Jack got up to on a Southwest Airlines' flight in December 1990. But it must have been pretty awful. So bad, in fact, that he later wrote a letter of apology to the flight attendants. The childish hand suggested that it may have been his parents' idea to write: 'I'm sorry for the way I acted on the plane. I was very tired. I know how to act better. I'm usually very good.'

Southwest has also received letters from older passengers expressing regret. Some customers have sent in wads of money when their consciences have pricked them after buying a senior citizen's discount ticket when they are too young to qualify. One letter enclosed $118 in cash. The passenger was returning a refund mistakenly received from Morris Air, an airline which Southwest bought in 1993. The unsigned letter accompanying the money explained the situation: 'I knew this money didn't belong to me. I haven't had the extra money until just now. I knew I needed to return this money to you since you own Morris Air and if I didn't return it now I would never have the extra money to do it later.'

You cannot get one nickel for commercial flying.

– INGLIS M. UPPERCU, FOUNDER OF THE FIRST AMERICAN
AIRLINE TO LAST MORE THAN A COUPLE OF MONTHS,
AEROMARINE WEST INDIES AIRWAYS, 1923

Spending a Bit More Than a Penny

Imagine the scene. There you are in the toilet of a Boeing 747 attending to a call of nature, when suddenly the door is kicked in and you are dragged half naked from the cubicle. Not a regular feature of a visit to an aircraft's bathroom, thankfully, but that's what allegedly happened to one unfortunate passenger on a flight from Paris to Newark Airport, New York, on 19 May 1997. Such was the distress caused to the passenger that he felt compelled to launch a lawsuit against Air France in the Supreme Court of the State of New York demanding damages.

The court papers tell the story: '... while plaintiff was on said plane, at approximately 11.30 a.m. during the flight, the plaintiff was in one of the lavatories using the lavatory which was locked by him from the inside. The plaintiff was properly and lawfully using the lavatory, with his pants and underpants down and in the process of going to the bathroom, and while the plaintiff was naked from the waist down, the defendant, the airline, its agents, servants, and employees, wrongfully, wilfully, maliciously, unlawfully and without any cause or justification or warning smashed open the door of the lavatory. Plaintiff, while still in the lavatory, was then viciously, wilfully and maliciously assaulted, battered and physically struck by multiple crew members of the plane. The crew members then, while the plaintiff was naked from the waist down, dragged the plaintiff outside the lavatory, exposing his genitals and other body parts to many seated passengers, both female and male. Plaintiff pulled away from crew members and re-entered the lavatory and pulled up his underpants and pants.'

It didn't stop there, though: '... after plaintiff again left the lavatory he was maliciously, wilfully and verbally abused, humiliated, profaned and denigrated for a considerable period of time by crew members. That the plaintiff, a non-smoker, was on a non-smoking flight and was at no time smoking in the lavatory or engaged in any improper activity in the lavatory whatsoever. Solely as a result of the actions of the defendant, the airline, its agents, servants, and employees and their assault and battery of the plaintiff, the plaintiff was injured and subjected to extreme humiliation and mental and physical distress and injury and damage to his reputation...'

The case also alleges a second cause of action, noting that the Plaintiff was the alleged victim of '... violent trespass and intrusion on his privacy... causing him to sustain injury, extreme humiliation, mental and physical distress and injury, and damage to his reputation.'

The case concludes with the sums demanded as damages as a result of these alleged wrongs done to the passenger: '... plaintiff demands judgement against the defendant on the first cause of action for assault and battery for compensatory damages in the amount of $3,000,000, and punitive damages in the amount of $3,000,000 and on the second cause of action for trespass against the defendant, plaintiff seeks compensatory damages in the sum of $3,000,000, punitive damages in the sum of $3,000,000, plus pursuant to New York Statute RPAPL 853, plaintiff seeks treble damages, together with costs and disbursements of this action.'

So that's a case demanding $36,000,000 compensation for being (admittedly extremely forcefully) interrupted while 'on the job'. Next time you go to the toilet on a flight you might want to take your lawyer with you.

> *A recession is when you have to tighten your belt; depression is when you have no belt to tighten. When you've lost your trousers – you're in the airline business.*
>
> – SIR ADAM THOMSON, CHAIRMAN OF BRITISH CALEDONIAN AIRWAYS

China Syndrome

There is an old saying when confronted by something weird and whacky – 'only in America'. Well it seems that we may now have to switch that to 'only in China'. Recently an eight-year-old Chinese boy was duped by what appears to be an unscrupulous Chinese airline.

Travelling alone, he bought a ticket from a Chinese airline to travel from his home city of eastern Ningbo to the southwestern city of Kunming during January's Lunar New Year festival. When he was airborne he looked at the back of his ticket to discover that he was entitled to a 50 per cent discount owing to his age. When he reached his destination and enquired of the airline why he had been charged the adult price he was told that he did not look young enough to merit an airfare discount. Before we all jump to conclusions, maybe he was tall for his age.

Now the precocious legally smart lad has decided to sue the airline as well as a Ningbo travel agency, asking for compensation and a public apology in a local newspaper.

FLYING FACTS

Boeings Still Going

The first Boeing 727 entered service with Eastern Airlines in February 1964. Ultimately they built 1,832 of this workhorse of the US and the world's airlines.

Bare-Faced Cheek

A Canadian man at Los Angeles Airport wanted to fly to Australia. He was frustrated to be refused a ticket when his credit cards were found to be invalid. Such was his desperation to get 'Down Under' that he decided to take the perfectly reasonable step of stripping naked and running over the tarmac before leaping into the wheel compartment of a moving Boeing 747 Jumbo.

The aircraft stopped and the man was arrested. Nancy Castles, a spokesperson for the airport, noted that he could have been sucked into an engine, crushed when the landing gear retracted or frozen to death naked at 30,000 feet. 'This was an extremely dangerous thing for him to do', said Nancy. Quite.

Controller: *'USAir 353 please contact Cleveland Center 135.60.'*
Pause...
Controller: *'USAir 353 contact Cleveland Center 135.60!'*
Pause...
Controller: *'USAir 353, you're just like my wife, you never listen!'*
Pilot: *'Center, this is USAir 553, maybe if you called her by the right name you'd get a better response!'*

Order, Order!

Drinking on planes has even reached the hallowed halls of the Houses of Parliament. Tom Harris, MP for Glasgow South, spoke about some of his personal experiences regarding the effects of drink on aircraft. Before becoming an MP he worked as a reporter on the Paisley Daily Express, during which time he spent a fair amount of time at the local sheriff court. On an almost daily basis, according to the MP, cases were brought before the court: 'Businessmen and people from all walks of life were brought before the sheriff and fined and jailed for some of the most appalling deeds of misbehaviour that one can imagine.' Paisley Sheriff Court has jurisdiction over Glasgow Airport you see.

Not that this was a situation that truly worried Mr Harris as he regularly sold the stories to the national newspapers. What sold best were the stories of 'air rage' – according to Mr Harris: 'It's one of the phrases much beloved of tabloid headline writers.' Mr Harris made a passionate case for why (excessive) alcohol and planes don't mix during a debate on a bill to ban the sale of alcohol on airliners that was receiving its second reading in the House of Commons. To illustrate the awfulness of drunken passengers he regaled the House with an incident that he witnessed.

'I can speak from personal experience. The first time I ever flew on a plane I jumped out when it reached 3,000 ft, although that is not entirely relevant to the debate. I can confirm that I was wearing a parachute, and I mention that experience only because I suspect that few people have done it. However, my first experience on a commercial flight was on a journey from Glasgow to London. I was employed as a press officer by the Labour Party in Scotland at the time and I had to attend a meeting in London during my first week in the job. On my return journey, I was seated in front of a gentleman and as soon as he entered the plane and sat behind me, I could smell the stink of strong alcohol on his breath.

Being a novice of airline flights I said nothing until, at about 30,000 feet, he threw up – mostly on the seat, the back of the seat in front of him and the floor, but a good portion hit me on the shoulder.'

Mr Harris went on to say that the experience didn't really put him off flying but it had made him think of the absurdity of the actions of the cabin crew. The British Airways staff apologised and helped him clean up his jacket and shirt and then, by way of compensation, they offered the future MP a large bag of miniature bottles of whisky and vodka. Naturally he accepted them.

Mr Harris concluded by saying it was the airline's responsibility to stop people who were intoxicated from getting on a plane. He also felt that the sale of booze on planes should not be completely banned for one simple reason. 'My wife would never get on a plane without having at least one G-and-T beforehand because she is not a good flyer. We travel separately, of course, so I do not know whether she has ever been involved in an air rage incident – she probably would not have told me if she had.'

Not a lot of people...
An anagram of Southwest Airlines is:
Lawsuits on the rise

The Tartan Army

Back in 1986, when Scotland were still a footballing force to be reckoned with, their national team were in the World Cup in Mexico. This was the tournament when the infamous 'Hand of God' played a part in England's downfall. Scotland made an early exit from the group stages after finishing bottom. They did give West Germany a fright when wee Gordon Strachan opened the scoring after 18 minutes. It caused wild celebrations among the Tartan Army in Queretaro and Gordon got pretty carried away as well. He raced towards the crowd and only had an advertising hoarding to clear to stand triumphant in front of the TA. Unfortunately at his height of five feet five inches it was a hoarding too high for Strachan. He stopped short of jumping and instead stood and lifted his leg as though he was going to hop over delicately. It was one of the enduring images of the tournament but West Germany still won 2–1.

What's all this got to do with airlines? Well there were vast numbers of the Tartan Army who needed to get to Mexico and Continental Airlines had a daily service to Houston from London and then numerous flights from there to destinations all over Mexico. Continental became the airline of choice for the Tartan Army. The kilted horde flew out over a number of days filling the terminal building with their flags and singing the Scotland World Cup song – Big Trip to Mexico. Once they were aboard the DC-10 it was the cabin staff who were responsible for trying to keep order. They had never seen anything like it. To be fair the vast majority of the fans were wonderful, and there were no real incidents of bad behaviour, with one exception.

Among the supporters was another diminutive Scot who was obviously out to have a good time. He had been drinking before he got on and then once airborne he carried on. Eventually he grew tired of sitting in his seat and climbed up into one of the overhead lockers where he took off his false legs and refused to come down. This incident resulted in one of The Sun's greatest headlines – 'Legless at 30,000 feet'.

Incidentally Continental, like the other airlines, flew home many fewer fans than it took out to Mexico. At last count there were thought to have been as many as 200 members of the Tartan Army still languishing in Mexico. Maybe someday there will be a lost tribe of light-skinned, ginger-haired youngsters discovered deep in the Mexican jungle – see you gringo.

'*As you know, birds do not have sexual organs because they would interfere with flight. (In fact, this was the big breakthrough for the Wright Brothers. They were watching birds one day, trying to figure out how to get their crude machine to fly, when suddenly it dawned on Wilbur. 'Orville', he said, 'all we have to do is remove the sexual organs!' You should have seen their original design.) As a result, birds are very, very difficult to arouse sexually. You almost never see an aroused bird. So when they want to reproduce, birds fly up and stand on telephone lines, where they monitor telephone conversations with their feet. When they find a conversation in which people are talking dirty, they grip the line very tightly until they are both highly aroused, at which point the female gets pregnant.*'

– DAVE BARRY, SEX AND THE SINGLE AMOEBAE

Get Me to the Plane on Time

A veteran member of the ground staff at Atlanta Airport was about to close boarding for a flight and was going through his final check when a man came dashing up to him, sweating and out of breath after what seemed to be a long run. The passenger gasped, 'Am I going to make the flight?'

'Yes sir, that's your ship right there,' replied the gate agent, pointing down the jetway. The man stopped dead and exclaimed, 'But I'm not going on a ship, I'm going on a plane!'

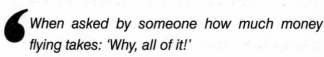

When asked by someone how much money flying takes: 'Why, all of it!'

– GORDON BAXTER, COLUMNIST FOR FLYING MAGAZINE

Is Nowhere Sacred?

In the mid-1980s a lady of ample proportions was answering a call of nature on board a flight in the USA. As she relieved herself she accidentally pressed the lavatory flush button. Now this would have given anyone a fright given the noisy and enthusiastic suction which aircraft toilets employ during flushing. In this case, unfortunately, the woman's generous curves created a perfect seal around the rim of the lavatory bowl, causing the toilet's suction to vacuum-seal her to the loo.

After several minutes of increasingly frantic heaving to no avail she shouted until a flight attendant came along. Rather embarrassed, she unlocked the door and the attendant tried to haul her free. Again the power of the vacuum was too great. Even the entire flight crew hauling on the poor lady's arms failed to dislodge her.

There was nothing for it but to land the aircraft with her still 'engaged'; there was no doubt that she was firmly connected to her seat. Once the plane was on the ground and the other passengers were deplaned efforts to free her began in earnest.

Matters were not helped by the greater air pressure on the ground increasing the grip the convenience had on her behind. The fire crew couldn't un-stick her either, until one enterprising fireman drilled a hole through the metal toilet bowl allowing the pressures to equalise and the victim, her mortification complete, to rise from her unwanted throne. And yes, she sued.

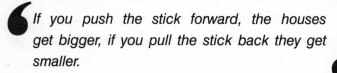

If you push the stick forward, the houses get bigger, if you pull the stick back they get smaller.

– ANON.

Hooligan Air

High-spirited travellers can be a handful for aircraft cabin crew, and soccer fans are preceded by their reputation. It's a rare flight, however, on which the situation gets so out of hand that the captain issues an emergency Mayday call. That was what happened in December 2002 when violence broke out on a chartered Astraeus Boeing 737 carrying 158 Celtic fans back to Glasgow after a game against Spanish club Celta Vigo in the UEFA Cup.

What was described as a 'riot' broke out, sparked by a row over smoking in the aircraft toilets. The fracas escalated and two stewardesses were assaulted before the pilot diverted to Cardiff Airport as a state of emergency was declared.

Armed police boarded the aircraft upon landing and arrested a number of passengers. The interior of the aircraft had been damaged and Superintendent Colin Jones of South Wales police described the incident as a 'serious outbreak of public disorder'. Six men were arrested on suspicion of assault and criminal damage offences. Celtic said they were 'extremely concerned' about the incident.

But that didn't stop another incident two months later involving Celtic fans smoking in the toilets of an aircraft on a flight to Germany to attend their next UEFA Cup game. History repeated itself when 40 minutes into the flight fans were discovered having a sly drag in the WC. The furious captain warned the passengers in an intercom address that, 'The consequences of a fire at 25,000 feet are too horrible to contemplate. This is something we, as an airline, take very seriously. In fact we have had several people jailed for this in the past. Please refrain from smoking.'

The MyTravel Flight 6703 from Glasgow continued the remaining 40 minutes to Stuttgart. John Wilson, the head of Cambuslang Travel, which had arranged the flight, was on board and noted, 'We are just lucky we have a more tolerant captain than the one who took the flight to Wales.'

Glasgow-based flight crews probably watch Celtic's progress in European competitions with great interest, and maybe even take annual leave to avoid being rostered.

 We're going to make the best impression on the travelling public, and we're going to make a pile of extra dough just from being first.

– C.R. SMITH, AMERICAN AIRLINES, ON THE INTRODUCTION
OF THE BOEING 707

The Band Plays On

After rowdy, drunken behaviour that got a Russian orchestra thrown off a trans-Atlantic flight, they acquitted themselves wonderfully the next night in a concert of Prokofiev and Shostakovich. But then, this wasn't the first time this group of musicians have behaved like a bunch of rock stars.

They were on a flight from Poland to the United States several years ago during which the musicians broke out food, cigarettes and alcohol even before the plane took off, creating a raucous scene that exasperated the flight attendants. The next evening at Carnegie Hall, a critic wrote, Russia's oldest and most elite orchestra – its players young and old, men and women – gave a magnificent concert of stirring, soulful Tchaikovsky.

In the current atmosphere of zero tolerance for in-flight disturbances, however, such antics are no longer acceptable. More recently, on the first leg of a flight from Amsterdam to Los Angeles for the start of a month long tour, United Airlines threw the orchestra off the plane in Washington and would not allow the musicians to continue their trip, threatening the concerts. They were eventually allowed to proceed after the orchestra apologised to the airline.

And then? 'And then, just as it did years ago in New York, the rowdy bunch put on a magnificent concert,' a critic noted. In Shostakovich's Fifth he added, 'Details took hold, yet the orchestra played with gripping unanimity.' He concluded: 'Let them have their vodka; they earn it the hard way.'

It's not a testosterone-driven industry any longer. Success is making money, not in the size of the airline.

– GORDON BETHUNE, CHAIRMAN AND CEO OF CONTINENTAL AIRLINES

> *This entire industry is in a death spiral, including this company, and I can't get us out of it. Deregulation is an abysmal failure and we have no more furniture left to burn.*
> – BRUCE LAKEFIELD, CEO OF US AIRWAYS, WHILE BETWEEN BANKRUPTCIES AND BEFORE BEING TAKEN OVER BY AMERICA WEST, OCTOBER 2004

The Great Unwashed

Even ordinary members of the public sometimes indulge in extraordinary behaviour on board planes; a plumber caused £30,000 of damage to an aircraft when he became violent on a flight from South Africa to London. He tried to bite and head-butt a cabin crew member after being asked to stop looking at pornography on his computer. An ex-soldier who stepped in to help restrain him was asked by the plumber to 'step outside' – an invitation which he declined seven miles up over Africa. He was jailed for three years.

Another passenger was jailed for three years and ordered to pay his victim £6,000 after he attacked her with a vodka bottle. He was drunk when he boarded the Airtours flight to Malaga in 1998 and was then abusive throughout the flight. When the stewardess informed him that Spanish police would be meeting the flight he hit her in the face with the bottle.

One drunken passenger had even more cause to regret his misbehaviour during a flight from Singapore to New Zealand. He was abusive to a female passenger and became violent when another passenger stepped in to defend her. The stewards on the

Air Singapore flight were having difficulty in subduing the man until they asked for help... from the 30 members of the British Police Rugby League team, who were travelling on the flight as part of a rugby tour, which was gleefully supplied. He was quickly brought under control and handed over to the New Zealand police upon landing and has no doubt mended his ways in the wake of the experience.

> *Things which do you no good in aviation: Altitude above you. Runway behind you. Fuel in the truck. A navigator. Half a second ago. Approach plans in the car. The airspeed you don't have.*
> – ANON.

Love Is in the Air Again

Long flights can be bad enough, but the experience can be infinitely worsened by the 'next seat neighbour lottery'. Will it be the screaming child, the hysterical woman, the angry businessman, the chronic snorer, the obese religious maniac or any one of thousands of people you'd rather not be tethered beside for the endless hours until you get to your destination? Why is it always a seat three rows away that the man/woman of our dreams takes as we watch hopefully when they walk along the aircraft aisle?

Help may be at hand. Peter Shankman has launched an internet matching service, which allows passengers to search for like-minded souls on their flight and sit next to them. The concept's father fondly recalls: 'A little while ago I was on a flight between Houston and New York when Miss Texas sat down next to me. She was lovely. The flight was five hours, but it felt like about 11 seconds. I asked myself why every flight couldn't be that way.'

Members of the airtroductions.com service are asked to complete a profile of themselves and of the person they'd like to sit next to. They visit the website before check-in to see if any other members are on the flight and if a match is found they are paired up for a small fee. It's not all high level dating – some members look for cooks or sports fans to while away the flight with. Some even ask for a companion who doesn't want to talk. Whatever your preference it could be the answer to a lot of people's prayers.

It would certainly have helped to avoid the plight of one poor passenger. On a two-hour flight on a US airline his seat assignment was changed so that he was placed next to an obese passenger, who allegedly occupied half of his neighbour's seat in addition to his own. For the duration of the two-hour flight they were pressed tightly together resulting in the poor squashed passenger disembarking wet with the man's sweat and with a tingling elbow.

Later the victim proceeded to sue the airline for the cost of surgery to correct the tendonitis in his elbow, alleging negligence and breach of contract. Continental refused his request for a temporary employee to aid him in computer work while the elbow healed. While he recognised that the airline shouldn't discriminate against larger passengers by making them buy two seats, he hoped that they might find a better way of accommodating them as a result of the case.

PLANE SPEAKING

New York controller: *'Federal Express 235, descend, maintain three one zero, expect lower in 10 miles.'*

FedEx 235: *'OK, outta three five for three one oh, FedEx two thirty-five.'*

New York controller: *'Delta fauve twuntee, climb one ninah zeruh, dat'll be finah... '*

Delta 520: *'Uhh... up to one niner zero, Delta five twenty.'*

New York controller: *'Al-italia wonna sixxa, you slowa to two-afifty, please.'*

Alitalia 16: *'HEY! You makea funna Alitalia?!'*

New York controller: *'Oh, no! I make-a funna Delta anna FedEx!'*

Hendrix Lives

As their Boeing 727 sat on the tarmac waiting to push back from the terminal, a flight attendant noticed a passenger in row 45 was staring out of the window and looking very glassy-eyed. She spoke to him to check if he was OK, and quickly realised that the man was stoned out of his mind. When the flight attendant asked the aging hippy what he was looking at so intently out of the window, he said, 'It's like wow, look, there's Jimi Hendrix on the back of that plane.' She looked out of the window and saw the reason for his confusion.

'It's not Jimi Hendrix, it is an Inuit, the usual tailplane logo of Alaska Airlines', said the stewardess.

'Man, what it is... is what it is,' replied the dazed and confused passenger.

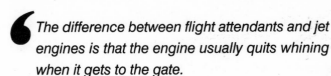

The difference between flight attendants and jet engines is that the engine usually quits whining when it gets to the gate.

– ANON.

High and Dry

A few years ago high spirits got the better of three men on a flight from Glasgow to Ibiza for a Club 18-30 holiday. Because they were already inebriated when they boarded the flight, the cabin crew refused to serve them more alcohol. The trio refused to take 'no' for an answer and proceeded to pilfer several bottles from the drinks trolley. Their clumsy attempts to conceal their crime were soon exposed when the booze was found under their seats. Their bubble was comprehensively burst, however, when the airline's strict zero tolerance policy was invoked and they were banned from boarding their return flight, leaving them to find their own way home.

 No one expects Braniff to go broke. No major U.S. carrier ever has.

– WALL STREET JOURNAL, 30 JULY 1980

(BRANIFF WENT BUST AND CEASED OPERATING IN 1982)

People Come First

Airlines try very hard to make their passengers feel important and to give the impression that they really care about us; after all it would be bad PR to confess that what they really care about is our money. It takes a pilot to come clean about the relationship the crew enjoy with the passengers when he referred to them as 'self-loading cargo'.

To comfort the disgruntled 'cargo', it's good to know that airline management can be similarly clinical about their staff; a senior executive of a major airline recently referred to their staff as 'one element of the cost base'.

PLANE SPEAKING

Tower: *'… and for your information, you were slightly to the left of the centreline on that approach.'*

Speedbird: *'That's correct; and my first officer was slightly to the right.'*

Flying Ducks

While waiting to board a flight between Sydney and Canberra, a man was surprised to see a large yellow duck waddling about in the departure lounge making 'quack quack' noises. He was even more surprised to find the same duck join the queue of passengers boarding the flight. When the man in the fluffy suit came to get onto the plane he had to remove his duck head and settled in his seat with the head in the luggage bin. Curiosity got the better of the other passenger after a few minutes and he leant across the aisle to where the duck/man was sitting and asked him why he was dressed in such an unorthodox manner. 'I was at a party dressed in this when someone bet I couldn't fly in it. You're on, I said.'

> *The three best things in life are a good landing, a good orgasm, and a good shit. A night aircraft-carrier landing is one of the few opportunities to experience all three at the same time.*
>
> – ANON.

Travellers' Tales

A large, blue-rinsed American lady was heard to exclaim, after landing at Da Vinci Airport in the Italian capital, 'When did they rename this place "Roma"?'

A man struck up conversation with his neighbour, a slightly intoxicated Irishman shortly after take-off from London en route to Sydney via Bombay, when his new friend asked, 'What time are we due in Dublin then?' How they laughed.

> *We have to make you think it's an important seat – because you're in it.*
>
> – DONALD BURR, FOUNDER OF PEOPLE EXPRESS

Travel Agents' Tales

Travel agents sometimes get to speak to people who shouldn't be let out in public unsupervised, and are expected to sort out travel plans for these folk. Their patience and understanding in the face of adversity is quite extraordinary. Here are a few tales to illustrate what they have to deal with before the passenger has even got near a plane.

A customer enquired about a package holiday in Hawaii. After going through all the costs, she asked if it might not be a bit cheaper to fly to

California and then take the train to Hawaii.

A businessman was booking a trip to China when the agent reminded him that he would need a visa. 'Oh no I don't, I've been to China before and they took American Express', replied the seasoned traveller.

An angry customer telephoned his travel agent to complain that his hotel room in Orlando didn't have an ocean view. The agent patiently explained that since Orlando is in the middle of the state of Florida, rather than on the coast, it doesn't have any ocean view hotel rooms. The man was still cross and wasn't going to fall for that one; he exclaimed, 'Don't give me that, I've looked on the map and Florida is a real thin state!'

A man rang his agent from the airport in a panic and said, 'I am on Flight 823, but how do I know which plane to get on when none of them have any numbers on them?'

A lady rang her agent to complain about her treatment by the airline she'd just flown on. 'They put a label on my bag saying "FAT". Now I may be overweight but there's no need for that!' she raged. After taking a moment to compose herself, the travel agent explained that FAT is the airline baggage system code for Fresno.

A lady caller asked to 'fly to Pepsi-Cola on one of those computer planes'. The agent asked her if she meant to fly to Pensacola on a commuter plane. 'Yeah, whatever,' replied the customer.

A man rang to ask if he should rent a car in Dallas. The agent noted that he only had a one-hour stop in Dallas between flights. When the agent asked him why he thought he might need a car, he replied that he had heard Dallas was a big airport and he would need a car to get between gates.

A woman called to discuss flights to Cape Town. When the agent began to detail the flight time and passport requirements the client broke in to inform her that since Cape Town is in Massachusetts, why would the flight be so long and a passport be necessary... ?

A lady called her agent to say that she'd just got her tickets and couldn't see how her flight from Detroit leaving at 8.20 a.m could arrive in Chicago at 8.33 a.m. The agent tried without success to explain the one-hour time difference. Finally she gave up and told the lady that the plane was just very fast, and she went away quite happy.

A woman called to make reservations and said; 'I want to go from Chicago to Hippopotamus, New York.' The agent was at a loss but finally said, 'Are you sure that's the name of the town?' 'Yes, what flights do you have?' replied the customer. After some searching, the agent came back with, 'I'm sorry, ma'am, I've looked up every airport code in the country and can't find a Hippopotamus anywhere.' The customer retorted, 'Oh don't be silly. Everyone knows where it is. Check your map!' The agent scoured a map of the state of New York and finally offered, 'You don't mean Buffalo, do you?' 'That's it! I knew it was a big animal.'

A lady called up a travel agent and asked, 'How long are your flights from Los Angeles to Phoenix?' The agent answered, 'Just a minute.' At which, the lady thanked him and hung up.

The managing director of a large travel agency had apparently been playing fast and loose with his company's money for a number of years. It was such a serious situation that when it came to the notice of the shareholders, of which he was not one, they decided to terminate his employment. When the chairman of the company was asked to comment on the departure of the MD he said. 'He has had to leave us because he unfortunately sustained an industrial injury – his fingers were caught as the till slammed shut.'

'*Governments have supported airlines as if they were local football teams. But there are just too many of them. This is the only industry I know that has lost money consistently and makes money infrequently.*

'

– RICHARD HANNAH, AIRLINE ANALYST WITH UBS

Tough Handle

If the three-letter airport identifier appearing on baggage tags and tickets for Fresno (FAT) caused problems with one overweight passenger, the identifier initially assigned for Sioux City, Iowa, caused even more trouble. It came under attack from state officials until the Federal Aviation Administration agreed that SUX was an unacceptable abbreviation for the facility.

'*So long as the airlines preserve their magic quality – including, above all, their safety and reliability – they will be guaranteed a significant role in the workings of the world. Science will never digitalise an embrace. Electronics will never convey the wavering eye of a negotiating adversary. Fibre-optic cable can do many things, but it cannot transport hot sand, fast snow, or great ruins.*'

– WALL STREET JOURNAL COLUMNIST THOMAS PETZINGER, JR.

Sheriff's Flight of Fancy

Even holders of high office are not above the law and should think twice before making 'jokes' on board aircraft.

In March 2005 Raj Jandoo was flying to Scotland's Western Isles to sit in judgment at a sheriff court on the island of North Uist when he began talking about a bomb. While on a stop at Inverness Airport for the Saab 340B aircraft to pick up and drop off passengers, he made a mobile phone call and in a loud voice remarked, 'Bloody repressed people up here are not used to seeing a black man and think I am a terrorist going to bomb their plane.'

His future was in doubt after he was convicted of breach of the peace and contraventions of air safety regulations and fined £2,500. Jandoo, 47, was the first black lawyer to practise at the Scottish bar and had become a well-known figure in legal circles.

He was larger than life, with a wicked sense of humour, and was a great friend.

– SIR RICHARD BRANSON AFTER THE DEATH OF SIR FREDDIE LAKER IN 2006

What's in a Name?

As the world shrinks, with air travel available to almost every corner, the scope for confusion over place names is increasing. The emergence of ticket purchasing on airlines' websites has removed the 'safety net' of the travel agent double-checking with the customer whether it is Dulles Airport serving Washington, DC, or Dallas Airport in Texas they want to travel to. Or Amman, capital of Jordan or Oman. Or Dakar in Senegal as opposed to Dhaka in Bangladesh.

Spare a thought, then, for two students who booked online for their trip to Sydney, New South Wales, Australia in 2002. Imagine their surprise when they arrived at Sydney, Nova Scotia, in Canada. There's not much difference between Sydney NS and Sydney NSW on the screen but they are literally a world, rather than just a W, apart.

Back-Handed Compliment

In the early 1960s, when Britain still had an aircraft manufacturing industry that could build aircraft without joining a European consortium, the British Aircraft Corporation designed and built the small, 79-seat, twin rear-engine BAC 1-11. The aircraft was a major investment for the company and they desperately needed a launch customer to buy the aircraft. At the time British European Airways favoured the Trident, and so the prime target was British United

Airways whose managing director was Sir Freddie Laker.

Negotiations were long and hard-fought, especially given Sir Freddie's tenacity in procuring guarantees from the manufacturer and getting the price reduced at every opportunity. Eventually, after months of negotiations, a price of around £10 million for the 10 aircraft was agreed. At the conclusion of the last meeting, at which the price was settled, Sir Freddie asked to see the chief BAC negotiator in his office, prior to the signing of the agreement on the following day. At this meeting he asked the BAC sales engineering director, John Prothero-Thomas, what BAC intended to do for Sir Freddie Laker personally, especially given the fact that he had committed so much of his personal energy into concluding the deal. John was put on the spot with this question because Freddie was effectively asking for a back-hander.

John went back to the head of BAC and they agreed he could tell Sir Freddie that they would pay him £10,000 – no small amount in the early 1960s. Sir Freddie was happy. At the signing ceremony later that morning in the BUA boardroom Sir Freddie was presented with the contract showing the previously agreed price. As he was about to sign it he stopped and said, 'There's a mistake here, there's the £10,000 you agreed to pay me, let's just knock it off the price BUA is paying for the planes.'

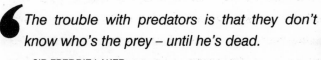

The trouble with predators is that they don't know who's the prey – until he's dead.

– SIR FREDDIE LAKER

Travelling Steerage

A Colombian student called Guzman astonished the Miami Airport staff when he arrived in the wheel well of a cargo aircraft. He survived the intense cold and altitude and to everyone's astonishment arrived in reasonable health. Despite his claims that he wanted to escape his mother, who didn't want him, and his stepfather, who beat him, he was deported immediately. However, he continued to harbour a burning desire to live in the US.

Undaunted by his previous experience he embarked on another attempt, but this time was discovered after only half an hour when the Arca Airlines plane landed in Bogotá. He had stowed away in the wheel well in Cali better prepared than previously: 'He had two pairs of pants, two shirts (and) a sweater,' reported Captain Hernando Guiterrez, owner of Arca Airlines.

Guzman vowed to continue his efforts to enter America, but his record may hamper his application for a student visa; the US authorities will need to be confident that he will return to Colombia when he completes his studies.

PLANE SPEAKING

ATC: *'Cessna Gulf, Alpha Bravo, Charlie Delta. What are your intentions?'*

Cessna pilot: *'To get my commercial pilot's licence and instrument rating.'*

ATC: *'I meant in the next five minutes, not years.'*

Free Upgrade? Certainly!

The great question on the minds of many travellers is, 'How can I get upgraded to business (or first) class?' Check-in agents are allowed to grant upgrades in some circumstances – typically when the cheaper cabin is overbooked and there is space in the class above. Occasionally they may do a favour for a particularly deserving customer, say a couple on honeymoon, but it's pretty rare. That doesn't stop thousands of people trying it on every day.

A survey in 2003 revealed that of the 1,000 travellers questioned men aged between 45 and 54 were 50 per cent more likely to succeed. Being well dressed is very helpful (in fact British Airways won't upgrade a passenger to business class unless they are smartly attired). The best way to help your chances is to approach a check-in agent of a similar age, and above all to be charming and courteous.

That advice didn't stop the 10 per cent of people in the survey who admitted impersonating a celebrity, the 20 per cent who faked pregnancy or the 13 per cent who confessed to trying bribery.

Ten Ways to Get an Upgrade – Perhaps

1. Be very polite to the check-in agent.
2. Be smartly dressed.
3. Be very famous (but why didn't you buy a first class ticket in the first place, you cheapskate?).
4. Be a bit of a celebrity, but if you have to tell them who you are then you've blown it.
5. Work for an influential company; even say you're a travel writer for Harpers and Queen.

6. Fly with the airline often enough to qualify for a high-level frequent flyer membership. Taking very full flights helps, too.
7. Bring cakes for the check-in staff.
8. Stress your medical condition, which is alleviated by your having lots of legroom.
9. Wring your hands in exasperation that your secretary has booked the wrong class of travel. But be prepared to have your bluff called and to pay for the upgrade.
10. Beg. This is demeaning, but can be effective.

Ten Ways to Ruin Your Chances

1. Be rude to the check-in agent.
2. Wear a tracksuit (unless you're a well known sportsperson).
3. Have children with you.
4. Pretend to be a celebrity.
5. Act like you've never travelled business/first class before.
6. Push the point.
7. Be drunk.
8. Try to bribe the agent. Unless it's for far more money than the first class ticket would have cost in the first place.
9. Act like it's your right to be upgraded.
10. Travel on charter flights which only have one class of service.

It Takes All Sorts

El Al Israel Airlines carries a great many passengers each year, most of whom are unremarkable, but a few manage to stand out from the crowd, not for bad behaviour, but for their very unusual requests to the airline's staff.

One regular passenger from Georgia in the US is so superstitious that she insists that the number 13 must not appear anywhere on her ticket.

Another passenger requested a window seat so that she 'could open it from time to time to get some fresh air'.

One passenger on an evening flight requested a morning paper with breakfast. The flight attendant informed him that, sadly, they weren't expecting a mid-air delivery of the New York Times.

A dog owner applied for her pet to join the airline's frequent flier programme. El Al refused on the basis that the animal was under 12 years of age and thus didn't pay full fare.

The airline received a parcel from a guilt-ridden passenger, whose conscience wouldn't let them keep a pilfered airline blanket.

A lady bought a ticket from the El Al desk and then asked for some scissors, so that she could cut into the lining of her coat to retrieve the money.

They have even had a very nervous first time flier who handcuffed himself to his seat for the duration of the flight.

If Richard Branson had worn a pair of steel-rimmed glasses, a double-breasted suit and shaved off his beard, I would have taken him seriously. As it was I couldn't...

– LORD KING, CHAIRMAN OF BRITISH AIRWAYS

Air Rage

The phenomenon of air rage has arisen over the last decade or so as passengers are squeezed into smaller and smaller spaces, airlines competing on price stretch their service thinner and crowded airports cause more delays. Wider society has become less inhibited and episodes of violence and abuse, which would have been unheard of a generation ago, are familiar to all of us.

Bad behaviour is very problematic in the confines of an aircraft. The issue is often exacerbated by the availability of alcohol. Even if the crew see a problem coming and stop serving the passenger, they have had hours in the departure lounge to take in booze, and been offered it for purchase at discount prices every step of the way from the check-in desk to the plane.

Passengers travelling to under-30s package holidays in the sun, and groups of lads in particular, are notorious for causing mayhem on the aircraft taking them off for their two weeks in the sun. Four men from Glasgow took things to extremes, though.

The group had been drinking heavily before and during the Futura Air flight from Aberdeen to Malaga, Costa del Sol, but that was nothing unusual. The trouble started when the plane was preparing to land. One of the group lit some whacky baccy, and when asked by a flight attendant to put it out he grabbed her breast and knocked her to the floor.

The pilot radioed Malaga Airport and the police were there to meet the flight. They sealed off part of the ramp and riot police boarded the Boeing 737 expecting to deal with the assault on the crew member, but faced a battle. In the fight which ensued one of the police was left with serious facial injuries. The hooligans were finally subdued and they found themselves in Alhaurin de la Torre prison charged with sexual assault and assaulting a police officer respectively.

Two of the group were deported and banned from visiting Spain for five years. After speaking to his son, who had arrived in London after his deportation, one of their fathers noted, 'They said it was another lad who smacked the copper and they thought the police were going to let them carry on with their holiday. We don't really know the whole story and I doubt very much if the boys will tell us.'

> ‘ *If forced to travel on an aircraft, try and get in the cabin with the captain, so you can keep an eye on him and nudge him if he falls asleep or point out any mountains looming up ahead...* ’
>
> – COMEDIAN MIKE HARDING

Soffer So Good?

In the pantheon of problem passengers, one lady is very near the top. On 20 September 2002 she boarded a US airline's flight from Miami a free woman and got off facing a 20-year jail sentence. She only recalls complaining about the quality of the catering; the FBI's version of events is somewhat different.

They record her sitting on the lap of a fellow passenger, pretending her hand was a gun and taunting him. She threatened flight attendants with a hail of foul language and threw herself on the floor of the cabin yelling 'Hail Allah, hail Allah!' before trying to wrench open a cabin door. Tired after her exertions she then sat down and ate a banana before taking a dose of Depakote, a drug used to control manic episodes in patients with a bipolar mood disorder. Perhaps the dose was overdue.

The lady was charged with the misdemeanour of assault and the federal felony of interference with flight crew. The computer programmer with a drink problem said she had been going to California to enter the Betty Ford Clinic for alcoholism treatment. After psychiatric evaluation she pleaded guilty to the misdemeanour and was sentenced to a year's probation and will continue to have psychiatric treatment in Florida. She is required to give any airline she plans to travel on 60 days' notice.

Rick Musica, Miami area vice-chairman of the Association of Professional Flight Attendants was spot on when he observed that the unofficial flight attendants' job description is 'part psychologist, part bartender, part Special Forces'.

> *There is not much to say about most airplane journeys. Anything remarkable must be disastrous, so you define a good flight by negatives: you didn't get hijacked, you didn't crash, you didn't throw up, you weren't late, you weren't nauseated by the food. So you're grateful.*
>
> – PAUL THEROUX, THE OLD PATAGONIAN EXPRESS

Boys Will Be Boys – Or Not

Most people are convinced that the photograph in their passport looks nothing like them, and customs staff certainly have their work cut out to determine whether the person in front of them is in fact the blurry face in the picture. It's not often that the passport holder appears to be a different gender than that listed in the details but it does happen.

A British transsexual sued United Airlines after they refused to allow him to fly while wearing women's clothing in 2001. He was escorted off the flight in Nebraska and told he would not be allowed back on until he dressed like a man and more closely resembled the picture in his passport.

His lawyer noted that although a 'biological male', the passenger (who had been living in London for six years with a woman's name) was wearing make-up, a wig and a dress at the time of the incident. The airline staff were alleged to have told him/her to put on a pair of trousers as well as taking off the make-up and long hair, leaving him feeling 'totally humiliated'.

This was the first time in many flights as a woman that he/she had experienced a problem. There is a mechanism for changing passports to accommodate people who have gone through a sex change, although it may not always be able to keep pace with the changes in the person. Customs staff are familiar with the intricacies of such situations and saw no need for the airline to impose such requirements.

Claire McNab of the Press for Change organisation, which campaigns for transsexuals' rights, observed: 'If United Airlines does have a gender dress code for passengers, I would hope that they would publish it promptly, so women wearing trousers, men wearing kilts, and others can be forewarned.'

The plight of the transsexual is not limited to airline passengers. A 44-year-old Scot surprised his colleagues when he started to wear earrings and long hair to work. He had been going to work as operations controller for a British airline as a man, but, unknown to his colleagues, was living at home as a woman.

The man, who now goes under the name of Marlene, claimed unfair dismissal and sex discrimination at a tribunal in 2004 after she was allegedly passed over for promotion and humiliated when her sex change became public. The airline's personnel manager denied the claim. 'This employee was not singled out because they were different. We did not know she was different at the time. It was quite a shock when it was revealed. I was dumbfounded.'

FLYING FACTS

Air Miles and Miles

The first Airbus entered service with Air France in May 1974... It's amazing just how long some of these aircraft have been flying.

 I didn't take this job to preside over a bankruptcy. I refuse to accept that United Airlines is collateral damage from September 11.

– JACK CREIGHTON, NEW CHAIRMAN AND CEO OF UAL
CORPORATION, 28 OCTOBER 2001; UAL ENTERED BANKRUPTCY
ON 9 DECEMBER 2002

Nun on the Run

A nun was banned from boarding a British Airways flight from Shetland to Aberdeen thanks to the abuse she directed towards staff. She was barred from the flight because she was carrying a two-foot-high statue of the Virgin Mary. The 64-year-old nun had been travelling around the world spreading the Christian faith, but had to endure a boat ride to get back to the mainland after the nun's run-in with the airline.

Speaking about the incident, she was unbowed: 'When they said I couldn't take the statue on the plane I said I'm reporting you and it's disgraceful behaviour. I don't call that rude, I call it self-defence against tremendous, unjust and cruel treatment, which is disgraceful.'

'*In my own view, it was not merely uncomfortable, it was intolerable. It might perhaps have been endurable for a two-hour flight but an eight-hour flight is a totally different matter.*

– JUDGE GARETH EDWARDS QC, REGARDS JMC'S 29-INCH SEAT PITCH. THE JUDGE UPHELD A COMPENSATION AWARD MADE TO BRIAN HORAN AFTER HE SUFFERED DEEP-VEIN THROMBOSIS (DVT) ON HIS JOURNEY FROM MANCHESTER, ENGLAND, TO THE CANADIAN SKI RESORT OF CALGARY. CHESTER COUNTY COURT, 17 APRIL 2002'

It Takes All Sorts

Passengers from different countries can have characteristic traits and common habits that entertain the cabin crew, up to a point that is. One flight attendant recalls a period of time he spent working on a regular flight from the US to Santiago in the Dominican Republic for an American airline.

He was taken aback when a lady in first class bit into a hot towel, trying to eat it. Unfazed, he returned a few minutes later to offer her a drink. She asked for red wine, with sugar. He wasn't surprised – having worked on the route for a while he was familiar with requests for extraordinary amounts of sugar from Dominican passengers, often 10 sachets going in a cup of coffee. The issue could become awkward for the crew, however, when the passengers would feed sachet after sachet to their children, rendering them frenzied and uncontrollable on a sugar high.

PLANE SPEAKING

O'Hare Approach: *'USA 212, cleared ILS runway 32L approach, maintain speed 250 knots.'*

USA 212: *'Roger approach, how long do you need me to maintain that speed?'*

O'Hare Approach: *'All the way to the gate if you can.'*

USA 212: *'Ah, OK, but you better warn ground control.'*

Castaway

With all the incidents of passengers behaving badly when they're the worse for drink, drugs or both, and the serious risk that such antics can pose to the safety of the aircraft and its occupants, it's only surprising that it has taken so long for one pilot to decide enough is enough. The hapless individual who is an example to other would-be airline carousers was on board Monarch Airlines flight ZB558 on 27 December 2005 from Manchester to Tenerife and doubtless looking forward to some winter sun.

He was keen to get into the holiday spirit and had been drinking heavily. Some way into the flight he launched a foul-mouthed torrent of abuse at the cabin crew. Despite their best efforts the staff were unable to calm him down and he began to turn his attention to the other passengers. Usually in these circumstances a group of men subdue the miscreant, restrain him and he is arrested upon arrival at the flight's destination. Not this time.

The captain decided that the man's behaviour was so bad that it was a threat to safety and elected to divert the flight to the tiny island of Porto Santo where the unnamed man was delivered into the hands of the Portuguese authorities. The aircraft left shortly afterwards to carry the rest of the 210 passengers, who were supportive of the pilot's actions despite the four-hour delay they had suffered, to their destination.

The unwilling castaway spent New Year on the 10-mile-long island with a population of 4,000 working out how to get home. It is a two and a half hour ferry ride to the closest large settlement, Madeira. He would have been able to while away the time by walking around on its sand dunes and considering the fact that Christopher Columbus met his wife there, who was the governor of Porto Santo's daughter. One thing is certain; his journey home will not have been with Monarch; when asked what would happen to the man the airline's spokesperson Jo Robertson said, 'He certainly won't be flying back with us.'

 Twenty-five per cent of the passengers on almost any aircraft show white knuckles on take-off.

– COLIN MARSHALL, CEO OF BRITISH AIRWAYS

FLYING FACTS

Size Isn't Everything (But It Helps)

2005 total scheduled passengers carried:

American Airlines 88.2 million

Delta Air Lines 84.2 million

Southwest Airlines 77.7 million

United Airlines 66.1 million

Japan Airlines 58.2 million Air

France-KLM 53.8 million

Northwest Airlines 51.9 million

Lufthansa 45.4 million

All Nippon Airways 42.3 million

US Airways 41.3 million

Continental Airlines 40.0 million

British Airways 35.1 million

Ryanair 33.4 million

easyJet 30.3 million

Qantas 28.9 million

Iberia Airlines 25.1 million

Korean Air 21.7 million

America West Airlines 20.0 million

Air Canada 20.0 million

Scandinavian Airlines System 19.3 million.

Calling Time on On Board Duty-Free

Most airlines have policies controlling the serving of alcohol to passengers who appear inebriated, and many will refuse boarding to people clearly the worse for drink.

An incident in January 2006 highlighted the issue of passengers consuming their own duty-free booze bought in the terminal. A Polish man was on a Thomsonfly flight from Mexico to Manchester when he went berserk and smashed up one of the aircraft's lavatories and attempted to open one of the emergency exits. It finally required 20 men to subdue and restrain him and such was the rumpus that the captain diverted the flight to Orlando, Florida, where he was arrested and charged with 'interfering with flight crew'. It emerged that he had got into his drunken frenzy not by being served alcohol by the cabin crew or by drinking before the flight but by drinking alcohol from a Coca-Cola bottle, which he had brought on board with him.

The case adds to the statistics identifying an alarming trend in passenger air travel: 'air rage' is increasing dramatically. The Department of Transport listed a total of 1,486 reported incidents of disruptive behaviour on board British aircraft for the year to 31 March 2005. This is an increase of 59 per cent over the previous 12 months, and is causing aviation safety experts to call for stricter controls on passengers' access to alcohol. There are increasingly loud calls for any booze bought in the airport to be loaded into the cargo holds and returned to the passengers on arrival. The fact that passengers can simply drink their own alcohol if denied further service by the cabin crew deprives the staff of one of their main means of controlling drunken people.

While they do have the right to deny boarding to already drunken passengers, airline staff do not do so lightly. If they decide to stop a passenger from getting on a flight, the airline has to remove their luggage from the hold (suitcases are never carried without their owners being on board for safety reasons) which inevitably causes delay and will probably mean missing the flight's departure slot, which costs money. So, while safety is foremost in their minds, airline staff will always try not to delay departure unless the person is completely blotto.

The problem isn't confined to the economy cabin or the yob element. In February 2005 two unlikely individuals admitted themselves into the hall of shame for appalling in-flight conduct. A senior diplomat was accused of abusive behaviour towards passengers on a flight from Abu Dhabi to London after drinking heavily during lunch on the flight. He was handcuffed to his seat and arrested upon arrival. He was later acquitted of the charges.

The second incident involved a senior foreign bureaucrat who was arrested following a flight from Washington to London during which he allegedly attempted to grope a female passenger and exposed himself to the cabin crew after consuming duty-free alcohol.

I feel about airplanes the way I feel about diets. It seems they are wonderful things for other people to go on.

– JEAN KERR, AUTHOR AND PLAYWRIGHT

Out of the Blue

Bored with the in-flight movie? Wish there was something a bit more gripping to watch? How about tuning in to live TV coverage of the aircraft you are on coming in to crash land, ending possibly in your own death?

That's precisely what was on offer to the 140 passengers on a Jet Blue flight in September 2005. The Airbus A320 had taken off from Burbank, California, for a flight to New York when its nose landing gear failed to retract properly. The aircraft circled for several hours to dispose of fuel before coming in for an emergency landing at Los Angeles International Airport, and in the meantime the television networks had picked up the story and were broadcasting live coverage of the aircraft's plight. The passengers on board were able to watch the pictures and listen to the speculation about their fate on the televisions mounted in the backs of the aircraft's seats. Where else but LA?

'We couldn't believe the irony, that we were watching our own demise on TV – it was all too post-modern', commented passenger Alexandra Jacobs, a journalist at the New York Observer. The episode of brutal reality television ended happily when the aircraft made a safe landing and all occupants disembarked unharmed. The footage showing the plume of sparks coming from the crippled nose gear as it scraped down the tarmac made a compelling sight for the millions of television viewers watching the events. At least the passengers were spared the images of the aircraft sliding down the runway as the entertainment system was shut down, along with all other non-essential systems, four minutes before touchdown. But they doubtless had quite enough of the sensation.

IN-FLIGHT CONFIDENTIAL

A less reported aspect of this incident is how superbly the pilot handled the situation. He was praised for bringing the aircraft safely down with non-functioning nose gear, indeed he joked to the passengers that he was sorry that he missed the runway's centre line by six inches, but it was his actions prior to landing which really saved the day.

Alerted to a problem by warning lights after he retracted the landing gear soon after take-off, pilot Scott Burke contacted his colleagues on the ground and told them that he had an indication that the nose gear was still extended. They checked the records and found that the aircraft had been reported for maintenance with a gear retraction problem recently, but this had been rectified. They advised him that the problem was a faulty warning light and there was probably nothing wrong with the gear. They said he should carry on to New York, but if he was worried to return to Burbank Airport.

The pilot wasn't satisfied with this and, as the officer in charge of the aircraft, he is ultimately responsible for the safety of the people on board. He used the time available – there was no immediate threat to the plane – to consider his options and decided that he wasn't prepared to risk the possibility that the warning light was functioning correctly. He elected to bring the aircraft down for an emergency landing, but refused to return to Burbank. He preferred to use Los Angeles International because he felt the emergency services there were better equipped and because there was a side wind at Burbank; bringing an airliner down with no steering on the front in a cross wind didn't seem like a good idea. In the event he pulled off a text-book landing, but the happy outcome was not only due to his skilled airmanship but also to his calm, careful thinking and good judgement.

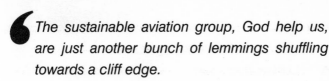

The sustainable aviation group, God help us, are just another bunch of lemmings shuffling towards a cliff edge.

– MICHAEL O'LEARY, CHIEF EXECUTIVE OF RYANAIR

Frequent Travellers

Had a busy travel schedule lately? Feeling a bit fed up with the grind of regular air travel, visiting the same airports day after day? You'll have to go some to earn the sympathy of Brother Michael Bartlett from the UK. He earned himself a place in the Guinness Book of Records for the most scheduled flight journeys in a 30-day period in 1993 by using a Sabena monthly Skypass to fly between London and Brussels a total of 128 times between 18 October and 17 November.

The poor, weary soul had travelled a total of 41,771 km (25,955 miles) by the end of his odyssey. He had stapled the individual tickets together, which in the end formed a 25.3-m (83-foot) ticket; the comments of the check-in staff when confronted by this monster are not recorded.

Brother Michael's marathon achievement does not match the intensity of Tae Oka, who holds the record for the most scheduled flights in a week. Oka, from Japan, took a total of 70 Thai Airways flights between 14 and 20 February 2001. The internal flights were all between the Thai cities of Chiang Mai, Chiang Rai and Mae Hong Son Airports.

Neither of these feats of endurance matches that of John Bougen and James Irving. Living out the dream of every gap-year traveller, they managed to visit 191 of the world's then 193 sovereign countries in under six months. Between 28 August 2002 and 12 February 2003 they set the record for the most sovereign countries visited in six months (167 days 15 hours and 39 minutes to be exact).

The 'all nations quest' started and finished in Auckland, New Zealand, and included travel on 104 different airlines, setting the record for the most airlines flown on in one year. They took 242 flights on 54 different aircraft types, setting another record for the most flights in a single journey. The rules required that they did not visit any of the 191 airports more than once and did not return to New Zealand until the end of the journey.

The record for the fastest circumnavigation of the globe using scheduled flights and visiting six continents is held by Michael Quandt. The German, editor of the travel section of a newspaper, managed the feat in a gruelling 66 hour and 31 minute trip in July 2004. He started and finished in Singapore and travelled via Sydney, Los Angeles, Houston, Caracas, London, Cairo and Kuala Lumpur.

At the other end of the commercial air travel record spectrum is that set by Fred Finn. A UK national, Fred had crossed the Atlantic on Concorde 718 times by February 2003. He started taking the flights on 26 May 1976 and still has the commemorative briefcase tag he was given on the flight.

If you're reading this on a long-haul flight and are feeling a bit cramped and bored (although we hope this book is going some way to help with the latter) then spare a thought for the passengers on Singapore Airlines' service between Singapore and New York City. The 16,600 km (10,300 mile) journey using an Airbus A340-500 takes its 181 passengers 18 hours, the longest commercial scheduled flight.

'*Flight Reservation Systems decide whether or not you exist. If your information isn't in their database, then you simply don't get to go anywhere.*'

– PLAYWRIGHT ARTHUR MILLER

Snakes on a Plane

People take some strange things onto aircraft in their hand baggage, although with heightened security the chances of something nasty slipping through are less and less. 10 years ago a six-year-old boy on board an Ansett flight from Melbourne to Perth in Australia, put his hand down under his seat to pick up a sweet he had dropped and was promptly bitten by a stowaway.

Almost immediately the boy became very unwell and tests later showed that a taipan snake had bitten him. The snake is particularly deadly and paralysis can set in fairly quickly. Luckily in this case the boy survived and so it seemed did the snake.

On landing snake catchers with sniffer dogs got on board to search for the snake. They found nothing and so the only alternative was fumigation. This produced no dead snake so it was deduced that a passenger had taken the snake on board in their hand baggage and taken it off again the same way.

Sick Obsession

One gentleman's hoarding instincts have found him a place in the Guinness Book of Records for his extraordinary collection. Niek Vermeulen of the Netherlands has amassed a collection of 3,728 airline sickness bags representing 802 different airlines since he began collecting in the 1970s. He started the collection as a bet with a friend to see who could get into the Guinness Book of Records. Explaining his achievement, Niek said, 'Somebody has to do it.'

Fellow collect-aholic Raghav Somani may not have started his collection for a bet, but since 1994 the Indian national has built up a world record hoard of airline luggage tags totalling 637 from 174 different airlines.

> *I don't think JetBlue has a better chance of being profitable than 100 other predecessors with new airplanes, new employees, low fares, all touchyfeely... all of them are losers. Most of these guys are smoking ragweed.*
>
> – GORDON BETHUNE, CEO OF CONTINENTAL AIRLINES

Chapter**EIGHT**

Excess Baggage

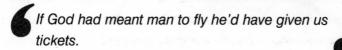

If God had meant man to fly he'd have given us tickets.

– ANON.

People who work for airlines are often fascinated by the whole business. In fact many of them seem to be nuts about aircraft and to have only a passing interest in making money. To be fair, in recent years this is something that has got an awful lot better and the industry now seems to display a finer regard for the bottom line than it once did.

This cavalier approach to the business of making money prompted one financial director of a British airline to comment: 'The trouble with our business is there's too much show business and not enough business', a remark that may have been prompted by a number of the airline's board members seeming to take more interest in the company's stable of sponsored golf professionals, than they did in the matter of increasing load factors. To justify the company's involvement with golf it was very important for that all important high-octane business fuel called corporate hospitality.

In this section we've gathered together all of the odds and ends which defy categorisation, the flotsam and jetsam of flying anecdotes creating a lost luggage office of assorted tales from the fringes of air travel. As one waggish graffiti artist amended the slogan on a poster advertising the then new supersonic Concorde service: 'Breakfast in London, Lunch in New York... Luggage in Hong Kong'.

PLANE SPEAKING

Pilot: *'Approach, Acme Flight 202, with you at 12,000 feet and 40 DME.'*
Approach: *'Acme 202, cross 30 DME at and maintain 8,000 feet.'*
Pilot: *'Approach, 202 unable to achieve that descent rate.'*
Approach: *'What's the matter 202? Don't you have speed brakes?'*
Pilot: *'Yup. But they're for my mistakes. Not yours.'*

Up, Up and Away

Mr Larry Walters, a resident of California, had long harboured a desire to fly. He joined the Air Force, but sadly his poor eyesight prevented him from training as a pilot. After leaving the armed services he decided one day in 1982 to satisfy his urge to fly like a bird. Lacking the traditional means, such as an aircraft, hang-glider or even parachute, he resourcefully decided to use balloon power.

Mr Walters purchased 45 weather balloons, tethered them to a plastic garden seat and set about filling them, one by one, with helium. He reasoned that eventually he would have sufficient lift to float up to the top of the trees in the garden, admire the view and enjoy the wonderful sensation of flying. A cautious man, he tethered the chair to his jeep with a 30-foot rope and he took with him his air pistol to shoot out some of the balloons when he wanted to go back down. He also thoughtfully took some beer and sandwiches to enjoy on the way. What could possibly go wrong?

Well, at first the adventure seemed to be a roaring success. He achieved take-off and began to climb. Once at his target height, the tree tops, he prepared to descend and looked down. And saw his friends cut the tether rope. He began to climb very fast. Petrified by the height and the danger of death if he got it wrong, he couldn't bring himself to shoot any balloons. So, transfixed by fear, he climbed further. And further. He levelled out at 16,000 feet and began to drift, cold and petrified for 14 hours.

Things began to get really out of hand when the air currents took him into the airspace of the approach to Los Angeles Airport. Several pilots reported seeing a man in a garden chair dangling below a cluster of balloons bobbing past them. Finally Larry summoned up the courage to start shooting balloons and effected a fairly controlled descent, until the dangling balloons caught on a power line, blacking out the Long Beach area for 20 minutes.

Unharmed by the current, Larry managed to climb down the pylon to safety and into the arms of the waiting police. As he was led away, Larry commented to a reporter, 'A man can't just sit around.' The authorities were not amused. Federal Aviation Administration Safety Inspector Neal Savoy commented, 'We know he broke some part of the Federal Aviation Act, and as soon as we know which part it is, a charge will be filed.' He was eventually fined $1,500.

PLANE SPEAKING

727 pilot, after being told to circle: *'Do you know it costs us $2,000 to make a 360 in this airplane?'*
Controller: *'Roger, give me $4,000 worth.'*

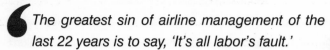

The greatest sin of airline management of the last 22 years is to say, 'It's all labor's fault.'
– DONALD CARTY, CHAIRMAN AND CEO OF AMERICAN AIRLINES

Returned Parcel

Airliners' occupants are used to the comforts of modern jet travel, including lavatories. While they might not be the height of spacious luxury, next time you feel like complaining spare a thought for the crew of a Falcon Jet coastguard spotter aircraft.

During one of their routine patrol flights a member of the crew felt very unwell with an upset stomach. The aircraft boasted a great range of equipment, but did not have room for a lavatory on board. The crewman's plight became so severe that he had to relieve himself in the cardboard box in which he had brought his lunch on board.

Inevitably, in such a small, cramped aircraft, things began to become a little smelly and the crew of five were finding it hard to concentrate. There was nothing for it but to jettison the noisome package. Fortunately the aircraft boasted a drop hatch for sending down emergency equipment to ships etc., so no problem.

As per procedure they reduced their height to 100 feet, slowed the aircraft's speed right down and the drop master prepared to dispatch the lunch box. On the pilot's command he gratefully dropped it through the hatch. Sadly, in their enthusiasm to be rid of the parcel, the crew had failed to check that it exceeded the 90lb minimum weight required to break through the airstream around the aircraft and descend to the sea. So the box was sent, spinning and bouncing, forcefully back into the cabin, coating the interior of the aircraft and its occupants with its unpleasant cargo. The mission was swiftly abandoned and the aircraft returned to base for a very thorough wash.

If you would look up bad labor relations in the dictionary, you would have an American Airlines logo beside it.

– US DISTRICT JUDGE JOE KENDALL

Flames in the Cabin

Normally the presence of fire in an aircraft is an event of the utmost seriousness. But not when that aircraft is carrying the Olympic flame to the start of the games. The true flame has to be carried from Athens to wherever the next games are being held and used to ignite the flame that will burn there throughout the event.

On the Delta Airlines Boeing 777 aircraft that was used to transport it to Atlanta for the 1996 Olympics, the flame was held in a specially designed safety canister attached to the bulkhead where it quietly burned during the flight. This not being a matter best left to chance, so did the other three back-up flames in their containers.

'*There always has been a mystique and a romance about aviation, but in terms of the principles involved of satisfying your customer there's no difference between selling airline seats and chocolate bars.*

– MIKE 'MARS BARS' BATT, BRITISH AIRWAYS' HEAD OF BRANDS (MARKETING) AND DIRECTOR OF NORTH AMERICAN ROUTES '

Glittering Glyndebourne

I was once being entertained by a major travel agent to a night of opera at Glyndebourne. Having watched the first half of the opera we settled down to our interval dinner. There were several other airline people at the table as guests of the generous travel agent. The convention at such affairs was that you kept business chat on a light-hearted basis and certainly never strayed into any kind of discussion about serious matters. Not least because I was working for an American airline and one of the other guests was working for our competitor British Airways, any talk about airfares was strictly off limits because of the anti-trust implications of such a conversation.

This didn't stop Mr BA from haranguing me about the fares he understood we were charging our passengers through the shady world of that 1980s airline phenomenon, 'the bucket shop'. I continually tried to change the subject and avoided responding to any of his increasing jibes about the need to 'raise our fares'. I understood that Mr BA had come from a consumer brand and so perhaps didn't understand the conventions, or the law. Perhaps because his jibes were not rattling me he got increasingly pointed. It was then I remembered what Rocky Cox, my old boss at British Caledonian Airways, once told me – I shared it with Mr BA. 'Never get annoyed with those who sell for less, they know what their product is worth.' He started to come back at me but was finally cut off by our host who brought the conversation back to more mundane matters.

 Why did God invent women when airplanes are so much fun?

– ANON.

Cannonball Run

Airlines don't just put people and cargo on an aircraft, shut the door and send it on its way. To allow the plane to take off safely it has to be trimmed, which involves a complex weight and balance procedure to distribute the load in the correct areas of the plane. This process applies equally to all freight aircraft and is slightly more complex in that it's often easier to move passengers around than it is freight. United Airlines operated a regular freight service from Chicago to Los Angeles and one night the staff were having a great deal of difficulty trimming the aircraft.

The staff were stumped as to how they were going to get the aircraft ready to fly without taking cargo off, which would have been a problem as they had contracts to fulfill. One of the cargo staff had a brainwave. Why not go around to Hertz and hire a car to use as ballast, then deliver it back to Hertz in Los Angeles and the only charge would be the minimum day rate rental. It was a perfect solution. Within 30 minutes the car was being loaded onto the aircraft and within an hour the aircraft was airborne en route for Los Angeles International Airport.

A few hours later the aircraft landed at LAX and the car was first off the plane. Within 30 minutes it was being driven round to Hertz to be handed in. The rental agent was flabbergasted that the car had made the cross-country trip so quickly, and with virtually no miles added on the clock. The United cargo person had to do a lot of explaining.

> *I'm not paid to be a candy ass. I'm paid to go and get a job done. I could have ended up with another job, but the job I ended up with was piecing together a bunch of companies that were all headed for the junk heap... I've got to be the bastard who sits around Eastern Airlines and says, 'Hey, we're losing $3 million a day or whatever the number is and bang, bang, bang, bang, what do you do?' So, some jobs are easier than others.*
>
> – FRANK LORENZO, CHAIRMAN OF TEXAS AIR CORPORATION

Rough Landing

Two young filmmakers had no idea what a storm they'd raise when they decided to make a home movie featuring an aircraft. Bruce Branit and Jeremy Hunt, both special effects experts, wanted to showcase their talents as directors. Using a borrowed car and camera, their home computers and an 80-year-old actress, they made a three-minute film called 405. The short film, showing an American Airlines DC-10 jet landing on top of a Jeep on Los Angeles' freeway 405, quickly became one of the top-rated videos distributed on the internet. The filmmakers chose American Airlines' livery for the aircraft model because of the 'attractive reflective qualities' of the red, white and blue stripes on the shiny polished aluminium body.

American Airlines had not given consent to the use of its trademarks and logos and was far from amused at the emergence of a film showing one of its aircraft landing on a freeway and crushing a car.

The film, which was made for $400, enjoyed a good deal of critical acclaim for the technical virtuosity of the action sequence, and quickly became a cult classic. Even the cars involved, a Jeep and Lincoln Continental, were shot sitting still and digitally inserted. This was not least because Angela Burns, the 80-year-old actress who featured at the end of the film being run off the road by the landing aircraft, did not have a driving licence.

'From a safety standpoint, we just hope that no one takes this film seriously and thinks this occurred. The company will be contacting the filmmakers regarding this movie. It is a very well done film, but we feel that in the light of the time and effort they put into this film, they could have just as easily used a fictitious brand', said John Hotard, spokesman for American Airlines. Branit and Hunt appear to have launched their careers as film directors with the film as they have been signed by the Creative Artists Agency.

‘*As a businessman, Frank Lorenzo gives capitalism a bad name.*’

– JOURNALIST WILLIAM F. BUCKLEY

Parking Incident

Forgetting to put the handbrake on the car and seeing it roll off is a staple of TV comedy writers. But as parked vehicle incidents go, a car is child's play.

In the early hours of June 2000 a 140-seat Continental Airlines MD-80 was being cleaned and checked ready for operations the next day. As the engine oil level was being checked, the aircraft lurched forward and its nose crashed through the wall of Newark Airport's Terminal C at Gate 115.

The aircraft's nose projected 20 feet into the terminal at a height of six feet and led to the closure of four gates for the day. The airport authorities did their best to conceal the embarrassing incident by arranging a number of potted plants around the scene. One flight attendant said they found it 'hilarious, just like in the movie Airplane'.

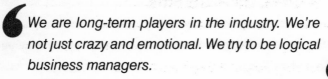

We are long-term players in the industry. We're not just crazy and emotional. We try to be logical business managers.

– FRANK LORENZO, CHAIRMAN OF TEXAS AIR CORPORATION

Slippery Customer

Smoking can damage your health, but it's not often that the packets can be regarded as dangerous. Imagine the shock when customs officials at Brisbane International Airport investigated a man wearing a suspiciously bulky jacket. They found a number of cigarette boxes concealed in his clothing, containing not smuggled fags but 19 pythons. Customs manager Tom Ramsay noted, 'When you see cigarette packs, you don't expect to find snakes inside.' The man was charged with importing regulated live species without a permit.

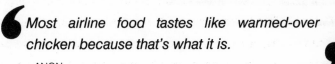

> *Most airline food tastes like warmed-over chicken because that's what it is.*
> – ANON.

Maintenance Problems

The US Air Force operates a system whereby the crew of an aircraft can log any problems, which they encounter for rectification by the ground crew; entries in this log are called 'squawks'.

Here are a selection of crew complaints and the maintenance crew's response in the log.

Problem: 'Left inside main tire almost needs replacement.'
Response: 'Almost replaced left inside main tire.'

Problem: 'Test flight OK, except autoland very rough.'
Response: 'Autoland not fitted on this aircraft.'

Problem: 'Something loose in cockpit.'
Response: 'Something tightened in cockpit.'

Problem: 'Evidence of hydraulic fluid leak on right main landing gear.'
Response: 'Evidence removed.'

Problem: 'DME volume unbelievably loud.'
Response: 'Volume set to a more believable level.'

Problem: 'Dead bugs on windshield.'
Response: 'Live bugs on order.'

Problem: 'IFF inoperative.'
Response: 'IFF inoperative in OFF mode.'

Problem: 'Friction locks cause throttle levers to stick.'
Response: 'That's what they're for.'

Problem: 'Number 3 engine missing.'
Response: 'Engine found on right wing after brief search.'

Problem: 'Aircraft handles funny.'
Response: 'Aircraft warned to straighten up, "fly right", and be serious.'

Problem: 'Target Radar hums'
Response: 'Reprogrammed Target Radar with the words.'

Problem: 'Radio switches stick.'
Response: 'Peanut butter no longer served to flight crew.'

Problem: 'Screaming sound in cabin at start-up.'
Response: 'Company accountant deplaned.'

Problem: 'Funny smell in cockpit.'
Response: 'Pilot told to change cologne.'

Problem: 'Aircraft 2,400lb over max weight.'
Response: 'Aircraft put on diet of 92 octane.'

Problem: 'Number 3 engine knocks at idle.'
Response: 'Number 3 engine let in for a few beers.'

Problem: 'Number 3 engine runs like it's sick.'
Response: 'Number 3 engine diagnosed with hangover.'

Problem: 'Brakes howl on application.'
Response: 'Don't step on 'em so hard!'

Problem: 'Radio sounds like a squealing pig.'
Response: 'Removed pig from radio. BBQ behind hangar tomorrow.'

Problem: 'Number 2 propeller seeping fluid.'
Response: 'Number 2 propeller seepage normal; Numbers. 1, 3 and 4 propellers lack normal seepage.'

Problem: 'Autopilot in altitude hold mode produces a 200 feet per minute descent.'

Response: 'Cannot reproduce problem on ground.'

Problem: 'Whole aircraft smells like BBQ.'

Response: 'Ground Checks OK.'

Problem: 'First class cabin floor has a squeak.'

Response: 'Co-pilot told not to play with toddler toys in the cabin anymore.'

Problem: 'Electrical governor is broke.'

Response: 'Paid off governor's debt to Jimmy "The Fish" Galvano.'

American aircraft mechanics' three favourite sayings: 'It's not a leak, it's a seep.'

'If it won't budge, force it. If it breaks, it needed replacing anyway.'

'If it's ugly, it's British; if it's weird, it's French; and if it's ugly and weird, it's Russian.'

– ANON.

Marketing Ploy

While this doesn't directly relate to the airline industry, the company concerned did make pasenger aircraft. This was posted very briefly on the aircraft manufacturer's website a few years ago. The company, of course, does not have a sense of humour, and made the web department take it down immediately.

Thank you for purchasing one of our military aircraft. In order to protect your new investment, please take a few moments to fill out the warranty registration card below. Answering the survey questions is not required, but the information will help us to develop new products that best meet your needs and desires.

1. ☐ Mr ☐ Lt. ☐ Citizen
   ☐ Mrs ☐ Gen. ☐ Der Führer
   ☐ Ms ☐ Comrade ☐ Il Duce
   ☐ Miss ☐ Classified ☐ Saddam Hussein
   First Name: Initial: Last Name:

2. Which kind of aircraft did you purchase?
   ☐ Fighter ☐ Bomber ☐ Electronic Mission
   ☐ Multi-role ☐ Classified

3. Date of purchase (Year/Month/Day): 19.. / .. /..

4. Serial Number:............... (Found on panel behind driver's seat)

5. Please indicate where this product was purchased:

☐ Received as gift/aid package ☐ Catalogue/showroom

☐ Independent arms broker ☐ Mail order

☐ Discount store ☐ Free gift with another purchase

☐ Government surplus ☐ Classified

6. Please indicate how you became aware of the product you have just purchased:

☐ Heard loud noise, looked up ☐ Store display

☐ Espionage ☐ Recommended by friend/relative/ally

☐ Political lobbying by manufacturer ☐ Was attacked by one

7. Please indicate the three factors that most influenced your decision to purchase this product:

☐ Style/appearance ☐ Speed/manoeuvrability

☐ Price/value ☐ Comfort/convenience

☐ Kickback/bribe ☐ Recommended by salesperson

☐ Company reputation ☐ Sales woman let you sleep with her

☐ Advanced weapons systems ☐ Backroom politics

☐ Negative experience opposing one in combat

8. Please indicate the location(s) where this product will be used:

☐ North America ☐ Iraq ☐ Central/South America

☐ Iraq ☐ Aircraft carrier ☐ Iraq

☐ Europe ☐ Iraq ☐ Middle East (not Iraq)

☐ Iraq ☐ Africa ☐ Iraq

☐ Asia/Far East ☐ Iraq ☐ Misc. Third World countries

☐ Iraq ☐ Classified ☐ Iraq

9. Please indicate the products that you currently own or intend to purchase in the near future:

☐ Colour TV ☐ VCR ☐ ICBM

☐ Killer satellite ☐ CD Player ☐ Particle beam weapon

☐ Kitchen appliance ☐ Air-to-air missile ☐ Space shuttle

☐ Home computer ☐ Thermonuclear device

10. How would you describe yourself or your organisation?
(Indicate all that apply):

☐ Communist/Socialist ☐ Terrorist ☐ Crazed

☐ Neutral ☐ Democratic ☐ Dictatorship

☐ Corrupt ☐ Primitive/Tribal

11. How did you pay for your product?

☐ Deficit spending ☐ Cash ☐ Suitcases of cocaine

☐ Oil revenues ☐ Luncheon Vouchers ☐ Personal check

☐ Credit card ☐ Ransom money ☐ Traveller's check

12. Your occupation:

☐ Homemaker ☐ Sales/marketing ☐ Revolutionary

☐ Clerical ☐ Mercenary ☐ Tyrant

☐ Middle manager ☐ Eccentric billionaire ☐ Retired

☐ Defence minister/general ☐ Student/trainee militant

13. To help us understand our customers' lifestyles, please indicate the interests and activities in which you and your spouse enjoy participating on a regular basis:

IN-FLIGHT CONFIDENTIAL

- ☐ Golf ☐ Boating/sailing
- ☐ Sabotage ☐ Airline Hijacking
- ☐ Flyfishing ☐ Propaganda
- ☐ Destabilisation/overthrow ☐ Default on loans
- ☐ Gardening ☐ Rape & pillage
- ☐ Crafts ☐ Black market/smuggling
- ☐ Collectibles/collections ☐ Watching sports on TV
- ☐ Wines ☐ Interrogation/torture
- ☐ Household pets ☐ Crushing rebellions
- ☐ Espionage/reconnaissance ☐ Fashion clothing
- ☐ Border disputes ☐ Mutually assured destruction

Thank you for taking the time to fill in this questionnaire. Your answers will be used in market studies that will help us serve you better in the future, as well as allowing you to receive mailings and special offers from other companies, governments, extremist groups, and mysterious consortia.

As a bonus for responding to this survey, you will be registered to win a brand new attack aircraft of your choice in our Desert Thunder Sweepstakes!

 Without doubt, Concorde died yesterday at the age of 31. All that will remain is the myth of a beautiful white bird.

– LE FIGARO EDITORIAL, THE DAY AFTER AF 4590 CRASHED AT TAKE-OFF FROM CHARLES DE GAULLE AERODROME, 26 JULY 2000

The Golden Years

On 15 May 1930, the first airline stewardesses boarded planes with the following instructions among items in their Flying Manual:

Keep the clock and altimeter wound up.

Carry a railroad timetable in case the plane is grounded.

Warn the passengers against throwing their cigars and cigarettes out the windows.

Keep an eye on passengers when they go to the lavatory to be sure they don't mistakenly go out the emergency exit.

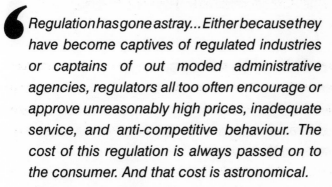

> *Regulation has gone astray... Either because they have become captives of regulated industries or captains of out moded administrative agencies, regulators all too often encourage or approve unreasonably high prices, inadequate service, and anti-competitive behaviour. The cost of this regulation is always passed on to the consumer. And that cost is astronomical.*
>
> – SENATOR EDWARD KENNEDY, OPENING REMARKS TO THE SUBCOMMITTEE ON ADMINISTRATIVE PRACTICE AND PROCEDURE, 6 FEBRUARY 1975

Get Me to the Match on Time

The loyal Colombian soccer fans travelling on a Run Air aircraft were not going to let the inconvenient fact that they were scheduled to be airborne get in the way of their seeing the country's youth team play. The crew of the aircraft used a fake fuel emergency as an excuse for an unscheduled landing at the city of Piura, instead of Lima, in Peru. By landing earlier and avoiding immigration procedures in Lima, the crew and 289 passengers on board were then able to watch the live television coverage of the Colombian side taking on Qatar in the World Under-17 Championship. Once the game had finished they continued on to Lima.

> *An aircraft which is used by wealthy people on their expense accounts, whose fares are subsidised by much poorer taxpayers.*
>
> – DENIS HEALEY, BRITISH LABOUR PARTY, REGARDING CONCORDE

The Skirl o' the Pipes...

British Caledonian was, because of its Scottish heritage, in love with all things tartan, which of course meant that the uniforms were just about the best there has ever been. The sight of a girl standing at the top of the aircraft steps, 'somewhere in Africa', in her crisp white blouse and her kilt has been known to make many an ex-pat go weak at the knees. Anyway I digress, because what BCAL also had was its very own pipe band. At the drop of a hat, or the start of a new route to some far flung corner of the world the pipers were dispatched to stir the hearts of everyone and hopefully make them buy more tickets.

When a new route was inaugurated the pipe band became a focal point of the airline's activities in the new destination city. The pipe band were clever, they always learned a new tune with particular links to the new destination so that they could play it at events around the new route start up. When BCAL began flying to Houston they played The Yellow

Rose of Texas while walking along the main street of the downtown area. Next thing you know they are all over the TV with local stations oooo-ing and ahhhhh-ing over this wonderful new Scottish/British airline.

When BCAL began flying to Atlanta I was asked to 'keep an eye on' the band during their time in the city while the more important BCAL employees got on with the job of schmoozing the local bigwigs and the guests on the inaugural service. A huge reception was planned in the ballroom of the Omni Hotel and the band and I went through what they would do. They planned to walk around the balcony area before descending the steps of the ballroom to entertain the thousand or so guests. We didn't talk about what songs they were going to play. That was my big mistake. That night, with the great and the good of Atlanta, including the Reverend Jesse Jackson, assembled in the ballroom, it came time for the band to enter. I was standing next to the BCAL chairman, Sir Adam Thomson.

First we heard the muffled strains of the pipes before the band entered the top level of the room proudly playing Scotland the Brave. As the band got to the steps and started to descend the chairman turned to me and said, 'Well done, aren't they marvellous.'

As I was about to reply the pipers began playing the special song they had learned for Atlanta. 'Oh my God,' was all I could say.

'What? What is it?' said Sir Adam Thomson.

'This song, you know what it is don't you? It's Marching through Georgia, the song the Union troops whistled and sang as they burnt Atlanta during the American Civil War.'

I thought he was going to have a seizure. I was lucky to survive that one, because somehow it became all my fault.

'*I think, historically, the airline business has not been run as a real business. That is, a business designed to achieve a return on capital that is then passed on to shareholders. It has historically been run as an extremely elaborate version of a model railroad, that is one in which you try to make enough money to buy more equipment.*'

– MICHAEL LEVINE, EXECUTIVE VP NORTHWEST AIRLINES, 1996

Meet Me in St Louis

When British Caledonian started flying to St Louis naturally the pipes were back. After the first flight had departed from the city all the BCAL staff, along with the pipe band and the crew that had brought the plane from London went to the nearby Ramada Inn, where the crew were staying, for a party in celebration of the BCAL airport manager's birthday. The party was going along really well, until that is the police appeared: 'Who's in charge here?' asked the cop.

'I guess that will be me,' I thought looking around the room, although I'm not too sure what I was in charge of at this point. 'Me. Probably.'

'Well you'll need to come with us, we've got some of your pipe band in custody along with three of your flight attendants. They've been playing their bagpipes in the hotel car park,' said the officer.

'Phew,' I thought, 'Is that all.'

'And, the flight attendants have been roller skating around them – topless!' It took a lot of persuasion for them not to press charges.

> *It was over in a blink of an eye, that moment when aviation stirred the modern imagination. Aviation was transformed from recklessness to routine in Lindbergh's lifetime. Today the riskiest part of air travel is the drive to the airport, and the airlines use a barrage of stimuli to protect passengers from ennui.*
>
> – NEWSPAPERMAN GEORGE WILL

Testing, Testing

One of the aircraft industry's main concerns is safety; vast amounts of time and money are spent trying to reduce accidents and aircraft manufacturers embark on extraordinarily rigorous ground testing programmes before even making a test flight with a newly developed piece of technology.

Jet engines produce vast amounts of power and operate to incredibly high reliability rates in a huge range of climate and weather conditions. However, one threat to which they are inevitably exposed is the ingestion of birds. Unfortunately birds are often attracted to the wide open spaces of airfields and despite all the efforts of the airport operators there can be flocks of them flying around as aircraft are taking off and landing.

A bird being sucked into an engine is a fairly common occurrence, and, while clearly fatal to the bird, this can also cause major damage to the engine and even make the aircraft crash. Therefore engine designers and manufacturers have developed a means of testing that their products are capable of withstanding such 'bird strikes'. They have come up with a gun for the purpose of launching dead chickens at the aircraft's maximum speed at an operating jet engine held in a test frame. If the engine can cope with that, it's another step towards being approved for use on an aircraft.

It is reputed that some railway engineers, upon hearing of the gun, were eager to employ it in testing the windscreen of a new high-speed train. However, on firing the gun, the engineers watched in shock as the chicken shattered the windshield, smashed through the control console, snapped the engineer's backrest in two, and embedded itself into the back wall of the cabin. Horrified, the engineers sent the aircraft manufacturer the results of the experiment, along with the designs of the windscreen, and asked the aircraft designers for any suggestions. The aircraft team sent back a one-sentence analysis: 'Thaw the chicken.'

The head of one aircraft manufacturer's testing department had heard about the mishaps involving his rail counterparts and chuckled. He used his customary procedure to ensure the test bird was thoroughly defrosted by leaving it in the gun overnight prior to performing the test in the morning.

The results were somewhat different from the expected. The anomaly was explained when, after close examination of the high-speed video footage, a very startled-looking stray cat clinging to a half-eaten chicken was observed as it exited the gun at Mach 0.7.

' *Today, the situation is exacerbated, with costs exceeding revenues at four times the pre-September 11 rate. Today, we are literally haemorrhaging money. Clearly this bleeding has to be stopped – and soon – or United will perish some time next year.*

– JAMES GOODWIN, CHAIRMAN AND CEO OF UNITED'S PARENT COMPANY UAL, 17 OCTOBER 2001 '

Three Men in a Boat

Some workers at the Boeing factory couldn't resist the temptation to 'borrow' for the weekend one of the life rafts, which was awaiting installation on a 747. They managed to smuggle the bulky and heavy capsule out of the factory and got it home. They took it down to their local river and excitedly activated the raft and watched it inflate. Gleefully they leapt aboard the orange craft and began a thrilling ride down the river.

Their revelry was somewhat curtailed when a Coast Guard helicopter swooped down towards them. They hadn't thought about the emergency locator beacon, which was activated when the raft was deployed. Once they got the raft back, Boeing decided it didn't need the joyriders' services any longer.

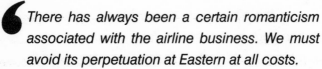

There has always been a certain romanticism associated with the airline business. We must avoid its perpetuation at Eastern at all costs.

– FRANK BORMAN, ASTRONAUT AND FORMER HEAD OF
EASTERN AIRLINES

Where Are We?

Navigation is a crucial skill for any pilot, and in the era of radar, GPS and collision avoidance systems it is easy to forget how recently pilots had to find their way by using physical features on the ground and other techniques based on maritime navigation. It wasn't long ago that a navigator devoted the entire flight to plotting the course and speed of the aircraft to keep tabs on its position. There is many a student pilot who has swooped down to read what it says on a road sign to confirm his position.

The pioneer of specialist charts for pilots was Elrey Borge Jeppesen, who died in 1996 at 89 years of age. He was born in 1907 and began flying at age 16. His pilot's licence was signed by Orville Wright, and he left high school to fly his war surplus JN4 'Jenny' biplane (which cost $500) as a barnstormer with Tex Rankin's Flying Circus based in Portland, Oregon.

Jeppesen later flew the night mail route between Cheyenne and Oakland, California. Fed up with the difficulties of navigating using a compass and the terrain below, he began making aerial surveys and taking photographs.

His charts featured elevations, landmarks and obstructions, which he had observed from the air. 'I invented something to prevent me from getting killed', he said. He sold his first charts to other pilots, at $10 each in 1934.

United Airlines began business in the 1930s, and Jeppesen became a pilot for them. His future wife worked for United as a stewardess. In 1936 they began a chart business – putting together the Jeppesen Airway Manual – in the basement of their homes in Cheyenne, Salt Lake City, and in Denver, where they moved in 1941. Jeppesen climbed obstacles such as mountains, water towers and the like, checking their elevations with an altimeter. He had charted most of the USA by the time his country entered the Second World War, and his 'Jepp' charts became standard issue to pilots in military service.

In 1954, pilot Jeppesen retired from United on medical grounds and put all his effort into the charting business. It was sold to Times Mirror Corporation in 1961, although Jeppesen served as chairman until 1988. The charts he pioneered continue to be the industry's standard.

Its operation in a world beset by fuel and energy crises makes no sense at all.

– SENATOR CRANSTON OF CALIFORNIA, REGARDING CONCORDE, 1974

Dead Dog Afternoon

A couple returning to live in Texas after working in the UK for a several years on secondment for an oil company shipped their dog home as cargo – nothing unusual in that. When the dog arrived at the British Caledonian Airways freight shed in Houston the warehousemen were upset to find the German Shepherd was dead. Being kindly as well as resourceful souls, the BCAL staff went to the local dog pound and got another German Shepherd, with identical markings. The couple flew from London to Houston the day after air-freighting their dog. Come the hour, cometh the couple and they were led into the warehouse where they were met by the dog, which the warehouse man had released from the kennel area. It jumped up and started to lick the lady, who promptly fainted. Her husband, who was equally in shock, somewhat falteringly, explained that their dog had died two days before they were due to travel and they were so distraught that they decided to ship the dead pooch so that he could be buried back in Texas... a small point that they had avoided telling anyone in London.

High Level Workout

The battle for passengers among low-cost US airlines took a new twist in 2004 when east coast operator Song started to offer its passengers the opportunity to have an airborne workout. For a nominal charge the seatbound passengers are provided with a large elastic band and a squeezy ball, which they can use in a workout guided by a handbook written by famous US gym owner David Barton.

Joining the battle to have bored and inactive passengers arriving in tiptop form is Song's rival for budget travellers JetBlue, which operates an in-flight yoga and Pilates programme.

' *United has little to fear from numerous small competitors. We should be able to compete effectively by advertising our size, dependability, and experience, and by matching or beating their promotional tactics... In a free environment, we would be able to flex our marketing muscles a bit and should not fear the threat of being nibbled to death by little operators.* '

– RICHARD FERRIS, CEO OF UNITED AIRLINES, 1976

Missing: One Boeing

Car theft is common throughout the world, but how often do we hear of an aircraft being stolen, and a Boeing 727 airliner at that? In May 2003 a 727 formerly owned and operated by American Airlines was stolen from the airport in Luanda in Angola. It's assumed that the plane was either taken by drug-runners or some kind of terrorist organisation. There was a mechanic on the plane and he has not been seen since. If you notice what appears to be an abandoned Boeing 727 (they are 153 feet long), please don't hesitate to contact your local police station.

PLANE SPEAKING

Pilot: *'Halifax Terminal, Nova 851 with you out of 13,000 for 10,000, requesting runway 15.'*

Halifax Terminal (female): *'Nova 851 Halifax, the last time I gave a pilot what he wanted I was on penicillin for three weeks. Expect runway 06.'*

We've Come a Long Way

The movement in recent years towards some airlines not offering any food service is in some ways a return to the grass roots of commercial passenger aviation. While the stimulus for not serving food nowadays is the fierce competition for passengers based on price, the offering of a spartan cabin and little comfort is reminiscent of what was provided in the 1920s.

The brave souls who tried the new means of transport might have been able to fly from coast to coast across the US in only 22 hours, but they endured some hardship on the way. The aircraft was not pressurised, so could only fly up to an altitude of 10,000 feet, and was not heated so it was often freezing cold inside. The air reeked of fuel fumes and the noise generated by the piston propeller engines was deafening. Passengers sat on either wooden benches or mail sacks. There were no crew members to attend to them as the pilot, co-pilot and navigator had their hands full keeping the plane in the air.

Despite these conditions 6,000 people had taken a flight by 1926, a year after the Kelly Airmail Act gave responsibility for the carriage of airmail and cargo, including passengers, to private airlines. The early days of flight offered real danger as well as great expense and discomfort. The frequent news of crashes did little to tempt the passenger traffic away from the familiar methods of the more comfortable train and more luxurious airship.

 The fascination of flight can't be expressed with words. But it really lies beyond the capabilities of human endeavour. Once you've experienced it, you'll never be able to forget it.

– FRIEDRICH OBLESSOR, 127 VICTORIES IN THE SECOND WORLD WAR

For a Few Dollars More

Since the deregulation (removal of government control over pricing and routes) of air travel in the US, and in many other parts of the world, the airline industry has witnessed a revolution. Others may argue that it's been in turmoil but there's no denying that the beneficiaries have been the passengers. Ticket prices have tumbled to the extent where promotional gimmicks have included seats for as low as $1 or £1, and the basic outcome of all this has been to cause havoc among the major carriers. The US was the world's first major market to deregulate and now sees an incredible 10,000 departures nationwide every day. The removal of control has allowed many small carriers to start up and challenge the 'majors' for market share – usually competing on price. This inevitably had the effect of cutting the profits of the big airlines with their high cost bases. The major carriers, lacking the nimble feet of the new entrant airlines, could do little to get their costs down. So enthusiastic have some of the small airlines been that they have failed after a few years, as the big boys managed to squeeze them out with the only muscle that they had – the marketing spend. Some new entrants have prospered, notably Southwest Airlines, founded in 1971, and others continue to flourish and make a profit.

When the effects of all this competition are added to the aftermath of the 9/11 attacks, with the interruption to revenue and changes wrought upon people's flying habits, the industry has been brought to the brink. By the end of 2005 airlines representing half of the available passenger seats in the USA were operating under bankruptcy protection legislation: United Airlines, US Airways (twice), Delta Air Lines and Northwest Airlines were all operating under Chapter 11. This law exists to allow a technically insolvent company to continue operating. It's not that this means that these airlines will cease to exist, far from it. When I joined Continental Airlines the company was in Chapter 11, it came out of it during the four years that I spent there, and went back into it after I left – the two acts being totally unconnected! Continental then came back out of Chapter 11 and remains so – at the time of writing.

Internationally the picture is little better. Many carriers such as Alitalia, Sabena, Scandinavian Airline System, Japan Air System, Air Canada and Ansett Australia have all declared or flirted with bankruptcy since 2000.

‘*America, the land of the free, is turning itself into the land of the free ride. (US airlines) are operating in protected markets. They are hoovering up public funds and they still can't make a profit.*

– ROD EDDINGTON, CEO OF BRITISH AIRWAYS, REGARDS COMPETING AGAINST SO MANY BANKRUPT US AIRLINES, 23 SEPTEMBER 2005 ’

Boats and Planes

The First World War brought great advances in aviation technology and training and this translated into the civil field in the period between the wars, which saw great development in passenger air transport.

In 1934 the Boeing 314 was launched, literally so since the Pan American Clipper Ship was an amphibian, a flying boat which took off and landed on water. Pan Am flew them across the Pacific and later, in 1939, the Atlantic.

It was a luxurious way to travel. With service reminiscent of that on cruise liners, up to 74 passengers had a lounge area and meals served on china plates. There were sleeping berths and breakfast was served in bed. Continuing the maritime theme, the crew wore naval-style uniforms and a bell was rung on the hour. It was an expensive business crossing the Pacific in such style; a ticket was about $10,000 in today's money.

In 1936 a new era of commercial air transport began with the introduction of the DC-3. It was safer than its predecessors thanks to its stronger all-aluminium-alloy construction. It had more powerful engines, which allowed it to cross the US in 16 hours, and to carry 50 per cent more passengers while doing it. Since it only cost 10 per cent more to operate than the planes that had been used hitherto it finally enabled an airline to make a profit flying people rather than cargo.

Suddenly passengers became more important than mail and competition for their custom led to greater interest in their comfort. Cabins were redesigned to resemble more familiar train interiors, with upholstered seats replacing wooden benches. The DC-3 also boasted sound insulation to deaden the engine noise and seats mounted in rubber to reduce vibration.

Meanwhile the concept of in-flight entertainment was emerging. The seductive new field of aviation had captured the public imagination and performers were eager to use the platform to publicise their talent. The media happily covered the event when an aircraft cabin was used as a stage to promote new movies. It was not long before movies were shown during the flight. In a publicity stunt, the movie Stagecoach was delivered to an aircraft on the runway at Idlewild Airport in New York by a horse-drawn stagecoach. The stewardesses put up a table and projector in the aisle and showed the film in-flight; between the reels they served refreshments.

Despite improvements over the next few years, air travel still had its drawbacks. Cabins were still unpressurised, so turbulence at the lower altitudes that the aircraft were forced to fly at meant that air sickness remained a problem. This was resolved around the time of the Second World War when Boeing adapted their military B-17 Flying Fortress into the civil Stratoliner and Lockheed began developing the Constellation.

These pressurised aircraft allowed passengers to be flown at 20,000 feet in greater comfort in the calmer air. But it was still very costly and air travel remained the preserve of the wealthy.

So few people flew that it was worthwhile for airlines to advertise for specific events. A 1937 advertisement for Imperial Airways was aimed at the dignitaries expected to travel to the coronation of King George V. This also illustrates how few countries had airlines and that it was not yet common for governments or heads of state to have private aircraft.

Other types of customers were also specifically targeted. An advertisement for TWA from 1951 shows a Lockheed Constellation in the background and was aimed at securing the 'grey dollar' – the caption ran 'Grandma leads a fast life... and loves it!'

Air travel was a very glamorous business and seen as the preserve of the successful. The chance of flying on a business trip was something to be aspired to and a great status symbol. Another advertisement from the 1950s shows a top salesman being rewarded by a flight as his delighted boss and admiring secretary look on – a far cry from today's weary 'road warriors' clocking up millions of air miles!

The jet engine changed everything. The British de Havilland Comet, launched in 1952, and the Boeing 707, arriving in 1958, ushered in an era when flying would become an option for the masses. The Comet's poor reputation for accidents led to the 707 becoming the jet aircraft of choice around the world. It could carry an – at the time – incredible passenger load of 181 at unheard of speeds of up to 550 miles per hour and opened up the world to an eager public in the 1960s.

Not only have aircraft become faster, larger and more efficient, the provision of entertainment has changed beyond recognition from the early days of stand-up comedians. From TWA launching the first dedicated in-flight entertainment system in 1961 to seat-back private screens with a choice of films, television and games, the provision of air phones and even internet access, there's never been more to occupy the passenger.

The stewardess as the sole provider of cabin service began to be phased out in the 1970s as more male staff were hired and the title was largely dropped in favour of the gender neutral 'flight attendant'. The 1970s also saw the US deregulate commercial air travel, which opened up the field to new airlines like People Express and Southwest, which made air travel affordable as they removed the frills in an effort to make a profit from lower and lower fares. Many airlines still compete fiercely for the premium market, offering all manner of comforts such as beds, massages and workouts for those who can pay top dollar, but the passenger at the back of economy may not feel too far removed from their predecessors sitting on mail sacks.

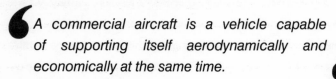

A commercial aircraft is a vehicle capable of supporting itself aerodynamically and economically at the same time.

– WILLIAM B. STOUT, DESIGNER OF THE FORD TRI-MOTOR

Getting Bogged Down

When British Airways began the first no-booking service in Europe, it operated between London and Glasgow. It was a dark day for its major competitor British Caledonian, which operated on the same route, except that it served Gatwick rather than Heathrow. The problem was not just that it provided an easy and convenient way to travel but from a marketing standpoint people just talked about the Glasgow Shuttle and even if the nearest airport was Gatwick, somehow the Heathrow route became the way to fly to Scotland. Things got worse when BA opened a Shuttle service to Edinburgh.

In the early 1980s I was given the job of trying to revive the loss-making services that BCAL flew within the UK; it was a daunting task. There were all sorts of issues that needed to be addressed but not the least of them was the whole image of BCAL's domestic routes. Also significant was the marketing of BA's Shuttle, quite a zippy little concept, as opposed to British Caledonian Domestic flights. I came up with the idea of rebranding the flights within the UK as BCAL Commuter, which was after all what many of our passengers were doing, and I involved some of the other small airlines that flew into Gatwick in the scheme. It was a co-operative marketing effort, which would hopefully benefit all of us.

Naturally one of the most important things to be done was to get people using the name as soon as possible. We did not have deep enough pockets to advertise the product to achieve our objectives and so PR was going to have to play an important role. I set about meeting some of the key journalists in the trade press as well as the nationals. One day I had a meeting with the editor of one magazine and spent a lot of time with him explaining our strategic moves, the benefits, the challenges that we faced and felt pretty pleased when I got to the nub of the matter.

'The thing is that BA's Shuttle is such a strong brand, we struggle to have any brand recognition. Let's face it, British Caledonian Domestic sounds like something you put down the toilet to clean it.' I'm sure I added that this was just for background and an off-the-record quote.

Well the inevitable happened, a week later out came the magazine with a banner headline. 'British Caledonian Domestic Can Clean Your Toilet.' Thirty seconds after I had seen the headline I knew I was in deep trouble. My phone rang; it was the chairman's secretary.

'The chairman wants to see you... now.'

I got no further than the door to his office. He tore me off such a strip that I was worried that if I got any closer I might suffer third-degree burns – that's how red in the face he was. I think I remember him saying something about me having to clean the toilets unless I was very, very careful.

FLYING FACTS

Blind Landings

It was in November 1964 that a BEA (a forerunner of British Airways) Trident made the first fully automatic landing in dense fog.

If Cars Could Fly

Today with the Channel Tunnel and the various ferry services taking the vast majority of cars between the UK and the Continent most people have forgotten that not that long ago cars used to be flown across the Channel. From their base at Lydd in Kent, which was evocatively known as Ferryfield, Silver City Airways flew Bristol Freighters on which it carried cars to and fro across the Channel. The airline began this 30-minute hop across the Channel in 1948 and by 1964 it had carried its 1,000,000th car, which, let's face it, is an awful lot of cars. The cars were loaded through the nose and on at least one occasion a car was so big that the man who drove it onto the aircraft had to stay put because the car door could not be opened once it had been loaded. These aircraft were affectionately known as Bristol Frighteners!

In 1959 a £10,000 prize was offered for the fastest trip between London and Paris to commemorate Bleriot's first cross-Channel flight. The winner went by helicopter and jet fighter but the fastest trip on a scheduled airliner was by Stirling Moss using a Silver City Bristol Freighter to get his Jaguar across the Channel. Back then it was £25 for the car and £4 for each passenger.

The flying cross-Channel car ferry service ended in 1970 when British United Air Ferries, the company that had taken over Silver City, made the last flight.

Total deregulation would allow anybody to fly any route, a situation that is unlikely ever to occur.

– NEW YORK TIMES MAGAZINE, 9 MAY 1976

What's in a Name?

The newly launched Embraer Phenom range of light jets was a gift to the industry's headline writers – Flight Evening News went with the predictable 'Phenom-enal' but where did they get the name from? It's no easy task coming up with the right designation for a new aircraft in a global market these days.

Many manufacturers stick to the safe pattern of a numerical code linked to the type and size of the aircraft – the Boeing 707, 717, 727, 737, 747, 757, 767 and 777, the Airbus A300 to A380 and the various Gulfstream models follow along the same lines. Some opt for a name, which can be useful in the business aircraft field when image is essential. The trouble is that many of the good ones have gone – Challenger, Hawk, Falcon, Puma etc.

Manufacturers are used to the pitfalls of naming their product; no doubt in the 1970s Nissan thought the 'Cedric' van would be ideally suited to the builders and plumbers of the UK. And Ford's 'Probe' never quite felt right. That's why the legions of international brand consultants and researchers are employed to get the name right and avoid language problems. However, Phenom could cause confusion in Vietnam...

> *Can the magic of flight ever be carried by words? I think not.*
> – MICHAEL PARFIT, SMITHSONIAN MAGAZINE, MAY 2000

Sky High

Surfing the web looking for a bargain flight? You might come across the skyhighairlines.com site. It won't help you get to where you want to go, but you'll have a good laugh as you explore the spoof site, which is actually highly original advertising for Alaska Airlines.

Advertising themselves as 'Saving you money at a price' and proud of 'The relentless pursuit of adequacy' the airline offers service from such popular hubs as Villages of Van Buren, Indiana, to Camp Crook, South Dakota, via Chalk Mountain, Texas, and Middleton, Delaware, in a nifty 18 hours and 44 minutes. You can choose between bench or cargo seating and are warned that it's more than likely you'll miss your connections and are advised either to speed walk or bribe a passing electric cart driver.

The site offers a range of travel products ranging from the 'Gotta Go' 94-ounce travel cup doubling as a portable lavatory, the 'Happy Baby' sonic isopod, a soundproof Perspex chamber to seal your screaming children into, and the 'Hiney Horn', a lever to force 'plus sized' passenger's behinds into the 'Execu-Miser Maxi-Slim' seating on the aircraft.

Fares are calculated online by a chicken pecking at a calculator (perhaps not so far from the truth in the opinions of some passengers). SkyHigh also offers a global baggage tracking service; just enter your name and discover that your luggage is in such exotic places as Moron, Mongolia, and you are invited to, 'check back tomorrow and see where those pesky bags of yours are off to next'.

Among the innovative operational procedures they offer is 'Challenge Seating' in which passengers are equipped with weapons and invited to fight for 'the seat they want, no, deserve'. The customer can also reduce the cost of a trip by using SkyHigh's 'Cohabi-Fares' service, which matches them to a family, with whom they can live with for the weekend, rather than staying in a lonely hotel room. Choices of location range from Deer Lick, Indiana, to Brainerd, Michigan, and the list of host family interests includes taxidermy and bead necklaces.

Not to be regarded as a low class operator, SkyHigh offers the revolutionary 'Cumulative Four-Star' holiday. Enter your departure date and a personalised itinerary of one-star operators is generated such as accommodation at the 'Emerald Acres Sod Huts', dining at 'Sweet Tooth's All-U-Can-Eat Pudding Place' and entertainment at 'Spikes

Clothing-Optional Volleyball Skills Camp'. Add this to SkyHigh's own one-star service and there's your four-star experience on a budget.

The Alaska Airlines connection is revealed down at the foot of the various pages, with suggestions that if you don't want to fly via half a dozen cities, have your bags lost or miss all your connections then perhaps you should use the link to the airline's website. All in all it's an admirable attempt to bring some refreshing self-deprecating humour to airline advertising.

Silver Birds on the Silver Screen

It is not unusual for filmmakers to need footage of aircraft or scenes to be shot on board airliners. Airlines are generally happy to co-operate and secure some exposure of their airline to the viewing public.

Over the years many airlines have had their operations shown in films, including:

Aeroflot: The Bourne Supremacy, Company Business, The Jackal, Birthday Girl, The Terminal

Air Canada: Airport, French Kiss, The Terminal, Wait Until Dark

Air France: Airport '79: The Concorde, Company Business, Kiss of the Dragon, L'Auberge espagnole, Moonraker, Sabrina, Transporter 2

America West Airlines: When a Man Loves a Woman (Andy Garcia played an America West pilot)

American Airlines: High Crimes, Home Alone, Home Alone 2, How Stella Got Her Groove Back, Passport to Paris, Stuck on You

British Airways: Bend It Like Beckham, Die Another Day, A Fish Called Wanda, GoldenEye, Mission Impossible, The Parent Trap, Three Men and a Baby

Iberia: The Pleasure Seekers

Lufthansa: The Lizzie McGuire Movie, XXX, EuroTrip, Diamonds Are Forever

Northwest Airlines: Bridget Jones's Diary, The Firm, Deception, Fargo

Pan Am: Blade Runner, Catch Me if You Can, Freaked, 2001: A Space Odyssey, Dr. No, From Russia with Love, Live and Let Die, Licence to Kill, Willy Wonka and the Chocolate Factory

TWA: The Aviator, Back to the Beach, Dumb and Dumber, Funny Face, Great Balls of Fire, Rocky III, Rocky IV, Salsa, Woman In Red

United Airlines: The Karate Kid Part 2, The Terminal, 13

Virgin Atlantic: Austin Powers: The Spy Who Shagged Me, Wayne's World

It can be a risky business for the movie maker if the film is set in the future, as they risk the film looking very dated if the airline ceases trading in the meantime; Pan Am is prominently featured in 2001: A Space Odyssey, and Blade Runner, set in 2019, but the airline went bankrupt in 1991.

Airlines are also very wary of being involved in any films showing crashes, for obvious reasons. Movie-makers then have to develop a fictitious airline, often using the name Oceanic Airlines. In-flight movies shown on planes are also vetted for this type of content and it is edited out. In the case of Get Shorty, a scene showing a plane crash was even replaced with footage of a train crash for the in-flight market.

Some lower budget films will use stock footage of aircraft taking off and landing – often doing so at the same airport – to give the illusion of travel without the expense of actually going anywhere. The aircraft is usually shown head-on, very conveniently avoiding the appearance of airline insignia.

It has been known for the sound effects of the engines not to match the aircraft type on the screen as the director mistakenly thinks all aircraft sound the same (in fairness, the majority of viewers probably do so as well). It is not unheard of on some less professionally directed films for the characters to take off in one aircraft type and land in another!

Flying is within our grasp. We have naught to do but take it.

– CHARLES F. DURYEA, 'LEARNING HOW TO FLY', PROCEEDINGS OF THE THIRD INTERNATIONAL CONFERENCE ON AERONAUTICS, 1894

Massaging Figures

In the race to attract premium-rate passengers airlines have offered more and more services, luxuries and inducements. The pampering has extended from the cabin to the departure and arrivals lounge with fine food, beauty treatments and beds available to those prepared to pay for first class travel.

Virgin Atlantic has been particularly innovative in catering for its upper class passengers' tastes, equipping its Heathrow Clubhouse with facilities for facials, manicures, massage, hairstyling and even a tanning bed. The 8,000 square foot space dubbed 'Cowshed at the Clubhouse' features a cocktail bar, a sushi bar, a floor to ceiling water wall and chandeliers made from Swarovski crystal.

In 2005, however, the airline had cause to regret offering customers shiatsu massage when a masseuse was awarded over £100,000 compensation for the repetitive strain injury she sustained while working on wealthy passengers. She was forced to give up her job and take a lower paying position in a call centre, then to take voluntary redundancy when she developed 'tennis elbow' and 'golfer's elbow'. The conditions were brought on by her performance of unorthodox 'forceful' massage on seated, fully clothed passengers, which would normally have been performed on undressed people, lying down with oil. This meant that the strain on the masseuse was unreasonable in the court's view and led to the award of compensation.

> *If you're ever faced with a forced landing at night, turn on the landing lights to see the landing area. If you don't like what you see, turn 'em back off.*
>
> – ANON.

Lions and Donkeys

British Caledonian's position as the chief competitor to British Airways, in those far-off days when government regulation stood in the way of competition, kept the two airlines from flying head to head with each other on just about every single long-haul route. That was until British Caledonian somehow managed to persuade the Civil Aviation Authority to allow it to compete with BA on the lucrative London–Hong Kong route.

Elaborate plans were laid for the start of the service and as usual there was an inaugural flight, on which the great and the good travelled with BCAL's chairman Sir Adam Thomson, to what was then still a British colony. To celebrate that first flight business leaders and diplomats, both British and Chinese, had organised a gala dinner at which those who had travelled from London were joined by the cream of Hong Kong society. Sir Adam gave a speech in which he told the assembled crowd about what had motivated BCAL to apply to fly to Hong Kong. 'Our planners and market research people saw a chink in the market', was his simple explanation.

One of Sir Adam's colleagues on the BCAL board on another occasion justified an increase in flights to West Africa by explaining that there had been a 'vast influx of Lesbian traders', into many of the countries along the coast. He meant Lebanese, and was totally unaware of his spoonerism.

A third member of the board of BCAL gave some wonderful insight into how an airline decides on what new destinations it should serve, or not, as the case may be. The company was in the process of thinking about flying from London to Denver and had done a great deal of research into the size of the market – the possibility was looking very attractive. Or it was until the company's sales director sent his opposite number on the BCAL board responsible for planning a memo with his views on the potential: 'I was returning from Los Angeles to London last week and our non-stop flight took us overhead Denver. We were at around 35,000 feet and it was a beautiful clear evening and I could see the whole of the city clearly. I must say it didn't look like a very big place to me and I would counsel against starting a new route, one on which we will inevitably fail to make any money.'

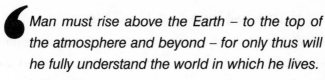

Man must rise above the Earth – to the top of the atmosphere and beyond – for only thus will he fully understand the world in which he lives.
– SOCRATES

The Throb of the Engines

When XL Airways went bust in 2008 it created a knock-on effect in the industry, one of the other casualties was none other than Throb Holidays.

Throb specialised in holidays for gay persons…discretion is our watchword. Unlike many of the passengers who were flying with XL Airways, Throb's customers had protection (so to speak) through the ATOL scheme. Throb had paid all their money to XL and could not recover their funds. This is the problem with tour operator to tour operator sales. Passengers remain protected through the bonding scheme, but the tour operator who has paid their money 'up front' (in this case to XL Leisure, as opposed to the airline) loses it and simply becomes a creditor.

You couldn't make it up…

The Boeing 747 is the commuter train of the global village.
– H. TENNEKES, THE SIMPLE SCIENCE OF FLIGHT, 1996

Ain't Nobody Here But Us Chickens

There's an old saying in the airline business that the great thing about air freight is that, unlike passengers, it tends not to answer back; although the people shipping it can often have a grasp of Anglo-Saxon that cannot be bettered. This was probably what motivated one cargo airline to take drastic action when faced by a pending disaster. They had a 36-ton load of chickens that were destined for Africa. Unfortunately the load was not insured and, after it was delivered to the warehouse, the aircraft went unserviceable. To avoid total financial disaster the airline decided to sell the chickens locally before they defrosted – but 36 tons is a lot of chickens.

Every supermarket was offered them at knockdown prices and many couldn't refuse. Some went to food manufacturers and it seemed like everyone at the airline was scouring the Yellow Pages looking for likely buyers. Needless to say there were a lot of cars leaving Gatwick Airport that day laden down with chickens for the freezer.

 The game we are playing here is closest to the old game of 'Christians and lions'.

– ROBERT L. CRANDALL, CEO & PRESIDENT OF AMERICAN AIRLINES

Toilet Techniques

It's sometimes hard enough to do what's needed in the cramped confines of an airline toilet, and men using the lavatory during unexpected turbulence have a hard time keeping things on target. Next time you are using one, be glad that your pilot doesn't fall back on his early experience.

One commercial airline pilot, who had spent many years prior to being a civilian flying for the US military, recalls that during his days flying C-130 Hercules transport aircraft full of cargo the question of needing to 'go' on a long flight would arise. The C-130 is a rugged piece of equipment, the workhorse of the military, and does not boast many refinements. It does, however, have a small urinal located by the loading ramp at the rear of the aircraft. Using this is a gymnastic feat, requiring the user to balance while holding a strut, keeping the lid of the urinal raised and doing what's needed. Rookie C-130 crew members usually learn the trick from a more experienced colleague.

On one particular occasion a C-130 was being used to transport fighter pilots along with a consignment of spares and cargo that they needed for a particular mission. Fighter pilots tend to be a confident bunch, very proud of what they do, and can be rather dismissive of those flying a lumbering, propeller-driven box car masquerading as an aircraft. Fighter pilots, of course, are no different from ordinary men and eventually they would need to visit the toilet.

The Hercules loadmaster, who travels in the cargo area, would direct each pilot to the urinal at the back. Once he was contorted into position and relieving himself, the word would go back to the pilot, who would disengage the autopilot and give the tail a good hard wag or two. The fighter pilot's urine-soaked trouser legs usually led to him keeping his low opinion of cargo planes and their crews to himself for the rest of the flight.

The Heart of Africa

In mid-1975 I was sent to Sierra Leone to do some research in preparation for British Caledonian beginning a cargo service along the West African coast from our base in London. I arrived in the former British colony from Dakar in Senegal, where I had stayed in a wonderful hotel run by a French company – the very epitome of French chic. But I was really looking forward to my stay in Freetown, the capital of Sierra Leone, because I was going to be staying at the Paramount, the hotel that had been immortalised in Graham Greene's novel The Heart of the Matter. On arrival I instantly realised it was a very different establishment from the one I'd left in Dakar.

After checking in at the Paramount, something that involved filling in more forms than it seemed possible for anyone to do anything with, I got to my room, which was nice, but far from luxurious; I decided to take a shower. There was no soap in the bathroom and having none in my wash bag I tried calling reception to ask for some; there was no reply. I went back downstairs from my room on the first floor to ask for some soap. After about 15 minutes a bar appeared, although it was not quite what I was expecting. It was half of a huge bar of carbolic soap.

Next day, scrubbed and clean, I was to take a trip on a Sierra Leone Airways flight to a couple of 'up country' places. I arrived at Freetown Airport where I was checked in for my flight, which was to be operated by a British built Trislander, a small commuter-type aircraft with three propeller engines. It was one of those aircraft that looked like it had no reason to fly at all, as the third engine was on the tailplane. I was seated next to the pilot – it only had the one. He turned out to have recently left the RAF and was working in the country to get flying time on his commercial pilot's licence before returning to the UK to find a slightly more glamorous position.

The first leg of our flight was to Bonthe in the south of Sierra Leone. From there it was a short hop, flying at 3,000 feet, to Gbangbatok. Watching from the cockpit as the runway comes closer and you prepare to land, is great in any aircraft; watching Africa roll by beneath you is even better. As we taxied towards the terminal building at Gbangbatok, which was actually not a building at all but a bus shelter surrounded by a white two-foot-high picket fence, we saw there was a man standing out front of the passenger facilities, saluting.

'I think I'll get out and stretch my legs for a couple of minutes,' said I to the pilot. 'OK, we have a 15-minute turn round here,' he replied.

As we pulled up in front of the saluting man, who was dressed in a khaki uniform with bright red epaulettes, and incidentally must have been six feet six inches and 20 stone, I said, 'Who's the guy?'

'He's the airport manager. He's currently under investigation on suspicion of cannibalism.' I never bothered about taking a closer look at Gbangbatok's terminal building.

> *A single lifetime, even though entirely devoted to the sky, would not be enough for the study of so vast a subject. A time will come when our descendants will be amazed that we did not know things that are so plain to them.*
>
> – SENECA, BOOK 7, FIRST CENTURY AD

The Name Game

The idea of using a famous person's name for an airport is not a new one. New York's LaGuardia Airport is named after the famous mayor of New York Fiorello LaGuardia (mayor 1934–45). Of course one of New York's other airports is John F. Kennedy International Airport and was so named in 1963 having originally been called Idlewild. Another American president who has been so honoured is Ronald Reagan whose name appends Washington's National Airport. How long before Little Rock's Airport becomes Bill Clinton International?

Columbus Ohio's Rickenbacker International Airport is not named after the guitar maker but Eddie Rickenbacker, a First World War fighter ace. Oklahoma's Will Rogers World Airport is named for the legendary cowboy and comedian. Another with a political connection is Las Vegas' McCarran International Airport in honour of the Nevada senator Pat McCarran. A favourite is New Orleans Airport, which is named Louis Armstrong International Airport.

In Canada they have got in on the act with Montreal naming its airport Trudeau International after the former Canadian Prime Minister Pierre. Toronto's Lester B. Pearson International Airport is named after the 14th Canadian PM. What price Thatcher International or Blairport? It's a shame that there is not an airport close to the Tayside village of Blairingone.

In Britain we have been slower off the mark but Liverpool has honoured one of its favoured sons in naming its airport after John Lennon. There appears to be no truth in the story that in alternate years it will be named Paul McCartney Airport – that was Yesterday's rumour. Perhaps most bizarre is Robin Hood Airport Doncaster Sheffield which is located at the former RAF base of Finningley... why? The French are less keen on the idea but did honour one of their former presidents when they named one of the Paris airports, Charles de Gaulle.

The former Belfast City Airport is one of the most recent re-namings. It was named after footballer George Best at a ceremony in May 2006. This followed on an earlier suggestion by former snooker star Alex Higgins who wanted the l, the f and the a removed from the city's name... Best is what it would have become but he couldn't get enough support for the idea.

> *The propeller is just a big fan in the front of the plane to keep the pilot cool. Want proof? Make it stop; then watch the pilot break out into a sweat.*
> – ANON.

Pulling Power

If all the tugs are out of action at the airport and the aircraft are therefore stranded, David Huxley is definitely the man to call. The Australian holds the world record for the heaviest aircraft pulled by a human. He started his career in 1991 by towing a 37-tonne (81,570lb) Boeing 737. He moved up to a 105-tonne (231,485lb) Concorde before, in 1997 at the age of 39, he managed to pull a Boeing 747-400 weighing 187 tonnes (412,260lb) a distance of 91 metres (298 ft 6 in) in 1 minute 27.7 seconds. There is no evidence to suggest that Mr Huxley has been hospitalised for a hernia operation but folks, don't try this at home – or even your local airport.

Two Left Feet

During the 1970s when the Nigerian economy was booming on the back of spiralling oil prices, the difficulty of getting cargo into the country was solved by the use of air-freight. The docks were completely clogged with ships, and there were also hundreds of container vessels lying off the coast of Nigeria waiting to dock. The use of air cargo reached airlift proportions, with hundreds of freighter flights going into the airports every month. This eventually led to the problem in the docks largely being transferred to the airports' facilities.

Ingenious ways of getting aircraft turned around in the shortest time were developed by all the airline operators – this of course mostly involved paying bribes to the loading staff. These people were more accurately unloading staff as the country was not exporting anything to speak of and were as often as not to be found asleep in the shade underneath the aircraft wings.

As well as bribes, the loaders, and those who worked in the huge congested freight sheds, were masters at the art of the disappearing consignment. For a while there was a monthly flight that consisted of nothing but 36 tons of shoes (that's an awful lot of shoes). Unfortunately these shoes were being liberated on arrival in prodigious quantities. Then someone came up with a novel solution. One month they would ship left shoes, the next month the matching right shoes. Unfortunately this didn't fix the problem, as Nigerians are apparently happy to walk around in two left shoes.

You've got to treat people as equals, and make them feel like it's their company. I don't know if I've had any impact or helped persuade Frank (Borman, to sell Eastern). But, I can tell you, there were many discussions on the subject.

– MICHAEL MILKEN, FINANCIER

Captive Audience

In 2005 a new phenomenon in airborne advertising was born: the in-flight sales pitch. On an Alaska Airlines flight into Washington passengers obeyed the standard security announcement requiring them to remain seated and fasten their seat belts for the final half hour of the flight. What they didn't expect was the ensuing announcement about the benefits of the Bank of America Visa card. Using the intercom the flight attendant urged the passengers to sign up for the card and colleagues went down the aisles distributing application forms. Airlines claim that they need the revenue offered by advertising in cash-strapped times, but it may be more than the passenger is prepared to bear for their cut-price ticket.

Alaska Airlines isn't alone. US Airways also pushes the Bank of America card (as with Alaska it is a joint card that earns the user air miles on the airline) and its cabin crew are paid $50 commission for each passenger they get to sign up.

Branding has even extended to food and drink service; Saab has paid to have its logo emblazoned on the napkins handed out to America West's passengers. Perhaps it won't be long before air-sickness bags are sponsored.

Big Is Beautiful

Commercial aircraft are getting bigger and bigger. The largest passenger aircraft currently being flown is the Airbus A380 which has a wingspan of 79.8 m (261 ft 10 in), a length of 73 m (239 ft 6 in) and a maximum take-off weight of 560 tonnes (1,230,000 lb).

The largest cargo aircraft by volume is the vast Airbus A300-600ST 'Beluga' Super Transporter. It has a cargo deck volume of 1,400 cubic metres (49,440 cubic feet). It is loaded through the front opening created when the entire section of the fuselage just forward of the wings is hinged upwards. It is used to transport sections of other passenger aircraft between Airbus' various factory locations.

 Deregulation will be the greatest thing to happen to the airlines since the jet engine.

– RICHARD FERRIS, CEO OF UNITED AIRLINES, 1976

Snappy Slogans

Airlines have long sought to come up with a punchy advertising line. Some have been memorable, others less so. Here's a few of each…

Fly the friendly skies. – **United Airlines**

Something special in the air. – **American Airlines**

To fly. To serve. – **British Airways**

The world's favourite airline. – **British Airways**

The Proud Bird with the Golden Tail. – **Continental Airlines,** pre-1983 bankruptcy

We never forget you have a choice. – **British Caledonian Airways**

We love to fly. And it shows. – **Delta Air Lines, replaced with You'll love the way we fly in January 1995**

Some people just know how to fly. – **Northwest Airlines**

How do we love you? Let us count the ways… – **Southwest Airlines**

The Wings of Man. – **Eastern Airlines**

Low Blows

Some airlines have gone further than a snappy slogan to attract passengers and have recently begun to attack their competitors rather than just emphasising their own merits. It is a traditional no-no for the advertising industry, but some ads have challenged protocol, such as the invitations appearing at airports for passengers to 'Enjoy your overpriced flight. Next time fly Virgin Express.'

Ryanair launched a more provocative advert for its service to Brussels. It pictured the iconic Mannekin Pis (the famous sculpture of the little boy relieving himself) with the question, 'Pissed off with Sabena's high prices?' Another low-cost carrier keen to tweak the big boys' noses was easyJet, which annoyed national carrier KLM when it advertised in the Netherlands with the Dutch line 'Koninkrijks Lowcost Maatschappij', translated as 'UK's Lowcost Airline'. More light-hearted advertising also abounds, for example Continental's billboards announcing its service from Manchester to the US with the line 'From the Mancs to the Yanks. Twice Daily.'

When I worked at Continental Airlines our first route from the UK was a daily non-stop flight from Houston to London; the other airline on the route was British Caledonian, my former employer. BCAL at the time were famous for their brilliant TV advertising campaign: 'I wish they all could be Caledonian girls'. This was sung by a lusty group of passengers to the tune of the Beach Boys California Girls, and the adverts had rightly won awards.

On the day of our inaugural flight we decided to throw a party for travel agents at the Lyceum located just off London's Strand. The reason was simple: there are few people who enjoy a good party more than a travel agent. Besides plying them with free drink we decided that a little entertainment was in order and among the on-stage activities there were four large ladies, the Roly Polys no less, who were dressed as Caledonian girls in very large kilts. The lyrics good-naturedly lampooned our competitor and amused the travel agents (I'm sure the free drink helped on that score).

When the party was over and we had congratulated ourselves on a fun evening it was back to the serious work of trying to fill aircraft with paying passengers. A day or so later I was sitting in my office when I had a call from the head of BCAL's advertising department, the larger than life Nicholas Boize. 'Ah fat garçon' – for some inexplicable reason he always called me that – 'I've been instructed to call you by the marketing director, you remember him, Mr Deller, and complain about your scandalous use of some ladies masquerading as Caledonian girls. He says that I am to tell you that we will sue you.' When I'd stopped laughing I suggested that Nic tell his boss that BCAL could get in line behind everyone else who was currently taking us to court. As a footnote they never did bother to sue.

> *More than anything else the sensation is one of perfect peace mingled with an excitement that strains every nerve to the utmost, if you can conceive of such a combination.*
> – WILBUR WRIGHT

Humble Beginnings

The international airline operating a large fleet of modern jet airliners and flying thousands of people every day to hundreds of exotic destinations may have started from very humble origins. As commercial aviation began to emerge in the 1920s and '30s many small aircraft operators started flying, some of which went on to grow into today's household names.

Aeroflot was born in 1922 with a service from Moscow to Königsberg, later extended to Berlin. The following year Russian civil aviation started in earnest when the Labour and Defence Council issued a resolution 'on empowering the Central Air Fleet Administration to handle technical supervision over airlines and founding the Civil Aviation Council'.

Alaska Airlines started life in 1932 when Mac McGee commenced flying a three-seat Stinson between Anchorage and Bristol Bay, Alaska. His operation merged with Star Air Service in 1934 and Alaska Airlines was on its way.

American Airlines records the start of the operation that was to become American as 1926, when Robertson Aircraft Corporation began a Chicago–St Louis mail service operated by a DH-4 biplane. One of the pilots was Charles A. Lindbergh, soon to become famous for his solo crossing of the Atlantic Ocean. The operation was part of the group that consolidated into American Airlines in 1934.

Continental Airlines traces its roots back to 15 July 1934, when Walter T. Varney and Louis Mueller started Varney Speed Lines to fly the 530 miles between Pueblo, Colorado, and El Paso, Texas, via Las Vegas, Santa Fe and Albuquerque. They changed the name to Continental in 1937.

Delta Air Lines had even more modest origins. It began in 1924 as Huff Daland Dusters, the world's first aerial crop-dusting operation, which changed its name to Delta Air Service in 1928 and started operating passenger flights in 1929.

KLM Royal Dutch Airlines was founded in 1919 to serve 'the Netherlands and Colonies'. Its first flight was from Amsterdam to London using a DeHavilland DH-16.

Lufthansa started flying in 1926 as Deutsche Luft Hansa Aktiengesellschaft, becoming Lufthansa in 1933 after a merger between Deutsche Aero Lloyd and Junkers Luftverker. Northwest Airlines had its beginnings in 1926 with the start of another mail service, this one between the Twin Cities and Chicago using two open cockpit biplanes, a Thomas Morse Scout and a Curtis Oriole. Qantas was formed back in 1920 with the creation of Queensland and Northern Territory Aerial Services Limited, which operated two war-surplus biplanes for joy rides and demo flights, based in Winton, Australia.

Turkish Airlines originated in 1933 as a division of the Ministry of Defence based in Ankara named the 'State Airlines Administration'. It then operated a fleet of four aircraft: one five-seat King Bird, two Junkers F-13s with four seats and a 10-seat ATH-9.

United Airlines also traces its history back to 1926 with the start of a mail service between Pasco, Washington, and Elko, Nevada, on 6 April. The owner of the business was Walter T. Varney again.

FLYING FACTS

Bend It with Boeing

The enormous Boeing 777 looks very graceful in flight. This is partly because the wings flex to a tremendous degree, giving them a smooth curve when cruising. In fact you could (theoretically at least) stretch a length of string from one wingtip to the other and it would clear the top of the fuselage.

A Chilly Wind

Next time you are sitting in an airliner hurtling through the earth's upper atmosphere at an altitude of well over 30,000 feet, at a speed something in excess of 500 miles per hour, pause for a second as you gaze out through the window to consider the fact that it is only the aircraft's 10-centimetre-thick fuselage walls which separate you from the rushing air stream. The air at this altitude is very, very cold, often many degrees below zero, and the wind chill at such speed is mind-numbing (literally). While not wanting to worry you, you'd conclude that it's pretty amazing that you didn't freeze to death shortly after take-off. The good news is that the physics of aircraft design and operation provide a reassuring explanation.

Firstly the wind chill factor isn't as significant on a smooth aircraft as it is on an un-aerodynamic surface such as human skin, so it's less efficient at removing heat. The lower density of the air at high altitude further diminishes it – for the same reason that there's less resistance to the plane because there's less air, it's less cooling.

There's also a counter to the cooling affect of the airflow; the friction caused by passing through the, albeit less dense, air at very high speed actually heats the aircraft's skin up. Concorde, as an extreme example due to its supersonic speed, heated up in parts by 200 degrees Centigrade during flight. Its dimensions increase as the aluminium skin expands due to the heating effect. This happens to a lesser extent with all aircraft.

Then there's the heating effect of packing so many hot human bodies together in the small space of the airliner's passenger cabin. All radiate heat in a practically sealed tube, so warming the air it contains. The cabin air is further warmed by the air-conditioning system, which takes off some of the enormous amounts of spare heat generated by the engines, and uses it to warm the circulating atmosphere.

Your comfort is finally assured by the aircraft designers keeping you separated from the freezing cold aircraft skin by lining the interior with plastic and filling the space between with common or garden fibreglass insulation. This not only helps with thermal insulation but also acts as acoustic insulation, deadening the deafening roar of the engines and wind noise.

 These days no one can make money on the goddamn airline business. The economics represent sheer hell.

– C.R. SMITH, PRESIDENT OF AMERICAN AIRLINES

Lighting Up Time

Next time you have to answer a call of nature in an aircraft, pay attention after you slide the bolt on the lavatory door into the locked position and note that the light automatically comes on after a delay of a moment or two.

Why does it not come on instantly? Has the airline been economising by installing cheap light bulbs? Not at all.

The delay is due to the low voltage fluorescent bulb building up the power to complete an arc through the gas in the tube and thus glow with light. For the technically minded, the mercury in the lamp needs to heat up sufficiently to start ionising.

The use of these slow-start low energy lamps is not to save money. Instant light bulbs, such as the traditional ones used in the home, demand a great deal of energy at the moment they light. This surge in demand for a few fractions of a second every time someone went into the lavatory would be very detrimental to the aircraft's other systems which need a smooth, constant electricity supply. Therefore aircraft are fitted with lighting systems which have a 'soft' start and avoid unwanted spikes in power demand.

PLANE SPEAKING

A United Airlines 747 captain tries to make light banter with Sydney, Australia, Approach Control:

Captain: *'Good morning, Sydney, this is United XXX, we're 50 miles out and have your island in sight.'*

Approach: *'Roger, United... you're cleared to circle the island twice, then it's OK to land.'*

Through the Square Window

As you gaze out of the window at the scenery and clouds during your next flight, your eye may wander to the glass (or, rather, Perspex) in front of your nose. You may ponder for a while the wonders of engineering that enable you to look out of the aircraft without fear of the window popping out of its frame, and you may also notice what looks like a small metal rod suspended in mid-air near the bottom of the window pane. It may well be surrounded by flecks of ice or condensation, and you might well wonder what it's doing there. It's not in fact a metal rod (despite its appearance) but a hole in the middle pane of the triple (or more) glazed window unit.

The layers of glazing are to insulate you from the cold, but they require a means of pressure equalisation between the layers, hence the small hole. The condensation, which forms near it, is the result of the inner air space becoming cooler as cold air from the layer next to the outside air moves through.

The position of the hole is very important; the designers have to consider leaving the best possible viewing area when condensation inevitably forms, preventing a crack forming between the hole and the edge of the window and avoiding the condensation covering the hole and then freezing causing a dangerous pressure difference between the layers of glass.

Up, Up and Away – An iPod Play list

A play list that runs for three hours and 14 minutes, ideal for a flight from London to Helsinki or New York to the Dominican Republic...

Freedom Flight	**Shuggie Otis**
Solo Flight Benny	**Goodman Orchestra**
Night Flight	**Joe Sample**
This Flight Tonight	**Joni Mitchell**
Flight 505	**The Rolling Stones**
Pan American	**Hank Williams**
5.30 Plane	**The Supremes**
Love Is in the Air	**John Paul Young**
Straighten Up and Fly Right	**Nat King Cole**
Outbound Plane	**Nanci Griffith**
Soaring	**Lee Ritenour**
Give Me Wings	**Michael Johnson**
I'm Mandy, Fly Me	**10cc**
Jet Airliner	**Steve Miller Band**
Jet Set	**Stephen Stills**
Las Vegas Turnaround	**Daryl Hall & John Oates**
Learning to Fly	**Pink Floyd**

IN-FLIGHT CONFIDENTIAL

Flying Sorcery	**Al Stewart**
Blues from an Airplane	**Jefferson Airplane**
Wooden Planes	**Art Garfunkel**
Something in the Air	**Thunderclap Newman**
Come Fly with Me	**Frank Sinatra**
In the Air Tonight	**Phil Collins**
Adiemus (Delta Air Lines Theme)	**Karl Jenkins**
Coming in on a Wing and a Prayer	**Eddie Cantor**
Flyin' High (In the Friendly Sky)	**Marvin Gaye**
To an Air Hostess	**Clifford T. Ward**
Flying	**The Beatles**
I'll Fly For You	**Spandau Ballet**
Clear Air for Miles	**Acoustic Alchemy**
Jet	**Paul McCartney & Wings**
Air Travel	**Chris Farlowe**
No Plane on Sunday	**Jimmy Buffett**
Fly	**Nick Drake**
Flying Home	**Lionel Hampton**
Airplane	**The Beach Boys**
Met Her on a Plane	**Jimmy Webb**
Up, Up And Away	**The 5th Dimension**
Gonna Fly Now	**Chuck Mangione**
Fly Away	**John Denver**
The Wing and the Wheel	**Nanci Griffith**
Fly Me High	**The Moody Blues**
Expecting to Fly	**Buffalo Springfield**
Trains and Boats and Planes	**Dionne Warwick**

Learning to Fly	**Tom Petty & the Heartbreakers**
Flying High Country	**Joe & the Fish**
Leaving on a Jet Plane	**Spanky & Our Gang**
One Day I'll Fly Away	**Randy Crawford**
We Can Fly	**The Cowsills**
One Day to Fly	**The Alan Parsons Project**

A Lick of Paint

Airline liveries have always been important in projecting a company's image and striving to give the right impression of professionalism and reliability. Often the country of origin's national flag or its colours are incorporated, as a government-owned air carrier displays its national origin to the wider world. Things began to change in the 1970s as more and more small airlines started up after deregulation and wanted to set themselves apart from the 'big boys' with their planes in variations of red, white and blue.

It wasn't only the 'upstarts' who got into lurid paint schemes; in 1997 British Airways famously decided to drop the Union Flag tail planes, which its aircraft had sported for decades in favour of a collection of lurid ethnic art from around the world. The idea was a PR disaster as it lost the cohesive brand image, which BA had worked so hard to forge, and caused outrage at the loss of the flag from the nation's flag carrier. Margaret Thatcher highlighted the problem when she draped a napkin over a model aircraft featuring an art tail at a function; her actions spoke volumes about national pride. Virgin Atlantic gleefully stepped into the breach and painted the Union Flag on its aircraft – they've never been shy of tweaking BA's tail! The idea was finally shelved in 2001 when all BA's aircraft paint schemes were returned to normal. This came as a huge relief to the specialist tail logo painters (although they missed the overtime) who no longer had to mask off and paint the hugely complex designs.

Some airlines, notably the USA's American Airlines, don't paint the aircraft's entire fuselage, instead they feature polished aluminium with stripes along the sides. Painting an aircraft is a very complicated business and a modern jet has about 400 pounds of paint on it. The complex and colourful liveries are costly to apply and can add significantly to the overall amount of paint used and consequently the aircraft weight. This has a negative effect on its fuel efficiency and such decisions are not taken lightly, at least by the airline's financial officer. Hence the reason why, when an aircraft needs a repaint, it is totally stripped back to the fuselage rather than have new coats of paint, and weight, added.

One of the most eye-catching examples of airliner art is the Boeing 737-400 (or 'Salmon-Thirty-Salmon') which was painted to celebrate the role Alaska Airlines plays in transporting Alaskan seafood to the continental US. It took a team of 30 painters 24 days of almost non-stop work to finish the image of a king salmon.

In Bed Together

The practice of airlines code-sharing is now worldwide, with practically every airline involved to some extent. A code-share allows one airline to offer a passenger flights and issue tickets while a different airline actually operates all or some of the route. Thus a particular flight may have passengers with tickets issued by one or more different airlines and the flight has several 'codes' (hence 'code-share') designating the operator.

The practice allows airlines to offer passengers seemingly seamless itineraries to destinations, which would be uneconomic to serve themselves. The airlines thus scoop up more customers, although there are plenty of people who have tickets for airline A who change planes mid-journey and are surprised to find they are on airline B for the rest of the trip and are not too happy about it.

 British Airways believes that it is intrinsically deceptive for two carriers to share a designator code.

– BRITISH AIRWAYS, COMMENT ON PDSR-85, NOTICE OF PROPOSED RULEMAKING, DOCKET 42199, 1984

Are You Sitting Comfortably?

An innovation by Qinetiq, a UK company, may revolutionise passenger safety if it catches on. They have designed a seat which is able to detect passengers showing signs of deep vein thrombosis, nerves or preparing for a terrorist attack.

The seats monitor movement and, via a display for the cabin crew, the pressure sensors reveal how the occupant is moving. This reveals if the passenger is asleep, staying still for too long (potentially exposing them to DVT) or nervous and jumpy. The passenger's seat number flashes up with a warning of any out of the ordinary movement, allowing the flight attendants to go and investigate.

The designers say the system could be enhanced with sensors to monitor temperature and skin moisture levels to give further indications of stress and anxiety; just the sort of symptoms a passenger who is terrified of flying, a potential air rager or terrorist preparing for an attack might exhibit.

PLANE SPEAKING

Pilot: *'Good morning, Frankfurt ground, KLM 242 requests start-up and push-back, please.'*

Tower: *'KLM 242 expect start-up in two hours.'*

Pilot: *'Please confirm: two hours' delay?'*

Tower: *'Affirmative.'*

Pilot: *'In that case, cancel the good morning!'*

No Business Like No-Show Business

Airlines are notorious for operating on the edge of insolvency and have to watch every penny of revenue. One of their eternal problems is seating capacity being flown without a passenger sitting in it – non-revenue operation. Given that, on average, one-third of all airline seating capacity is flown without a body in it, it's an area of great interest to airline planners. In an effort to minimise the number of empty seats, computer systems have been devised to forecast the likely number of passengers who have booked onto the flight who will not actually turn up and take it – these are known as 'no-shows' in the industry. This leads to the airline deliberately over-booking the flight to the appropriate degree to offset the problem.

Unfortunately people do not always behave in the way computers expect them to and the pesky souls sometimes go and turn up. This leads to the thorny issue of the gate or check-in staff having either to upgrade some people, usually frequent fliers who are unexpectedly given a seat in the first or business class sections, or having to 'bump' some people off the flight. This is usually accomplished by offering vouchers for discounts or cash for volunteers prepared to take a later flight, or if this doesn't make enough space having simply to deny boarding to some passengers and re-book them on another flight or even airline.

> ' *A plane is a bad place for an all-out sleep, but a good place to begin rest and recovery from the trip to the faraway places you've been, a decompression chamber between Here and There. Though a plane is not the ideal place really to think, reassess or re-evaluate things, it is a great place to have the illusion of doing so, and often the illusion will suffice.* '
>
> – SHANA ALEXANDER, THE FEMININE EYE, 1970

Please Sir, They've Stolen our Aircraft!

Aircraft are notoriously difficult to steal; especially airliners. That is unless you invade a country and set about removing them under the guise of 'war-booty'. Which is why the Iraqi government says it will pay $300 million in compensation to Kuwait Airways for claims related to Saddam Hussein's 1990 invasion of the neighbouring emirate; they apparently stole 10 aircraft including two Boeing 767. An Iraqi government spokesman says the Iraqi Cabinet, 'approved a final and comprehensive settlement.' But a spokesman for Kuwaiti Airways says the payment is by no means a 'final' settlement as the airline's total claim is $1.3 billion including interest… just the odd $1 billion different.

Too Overdressed to travel

There was a time, long ago, when male airline staff had to wear a jacket and tie, while female employees would be required to dress smartly, when travelling on a non-revenue ticket. However, it seems that the times-are-a-changin'. A US flight attendant is suing JetBlue

Airways and Delta Air Lines, saying a male employee denied her a work-related flight because she wasn't dressed provocatively enough. The 37-year-old Pittsburgh native, works for Delta and her employer has an agreement for JetBlue to ferry its flight attendants to job assignments on a standby basis. Her lawsuit states that a male JetBlue worker wouldn't let her on a flight in October 2007 because she wasn't dressed provocatively enough, then allowed other flight attendants with less seniority to board the plane.

'(She) changed into more provocative clothes, but (the employee) told her she was too late to board the plane and should have dressed like that before,' stated the lawsuit, which was filed in Pittsburgh federal court. 'He wanted her to change to a lower-cut shirt and tighter pants, and wear more make-up before letting her on the plane,' said the disgruntled flight attendant's attorney. According to the lawsuit, 'Delta and JetBlue officials refused to intercede when she complained.' Apparently she is losing income, because she has stopped taking JetBlue flights to job assignments so she can avoid harassment by the male employee.

Horny Story

As we were going to press Mike Kay – our man in Paris – sent us this:

When I was working in the West Indies in the 60's for BOAC, I took the companies 'Mini Moke' to a 'mechanic' to get the brakes repaired. When I went back a week later he said 'I could not get the parts, so I have fitted another horn...'

And in the End...

By way of conclusion let me tell you how I 'retired' from the airline business. I felt after 20 years that I needed to get a life. Jumping on and off aircraft may be fun for some but I got to the point where I hated it. In four years with Continental I flew across the Atlantic 96 times – in each direction! One of the problems with the business is that airline seats do not really cost the company money when they send employees off on business trips. People fly around the world at the drop of a hat for meetings and this situation is often exacerbated because airlines, through their relationships with hotels, get very big discounts for staff who are travelling on business. Reciprocal arrangements with other airlines means that staff can often travel on other carriers for free. This 'conspiracy' causes airline employees to behave like lemmings, flying around the world in search of meetings to attend.

One day my boss called me from Houston and said, 'We shall have our international division meeting this quarter in Guam.' Now I knew where Guam was and my heart sank. For those of you who don't, it's an island in the middle of the Western Pacific Ocean and it's a bloody long way from anywhere. To get there from London meant a flight to Los Angeles, another to Honolulu and then a seven and a half hour flight to Guam. Naturally I did as asked and made my way to the meeting, which was planned to last for just a day. I arrived the evening before and at the following day's get-together I spoke, in total, for 101⁄2 minutes! The day after the meeting I left Guam and flew home. I was scheduled to stop off in New York on the way back because a very close friend was getting married. I missed his wedding because of various delays en route and it was at that point that I thought, 'This is madness. Life's too short to be travelling the world like this.'

A few weeks later, having returned to London from a day trip to Houston, I got off the plane at Gatwick around 9.00 a.m., went to the office to have a quick shower and then drove to Peterborough for a meeting at Thomas Cook's head office. Driving back around the M25 afterwards, I thought, 'That's it, I really have had it.' I called Frank Lorenzo, the chairman of Continental, from my car phone.

'Frank, I'm going to leave.'

'Where are you going? Is it Pan Am, have they offered you a job?' said a surprised Frank Lorenzo. 'No, I'm just leaving. I want to have a life of my own.'

Was what happened to me in the airline business unusual? No, not at all. I have often said to people, since leaving the business, that I used to have a proper job. Writing this book has reminded me that it was far from that. It was mad! But guess what? I loved it.